THE IRISH LANGUAGE IN NORTHERN IRELAND

The Irish Language in Northern Ireland

The Politics of Culture and Identity

Camille C. O'Reilly
Lecturer in Social Anthropology
Richmond, the American International University in London

First published in Great Britain 1999 by
MACMILLAN PRESS LTD
Houndmills, Basingstoke, Hampshire RG21 6XS and London
Companies and representatives throughout the world

A catalogue record for this book is available from the British Library.

ISBN 0–333–71963–8

First published in the United States of America 1999 by
ST. MARTIN'S PRESS, INC.,
Scholarly and Reference Division,
175 Fifth Avenue, New York, N.Y. 10010

ISBN 0–312–21790–0

Library of Congress Cataloging-in-Publication Data
O'Reilly, Camille.
The Irish language in Northern Ireland : the politics of culture
and identity / Camille C. O'Reilly.
p. cm.
Includes bibliographical references and index.
ISBN 0–312–21790–0 (alk. paper)
1. Irish language—Political aspects—Northern Ireland. 2. Irish
language—Social aspects—Northern Ireland. 3. Language and
culture—Northern Ireland. 4. Language policy—Northern Ireland.
5. Group identity—Northern Ireland. I. Title.
PB1298.N67074 1998
491.6'2—dc21   98–19152
                                                          CIP

This book is printed on paper suitable for recycling and made from fully managed and sustained forest sources.

10   9   8   7   6   5   4   3   2   1
08   07   06   05   04   03   02   01   00   99

Printed and bound in Great Britain by
Antony Rowe Ltd, Chippenham, Wiltshire

For Herb

Agus do mo theaghlach. Is grá liom sibh uilig.

Contents

Preface

Born and raised in California, I decided to go to Northern Ireland to study for an MA in social anthropology. I arrived in Belfast in July 1991, in the middle of the marching season. I remember feeling a vague sense of unease at the sight of bowler-hatted Orangemen marching down the street in formation, but having only a basic understanding of the conflict I did not know the full meaning of what I was witnessing. The city seemed oddly quiet for mid-summer. I would learn in time that there is a mass exodus from Belfast every year around 12 July, the biggest holiday in the Unionist calendar. Many Catholics and some Protestants flee the tension of the season, which all too often results in violence as the Protestant marches attempt to pass through Catholic areas. In retrospect, I suppose it was an apt time to be introduced to Northern Ireland.

I felt slightly baffled as well when I first encountered the Irish language in Belfast. At the time I had no interest in the language, nor was I aware of any revival movement in the North. A new acquaintance of mine had asked me to attend a week-long intensive course in Irish which was put on as part of the West Belfast Community Festival, held in August each year. I knew almost no one in the city and was anxious to meet new people, so I obliged her by attending. I was also more than a little curious about west Belfast, having read quite a few books about Northern Ireland before my arrival. I was drawn both by its mystique and its infamy – the Falls Road is the heart of the working-class Catholic 'ghetto', the bit of Belfast that regularly appears in television documentaries on the North with its murals and graffiti, British army foot patrols and red-brick terraced housing. So we took a black taxi from the city centre up the Falls Road each morning at 10 o'clock for a week.

I remember especially one middle-aged woman in the class, named Bridie: she struggled along with the rest of us, and during the break I struck up a conversation with her. When I asked her why she was taking the class, she told me that she wanted to learn to speak her own language. Irish is the native language of Ireland, she said, and we really ought to speak our own language. This formulation of Irish as 'our own language' is what eventually led me to research the relationship between the language, identity and Nationalist politics in Northern Ireland today. The sentiment was repeated to me often, always in

English and in a surprisingly uniform way, by people from a variety
of backgrounds with different experiences of the language. As I was
to learn, however, this seeming uniformity masked a considerable
amount of variation and disagreement as to the meaning and relevance
of the Irish language to politics, culture and identity in the North.

This book is about the politics of language and culture in the
Nationalist community of Northern Ireland. My primary aim is to
unpack the phrase 'our own language', to get behind its mundaneness
and learn what has made Irish so compelling to these people at this
time, in this place. Many who have become involved with the language
have little formal education. A significant proportion identify themselves as working-class. Many come from socially and economically
deprived areas, like west and north Belfast, which have borne the brunt
of the violence over the last 30 years. Some have adopted the language
with a missionary zeal; others are satisfied to learn the *cupla focal* ('few
words') and send their children to become fluent at one of the Irish-
medium schools. Some have discovered the language through their
Republican politics; others are repulsed by Republicanism, coming
to love the language for 'cultural' reasons. Many have found a voice
through the politics of the Irish language, a means to represent themselves in a context where the political and cultural expression of an
Irish identity has been repressed. Quite a few have discovered that a
knowledge of Irish and participation in the revival movement provide
access to cultural and symbolic capital, and have used this to accrue
a certain degree of power and benefits for themselves and the groups
they represent.

There is no doubt that the Irish language revival movement has blos-
somed in Northern Ireland over the last three decades, and nowhere
so visibly and successfully as in west Belfast. However, there have been
other periods of growth in interest in the survival of the language which
have not been sustained for long, most notably in the heyday of the
Gaelic League at the turn of the century, and the heady days after the
Easter Rising in the South. How can anyone know whether the current
revival indicates real progress, or whether it is simply the last gasps of
a dying language? It is a question which perhaps can only be answered
at some point in the future, when all the bets are in and the race has
been either won or lost.

In the meantime, we can only look at the indicators and speculate.
Most of the people involved in the movement have a deep and driving
belief that Irish will survive and perhaps even prosper. To suggest
otherwise is considered defeatist, if not an outright betrayal. Outside

commentators tend not to be so hopeful, as the provocative title of Hindley's (1990) book, *The Death of the Irish Language: a Qualified Obituary*, suggests. Some Irish academics are somewhat less pessimistic, for example Maguire (1991) and Ó Huallacháin (1994).

While a dedicated minority are certainly not lacking in will, there are some obvious and serious problems in trying to create an Irish-speaking community where previously there was only English, not the least of which is the obstacle of learning the language. It is difficult to estimate the number of people who have attempted to learn Irish over the years. Because there are so very few native speakers of Irish in Northern Ireland, the 1991 Northern Ireland census statistics on the number of people with a knowledge of Irish could be taken as some indication of the number of people who have at least attempted to learn the language, however limited their success may have been.

On the census return 142,003 people, 9.5 per cent of the population of Northern Ireland, indicated that they had 'some knowledge of Irish' (Nic Craith 1995: 14); 22.15 per cent of Catholics in Northern Ireland gave the same answer (Nic Craith 1995: 19). Of these 37,253 people with a knowledge of Irish live in the Belfast Urban Area, just over 8 per cent of the population of the city (West Belfast Economic Forum 1993). Nearly half of the Irish speakers in the city live in west Belfast (West Belfast Economic Forum 1993). That means that roughly one in five people in west Belfast can claim some knowledge of Irish. In spite of the promising numbers, levels of spoken ability are low – less than a third of those who claim some knowledge of Irish in the Belfast Urban Area say they can speak the language (West Belfast Economic Forum 1993). While these numbers certainly are not meaningful in terms of fluency, they do tell us something about interest in the language and the number of people who have attempted to learn Irish at some point in their lives.

The census figures indicate a growth in knowledge of Irish. It is important to remember, though, that numbers do not tell us everything. As Mertz points out, the importance of a language to a community cannot be assessed by simple mathematics – 'it is the entire cultural-linguistic framework through which speakers actively interpret their linguistic experience which gives relative weight and meaning' (1989: 113) to language use. Positive feelings about the Irish language, fostered during the years of the Troubles, may well fade in more peaceful times as issues of identity become less pressing.

Whatever the future of the Irish language, it has taken on a new significance for Nationalists in Northern Ireland over the last few decades. As the profile of the language increases and the number of people who learn to speak it grows, its place in the identities of Irish people is likely to continue to shift and change. Both of the main Nationalist parties, the SDLP and Sinn Féin, promoted the Irish language as a key aspect of Irish identity in the negotiations on the future of Northern Ireland. The linking of the language to the idea of parity of esteem will have consequences for conceptualizations of Irish identity in the future, both politically and culturally.

Much of the research presented in this book was carried out before the IRA ceasefire of August 1994. It went through various incarnations during the first ceasefire, after it broke at the end of 1995, and through the second ceasefire and the start of all-party talks. To the best of my knowledge, the change in the political situation has not yet made a perceivable difference to the information and ideas presented here. In all likelihood, though, it will at some point in the future, particularly now that a settlement has been reached and the conflict may be coming to an end. This is just one question among many that must wait for the unfolding of events to be answered.

Acknowledgements

I am grateful to Graham McFarlane, Kay Milton and Joe Ruane for their advice and support. I would like to convey special thanks to the *Gaeilgeoirí* of west Belfast, and all the people I interviewed in the North and in Dublin, especially those I have quoted directly. My interpretation of their words is my responsibility alone. If I have unwittingly misrepresented anyone, I hope they will understand that it was not my intention to offend. Thanks also to May McCann, Hastings Donnan, Gordon McCoy, Seán Ó Muireagáin and Aodan Mac Póilin. I would like to extend my gratitude as well to the librarians in Belfast's Linenhall Library, especially in the political and Irish collections. Both library and librarians proved to be invaluable sources of information. I would also like to acknowledge the support of the ULTACH Trust, the Lawlor Foundation and *Bord na Gaeilge*, all of which gave financial assistance during the researching and writing of this project.

The poem *Fill Aris*, by Sean Ó Ríordáin is reproduced by permission of the author and publisher, Saírséal Ó Marcaigh.

IRELAND

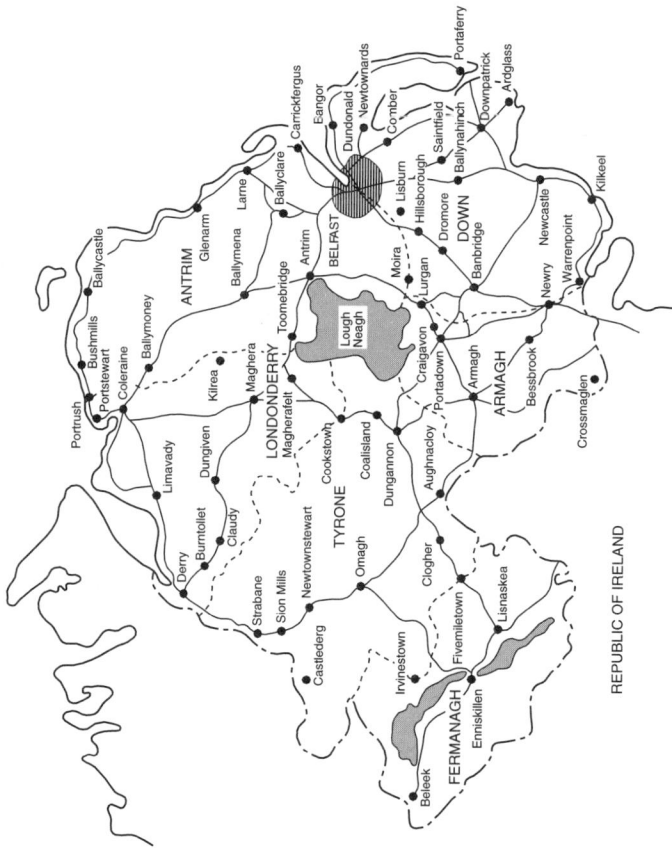

NORTHERN IRELAND

BELFAST

1. Cluain Ard
2. Cultúrlann & Meánscoil Feirste
3. Gaelscoil na bhFál
4. Bunscoil Bhreann Mhadagáin
5. Bunscoil an tSléibhe Dhuibh (Scoil na Fuiseoige not shown)
6. Bunscoil an Droichead

Areas of predominantly Catholic population

Oldpark · Cliftonville · Belmont · Sydenham · Ardoyne · Glencairn · Shankill · Falls · Springmartin · Ballymurphy · Turf Lodge · Windsor · Andersonstown · Lenadoon · Ballymacarret · Bloomfield · Knock · Castlereagh · Cregagh · Ballynafeigh · Braniel

HOLYWOOD ROAD · BELMONT ROAD · UPPER NEWTOWNARDS ROAD · KNOCK ROAD · BALLYGOWAN ROAD · SYDENHAM BYPASS · BEERSBRIDGE ROAD · CASTLEREAGH ROAD · UPPER KNOCKBREDA ROAD · WOODSTOCK ROAD · CREGAGH ROAD · ALBERTBRIDGE ROAD · RAVENHILL ROAD · ORMEAU ROAD · ORMEAU EMBANKMENT · ANNADALE AVE. · STRANMILLIS EMBANKMENT · STRANMILLIS ROAD · YORK RD. · LIMESTONE ROAD · ANTRIM ROAD · NORTH QUEEN ST · YORK ST · CORPORATION ST · OXFORD ST · VICTORIA ST · ST VICTORIA ST · CHICHESTER ST · MAY ST · CLIFTON ST · CRUMLIN ROAD · WOODVALE RD. · SHANKILL RD. · DIVIS ST · SPRINGFIELD ROAD · GROSVENOR ROAD · SANDY ROW · DONEGALL ROAD · UNIVERSITY RD · MALONE ROAD · LISBURN ROAD · STOCKMANS LA · M1 MOTORWAY · MONAGH BYPASS · KENNEDY WAY · GLEN ROAD · ANDERSONSTOWN ROAD · COLLEGE SQ EAST

River

Fill Aris

le Seán Ó Ríordáin

...

Téir faobhar na faille siar tráthnóna gréine go Corca Dhuibhne,
Is chífir thiar ag bun na spéire ag ráthaíocht ann
An Uimhir Dhé, is an Modh Foshuiteach,
Is an tuiseal gairmeach ar bhéalaibh daoine:
   Sin é do dhoras,
   Dún Chaoin fé sholas an tráthnóna,
   Buail is osclófar
   D'intinn féin is do chló ceart.

(Ó Ríordáin 1987: 41, lines 17–24)

1 Introduction

This book is an attempt to understand the emergence of the Irish language revival movement in Northern Ireland in the 1980s and 1990s. Starting with the premise that there is more to this than just the revival of a language in decline, how are we to understand the significance of this small, thriving social movement taking place in the midst of a sustained political conflict? Why have some people taken an interest in Irish, which has not been spoken as an ordinary means of daily communication in Northern Ireland for many generations,[1] at this particular time and place? And what can we learn from this movement about the politics of identity and culture in general?

The Irish language is one of a number of key features of Irish identity, but its significance as part of that identity has varied over time, as has its importance for different individuals. Over the last two decades it has become an increasingly important aspect of national identity for many people in Northern Ireland, especially in Nationalist enclaves such as west Belfast. Some consider the language to be the essential feature of Irish identity, even while others consider it to be unimportant. Cohen (1985, 1994) has suggested that ethnic identity is not easily generalized to entire populations. Rather, it is mediated by individual experience and continually reconstructed on a personal and collective level. The discussion which follows will illuminate this process as it occurs in relation to this one aspect of Irishness, among those who value the Irish language.

THE PROBLEM OF INTERPRETATION

Cohen suggests as a general principle that people tend to become more aware of their culture when they stand at its boundaries (1982: 3). In Northern Ireland, particularly since the start of the Troubles, people are continually reminded of these boundaries – between Catholic and Protestant, between North and South, between Ireland and Britain. It is not surprising, then, that people should be quite conscious about certain aspects of their culture. The Irish language is one such aspect, because it is taken by most (although not uncontroversially) to be a marker of Irish identity. This consciousness means that many people interested in the language have thought through issues of identity, and the meaning and importance of the language to that identity. Others, however, have not.

Even an articulate and well thought out statement can be difficult to interpret, particularly if it relates to abstract ideas such as identity and beliefs. To take at face value what is explicitly stated would severely limit the depth of our understanding. On the other hand, a sense of identity cannot be understood simply through the observation of behaviour. The challenge is to listen to what people say and try to understand this by examining it in the context of actual events.[2]

Contextual interpretation has a number of pitfalls, however. The range of context taken into account, and the manner in which it is seen, affect the interpretation. There is also the risk that the researcher might credit people – and the statement or concept – with a consistency they or it do not actually possess. As Gellner points out, the use of a particular concept often depends on ambiguity and a diversity of meanings which vary according to context, even though the concept may give the impression of consistency (1973: 42).

Another problem of interpretation is in attributing meanings which informants might not themselves see or agree with. Events in Northern Ireland, as anywhere else, contain various levels of meaning, and people are aware of and able to express the motivations and rationalizations for the actions they take to varying degrees. If asked, people will generally be able to give an explanation for most of what they do, but ordinarily such questions are not asked about conventional activities.

Giddens (1984) suggests a way of conceptualizing this problem by distinguishing between what he calls discursive and practical consciousness. He defines discursive consciousness as 'what actors are able to say, or to give verbal expression to, about social conditions, including especially the conditions of their own action', and practical consciousness as 'what actors know (believe) about social conditions ... but cannot express discursively' (Giddens 1984: 374–5). Essentially, it is the difference between what is said and what is characteristically simply done.

This framework helps us to understand some of the problems encountered when seeking out explanations for people's actions, particularly in relation to abstract concepts such as identity. In conversation, we can only gain access to what is on the level of discursive consciousness, or what people are able to give verbal expression to. However, Giddens argues that knowledgeability, or those things that people know or believe about their own actions and those of others, is based more on practical rather than discursive consciousness. In addition, many motivations are unconscious. Compounding the problem is that people are able (and willing) to articulate what they know on the level of discursive consciousness to varying degrees.

Charsley (1987) also addresses problems of interpretation, but from a different angle. While not everyone may be aware of the meaning or significance of certain events, there are often local experts or professionals who have views on the matter. Anthropologists often rely on these local experts for their own interpretations and sometimes go no further than the explanations they offer. This, however, limits the analysis to what exists in the discursive consciousness of the local expert. Charsley suggests that indigenous exegesis – explanation on the discursive level of consciousness – should not be taken as a guide to 'true meaning', but rather seen as an integral part of the phenomenon being studied.

I would concur with Charsley's assertion that it is the anthropologist's job to identify appropriate possible meanings whether or not those observed are making readings, or the same readings, themselves. Charsley suggests two main approaches to identifying and allocating meaning. First, people may mean things by their actions or by the objects they create. This can be understood both by looking at what people say they mean and by 'reading' the meaning in the context of the society itself. In Charsley's example, the sharing of the wedding cake and the cutting of it by the bride and groom together can be seen as an act of unity between the couple. The second way in which meanings are identified and allocated is symbolically or metaphorically. For example, the cake may symbolize the bride, while the cutting of the cake can be seen as a sexual metaphor (Charsley 1987: 103–4).

The difficulty is that people tend to act according to the set of specifications considered appropriate to the situation in their culture. As Giddens also notes, only occasionally are they pushed to explain what they are doing. When such explanations are made, often for the benefit of the anthropologist who is asking the question, they should be taken as only one of a number of possible meanings. But what of meanings which are not explicated in this manner? Can there be meanings apart from those of which the actors are aware? (1987: 108). This is a serious question, because much to which anthropologists are trying to attribute meaning is left unexplained by the actors.

Even with a good understanding of the sociocultural context, what people express on the level of discursive consciousness–what is explicitly stated – can be difficult to interpret. That which is on the level of practical consciousness – what is simply done – is also open to interpretation. The explanation of the indigenous expert, or the anthropologist, are just a few of many possible readings, ones with which the individuals concerned may or may not agree or accept. Charsley suggests that the outside observer should attempt to read the different elements – discourse, sociocultural context, symbolic and metaphorical interpretations – as if they were a text. Many different readings are possible, and new potential meanings may come into play as practices change. I intend my own reading of meaning and identity in the Irish language revival to be taken in this light, not as *the* reading, but as one interpretation among many possible interpretations.

ETHNICITY AND NATIONALISM

Since the 1970s, ethnicity has become an increasingly important concept in anthropology. The rise of ethnic identity as a basis for political activism in industrial states, and the importance of ethnicity in post-colonial politics, has led to a proliferation of studies on the subject. A number of recent volumes have dealt with current debates and issues.[3] I intend to make only a few points here that are of particular relevance to this discussion.

Ethnic groups are often treated as if they were culturally homogeneous. Cohen is critical of the idea that ethnicity can be generalized to all members of a group, and that the individual is in essence 'the nation writ small' (1994: 157). He has argued both that local experience mediates national identity (Cohen 1982), and that ethnicity is continually reconstructed on both the personal and collective level (Cohen 1994: 120). Ethnicity, like all social identities, is negotiated through the processes of daily life rather than being a static given. An examination of the discourses of the Irish revival highlights these points, showing how people, both as individuals and as members of collectivities, engage with the process of constructing and reconstructing ethnic identity.

It is important to be aware of the amount of variation that can exist within an ethnic group. Barth (1969) has suggested that the boundaries between groups are of primary definitional importance, but it cannot be taken for granted that the cultural content which those boundaries enclose is equally shared by all. Instead of thinking of ethnic groups in terms of a list of shared features, Mahmood and Armstrong (1992) suggest that it would be more useful to think of them in a prototypical manner. Recognized members share most, but not all, characteristics, while certain traits may not be considered of equal importance in people's minds (Mahmood and Armstrong 1992: 8).

This is an important consideration, since only a small minority of Nationalists are seriously interested in the Irish language. Political conflict has heightened people's awareness of their ethnic identity, but only some people have chosen to express this through an interest in Irish. According to Mahmood and Armstrong's idea of ethnic prototypes, it should not be considered problematic that some see Irish as an important emblem of identity, while others take no interest in the language and do not see it as an important ethnic boundary marker.

The relationship between ethnicity and nationalism is a complex one. Ethnicity tends to be bound up with nationalist ideologies, lending legitimacy to movements for self-determination, popular sovereignty and cultural diversity (Smith 1981; Edwards 1985). Ethnic consciousness may have always constituted an important element of human existence, but its social significance and political relevance have varied greatly throughout history (Smith 1981: 87). It is generally agreed that the modern concept of nationalism is in no way 'natural', in spite of the claims of ethnic nationalists. Smith argues that we should 'understand nations as a recent type of political formation utilizing an ethnic base and transforming the style and content of much older, and often dormant, ethnic ties' (1981: 85).

In Smith's view, a clear-cut distinction between ethnicity and nationality, and between ethnic sentiment and nationalism, is difficult to establish. Connor (1978) says that what distinguishes ethnicity from nation is essentially self-consciousness. While an ethnic group can be other-defined, a nation must be self-defined. He suggests, then, that nation be defined as a self-aware ethnic group, while the term ethnic group could be applied both to nations and 'potential' nations.

In this book, I will primarily use the terms ethnicity or ethnic identity, but with the understanding that by most, if not all, definitions the Irish constitute a nation. Under the political circumstances which prevail in Northern Ireland, the term 'ethnic' is less ideologically charged than 'national' or 'nationalist'. This being the case, I use the term 'Nationalist' only when I am specifically referring to those who hold political aspirations for a constitutional status which in some way incorporates a connection between Northern Ireland and the Republic. When discussing the Irish language as part of the identity of Catholics and Irish speakers, I will use the terms 'ethnic' and 'ethnicity' instead.

Throughout the text, capital 'N' Nationalism refers specifically to the ideology of Irish Nationalism, while lower case 'n' nationalism refers to the ideology or idea of nationalism in general. According to Anderson (1983), it is important to look at nationalism in the broader sense as a cultural system.[4] Using this approach, the Irish language movement in Northern Ireland can be seen as part of the much wider phenomenon of nationalism. It should not be viewed as anomalous or 'backward'. The behaviour and activities associated with the Irish language revival movement are rooted in large part in the ideas and ideals of nationalism, and are understandable in those terms as a wholly contemporary phenomenon.

The identification of ethnic and nationalist movements with language has been particularly prevalent since Herder equated the German language with the German nation. Many theories of ethnicity and nationalism still make this connection. Hobsbawm (1990) points out, though, that nationalism only became essentially linguistic towards the end of the nineteenth century. In the case of Ireland, for example, the Irish language was not an issue in Nationalist politics prior to the founding of the Gaelic League in 1893 (Hobsbawm 1990: 107).

Gellner suggests that the tie between language and an ethnic group is not nearly as strong as romantic nationalists tend to claim (1972: 165). Rather, language is one of a number of symbols, including other aspects of culture and genetically transmitted traits such as skin colour, which can be seized upon by underprivileged groups to highlight inequalities and claims to political power (Gellner 1983: 74). While in Gellner's view the cultural aspirations of nationalist movements tend to be relatively weak, Nairn (1977) and Kedourie (1960) have argued that they can be an important agent of social change.

Edwards (1984, 1985) expresses doubts about the importance of language to a sense of ethnic identity when compared to other factors, such as religion. In fact, he cites Ireland as an example of how a people can lose their mother tongue without losing their sense of ethnic identity. This opinion is shared by Wardaugh, who states that 'most Irish feel no need of any kind for the language and exist quite satisfactorily without it' (1987: 94).

As Smith suggests, language issues amplify rather than generate nationalist sentiments. A sense of being Irish generally precedes a desire to learn the Irish language, although this may in turn strengthen a person's sense of ethnic identity. Language, like religion or skin colour, takes its meaning from particular historical situations, even when they have an independent effect on that situation (Smith 1981: 51). Both language and religion have played a critical role in the history of Ireland for centuries, and have been imbued with unique meanings as a result. Irish people are Irish whether or not they speak the Irish language, but it does occupy a special position in the identity of many Irish people because of the history associated with it.

DISCOURSE AND IDEOLOGY, LANGUAGE AND POLITICS

I would like to take a moment to clarify some of the terminology that will be used in this book, particularly the notoriously slippery concept of 'discourse'. Although some theorists have used the terms 'ideology' and 'discourse' almost interchangeably, it could also be argued that they belong to two different theoretical approaches. For the most part, 'ideology' tends to be associated with the Marxist tradition, while 'discourse' belongs to a poststructuralist paradigm. The concept of ideology is rooted in action theory and is part of an attempt to grasp the way in which unequal power relations are maintained with minimal use of direct force or coercion. The concept of discourse, on the other hand, came into social theory from linguistics. It is part of an attempt to understand how language not only reflects or conveys social experience, but actually constitutes social subjects and social relations. Foucault (1972, 1982), who is largely responsible for developing the concept of discourse as it is used in social theory, quite self-consciously avoids the concept of ideology.

In the Marxist tradition, ideology is used in two different ways. In one sense, ideology implies false thought, illusion or the product of false consciousness. In Larrain's (1983) terminology, this is the 'negative' conception of ideology. The other sense in which Marx used the term was to refer to the set of ideas which arise from a class or group with a given set of material interests – Larrain's 'positive' conception of ideology. Foucault developed his theory of discourse in contrast to the first sense of the term in particular.

Purvis and Hunt (1993) prefer to label this distinction the 'critical' and the 'sociological' conceptions of ideology. The critical conception 'delimits a realm in which social knowledge and experience are constructed in such a way as to "mystify" the situation, circumstance or experience of subordinate classes or dominated groups' (Purvis and Hunt 1993: 478). The sociological conception 'focuses on a plural conception of ideology as the outcome or result of the specific social position of classes, groups or agents' (Purvis and Hunt 1993: 478). They suggest that the theory of ideology has been most elaborated upon in this second sense of the term, and that this has led to a tendency to blur the distinction between the concepts of ideology and discourse.

Purvis and Hunt argue that the concepts of ideology and discourse can be usefully used together, and that both have an important theoretical role to play in the analysis of social relations. They suggest that discourse be used to refer to process, and ideology to effect. What makes some discourses ideological is their connection with systems of domination: 'Ideological discourses contain forms of signification that are incorporated into lived experience where the basic mechanism of incorporation is one whereby sectional or specific interests are represented as universal interests' (Purvis and Hunt 1993: 497). This formulation goes ome way towards addressing a common criticism of poststructuralism: that it fails to show how discourses or texts fit into the hierarchical structure of society via unequally empowered agents.[5] The value of linking the two concepts of ideology and discourse is that it allows the incorporation of a view of power into poststructuralist analysis. I shall discuss the relationship between ideology, power and discourse in more detail below.

While Purvis and Hunt define discourse to include any system of linked signs, linguistic or otherwise, it seems to me that such a broad definition could lead to just about anything being considered a discourse, or part of a discourse. The problem of a clear and broadly acceptable definition of the term has been a serious one. The literature on discourse is complicated by many, often conflicting definitions and terminologies. In part, this is due to the transfer of the term from linguistic to social theory. In the process of adapting the concept, a confusing muddle of terms and definitions has ensued. The same terms are given conflicting definitions, different terms are used to describe what is essentially the same phenomenon, or the term 'discourse' is simply poorly or vaguely defined.

As a starting point, Milton suggests that it is useful to distinguish between a general and a specific definition of the term, something which is not done in many analyses (1996: 166). In the general sense, discourse is a communicative process. In the social sciences, most follow Foucault and use the term to refer to the way in which knowledge is constituted through communication.[6] Milton (1993) calls this the 'processual' conception of discourse. Seidel, for example, sees discourse as 'a site of struggle in which social meanings [are] produced (not reflected), sustained and challenged' (1989: 223).

More particularly, it is also possible to speak of 'a discourse' or 'discourses'. In this specific sense, discourse has been used in essentially two different ways. In the first, a discourse is defined simply in terms of its subject matter, for example scientific discourse or the discourse on organic food (James 1993) – what Milton calls the 'substantive' meaning of the term. Substantively, communication about the Irish language in Northern Ireland could be considered a discourse because it revolves around a particular theme: the language itself.

In the second specific sense of the term, discourse is a mode of speaking governed by certain frameworks which delimit meaning and influence what can be said and done. In this conception, discourses provide definite and distinguishable mediums through which communication takes place. Discourses do not so much control what can be said as facilitate certain possibilities and impede others. Peace (1993), for example, uses a similar definition of discourse when he examines competing moral and scientific discourses in debates over planning and industrial development in Cork.

In general, the term discourse refers to the way in which social reality is constituted through communication. Specifically, discourse can have a dual meaning, both processual and substantive (Milton 1993: 8). All of these definitions apply in my own analysis, although the second specific conception of discourse as modes of speaking with distinguishable frameworks will be most important.

In Foucault's work, 'professional' discourses are imposed on people from above, in the sense that people are inserted into subject positions through these discourses. Dominant discourses are seen as imposing their own frameworks and rationalities on people, limiting discursive possibilities. Little is said, however, about the contradictions which exist within discourses, and about other resources which give rise to the alternative discourses which challenge dominant discourses. My own conception of the way discourses are used is less rigid and 'top down'. While existing discursive frameworks do constrain what can be said and done, this does not preclude the possibility of a creative use of discourse by both professionals and 'non-professionals'. As Fairclough (1989) points out, social conventions enable as well as constrain, facilitate as well as impede. By exploiting the internal contradictions inherent in all discourses, and by the creative use and combination of different discourses, people can create alternatives which challenge dominant discourses and chip away at dominant ideologies.

In addition to the specifications outlined above, I would restrict the meaning of discourse to language only (in contrast to Purvis and Hunt, for example). I see discourse in both the general and specific sense of the term as a linguistic vehicle for thought, communication and ideology, as well as action. While language as a human faculty and as a channel of communication may belong to everyone, '*the* language, the institution, the apparatus of ritual, value judgement and so on, does not belong to everyone equally. It can be controlled by a small elite' (Cameron 1986: 145, emphasis in original).

Power is an important part of the exercise of discourse, and power relations need to figure in any analysis of the way in which social reality is constituted through language. In Bourdieu's conception, the political field is 'the site par excellence in which words are actions and the symbolic character of power is at stake' (Thompson, introduction to Bourdieu 1991: 26). To paraphrase Noam Chomsky, questions of language are in essence questions of power (Grillo 1989a: 2).

Power at the level of social institutions in society is at least in part the power to control discourse and through it, ideology. The relationship between discourse and ideology is key to understanding relations of power in society, and the way that discourses can both contribute to and challenge those relations. While for Foucault, power is inscribed within the discourses themselves, I prefer the conceptions of discourse and ideology suggested by Purvis and Hunt as providing clearer tools for the analysis of language and power. As part of our experience of social reality, ideology is constituted through discourse – it is expressed, reproduced and changed through discourse. At the same time, the frameworks which shape discourse are themselves formed with reference to existing ideologies. The use of both ideology and discourse in an analysis gives rise to a concept of directionality in the exercise of discourse, in the sense that ideology works to the advantage of some and the disadvantage of others in society. As Fairclough argues, discourses do not have inherent political or ideological values, but they may come to be invested with meaning in particular ways in different social domains or settings. Since meaning can be 'invested' in particular discourses, it follows that they can also be 'reinvested' with different meanings (Fairclough 1992: 67).

Control through consent rather than coercion relies on ideological power, and since discourse is the main vehicle of ideology, it is essential that those in power have a significant degree of control over various discourses. By using dominant discourses people legitimize particular power relations, usually without being conscious of doing so. On the other hand, certain power relations can be delegitimized or challenged through the failure to engage with dominant discourses, or through the conscious use of alternative discourses – what Halliday calls anti-languages (Halliday 1978: 164–82; Fairclough 1989: 91). If dominated discourses are successfully suppressed or contained, the dominant discourse may cease to be seen as just one position among many and come to be seen not only as legitimate, but as 'natural'. This sort of naturalization is the ultimate objective of proponents of a dominant discourse (Fairclough 1989: 91).

Frazer and Cameron (1989) identify certain alternative discourses as being 'languages of liberation', for example the 'feminist way of talking'. A language of liberation, they argue, 'is liberating by virtue of the *meanings* it makes available – meanings which are either illegitimate or at best unarticulated in competing discourses', as opposed to a 'language of power', which is the language of important public or institutional domains and is powerful by virtue of its association with currently powerful speakers (1989: 38, emphasis in original). Languages of liberation, then, are the site of hegemonic struggle, located as they are on the boundary between the field of opinion and the field of doxa – the field of what can be discussed and the field of what is 'natural' or just known – or to use Giddens's terminology, the boundary between discursive and practical consciousness. Languages of liberation are a means through which people can change or challenge dominant ideologies, by posing alternatives to languages of power.

Some of the discourses of the Irish language revival by this definition might also be considered 'languages of liberation', in the sense that they challenge certain dominant discourses which would be more associated with the institutions of power. However, it is not quite as simple as it might at first appear. In some ways the discourses of the Irish revival can be used to challenge the dominant ideology (or ideologies) in Northern Ireland, for example by contesting the constitutional position of Northern Ireland and the dominant British ethos of the state. In other ways, the discourses are used within acceptably defined parameters of debate, for example the issue of parity of esteem,[7] or comparisons between the status of Irish and other minority languages in Britain. Certain aspects of some Irish language discourses are being incorporated into dominant discourses, for example the incorporation of aspects of Irish language discourses into the discourse of community relations and cultural traditions. (This will be discussed in greater detail in Chapter 5.)

There is clearly a process of struggle and negotiation taking place between the different discourses as to which, or which parts, will be accepted. If, as a result of the current peace process, certain traditions and symbols of Irishness become 'officially' recognized, then even more of these discourses may be incorporated into the institutions of power in the North. As Brow suggests, 'the struggle for hegemony is always an open-ended process of contestation as well as incorporation, of negotiation and resistance as much as of accommodation and consent' (1990: 5).

From this discussion of ethnicity, language and politics, I would like to turn to a consideration of where this book fits into the anthropology of Ireland in general, and works on the Irish language in particular.

TRENDS IN THE ANTHROPOLOGY OF IRELAND

From Arensberg and Kimball's work of 1968 up until the mid-1980s, anthropological studies of Ireland have tended to focus primarily on rural areas and/or locality studies. Urban studies have been more common in other disciplines.[8] Following a wider trend in anthropology, however, an increasing amount of ethnographic research is being carried out in urban areas.[9] Rather than conducting specifically 'rural' or 'urban' studies, in recent years anthropologists in Northern Ireland have become more interested in engaging with problems such as violence, the sectarian divide, conflict resolution and broader issues of politics and identity.[10] This book is very much part of this trend.

Crozier (1985) and Curtin, et al. (1993) argue that there is an essential dichotomization of ethnographic research in Ireland into the 'dying community' camp, and the 'two tribes' or 'political and religious schism' camp. The South tends to be portrayed as a society and culture in decline. The North, on the other hand, is characterized as being made up of two diametrically opposed communities who manage to tolerate each other most of the time in spite of their differences.[11] Ethnographic studies of this type tend to focus on the question of how the two communities manage to share the same space in spite of intrinsic cultural differences.[12]

In a review of dominant trends in the anthropology of Northern Ireland up to the 1980s, Donnan and McFarlane (1986a, 1986b) argue that anthropologists have tended to project a different image of the North from academics from other disciplines. Until this time, at least, anthropologists portrayed Northern Ireland as an essentially balanced society which was periodically disrupted by violence. In other disciplines, the image tends to be one of a thin veneer of good relations covering much deeper divisions.[13]

This book focuses on just one of Northern Ireland's two 'communities', the Nationalists. It is not primarily concerned with the relationship between Protestants and Catholics. Instead, I investigate divisions and differences *within* the Nationalist community, looking especially at the section that is interested in the Irish language. In this sense, it does not fit in with the 'two tribes' trend of Northern ethnography.

However, the assumption of a certain degree of division between Protestant and Catholics is implicit throughout this work. On the topic of the Irish language, at least, there are clear differences in the views of both groups. The depth and nature of the division between Protestants and Catholics more generally has been the topic of much scholarly research, and will not be dealt with in any detail here.

THE IRISH LANGUAGE

The majority of research on the Irish language has focused only on the Republic of Ireland.[14] Of the research that has been carried out in Northern Ireland, most is in the area of linguistic studies or Celtic studies, with an emphasis on attitudes towards the language and educational issues.[15] The Irish language has not figured prominently in ethnographic studies of the North. O'Connor (1993) mentions the Irish language briefly, but only Maguire's (1991) work looks at the Irish language revival in Belfast in any depth. To my knowledge, only one anthropological study of the Irish language in Northern Ireland has been published: Kachuk's (1994) study of the Irish language and the Republican movement in west Belfast.

Sweeney (1987) conducted a survey into the Irish language in Northern Ireland which was of particular significance because, at the time, no census since 1911 had included a question on the Irish language. While the 1991 census does provide information about the number of people claiming some knowledge of Irish in Northern Ireland, Sweeney's survey supplies additional information. Of the 5,111 adults interviewed by Sweeney, only two gave Irish as a first language and, as might be expected, none was a monoglot Irish speaker. While Irish is commonly known in Northern Ireland, widespread knowledge of the language is restricted almost exclusively to Catholics. Sweeney reports that 23 per cent of Catholics were interested in gaining further knowledge of Irish. This increased to 34 per cent when considering only those under 25 years old (Sweeney 1987: 16). A quarter of all Catholics, and a third of the Catholics under 25, thought it important to have a knowledge of Irish (Sweeney 1987: 17). Almost half of the Catholic parents said that Irish was an important language for children (Sweeney 1987: 20).

Maguire's (1991) study of the Shaws Road *Gaeltacht* indicates that identity is an important part of parents' decision to send their children to *Bunscoil Phobal Feirste*, Belfast's first Irish-medium primary school. Her data on the families of pupils who attend the *Bunscoil* shows that they are not a homogeneous group in the sense of social class or economic status. Maguire believes that the source of their motivation and commitment lies within the realm of culture and identity (1991: 93), although she does not go into much detail about what she means by this.

What she does say is that 'Irish identity' was mentioned most frequently as the first single factor when considering the benefits of *Bunscoil* attendance (1991: 98). Maguire does not herself define this term. However, when 'Irish identity' was elaborated on by parents, they expressed the view that it represented a sense of belonging to the Irish nation, and of not simply allowing themselves to be seen as members of a British province. They felt that Irish distinguished them from mainstream citizens of the United Kingdom. Finally, the Irish language was seen as a way of becoming connected to a rich cultural heritage (Maguire 1991: 99).

Maguire writes that in the context of Northern Ireland, where the culture of the Catholic minority is not equitably treated, 'the shift towards bilingualism constitutes a conscious attempt to reinforce one's sense of identity' (1991: 99). This sentiment is echoed by McMinn (1992), who argues that if a state denies the legitimacy of a claim to national identity, people will tend to fight back with both political and cultural weapons. These points will be explored in some depth in the chapters which follow.

METHODOLOGY

I lived in west Belfast while conducting the research on which this book is based. The most intensive period of research was from June 1993 to January 1995, but my involvement in Irish language circles was ongoing from early 1992 until May 1997. I began without a word of Irish, but I have acquired a conversational level of fluency in the language over the years.

Participant observation was my primary research method, but as Jenkins (1993) points out, it has its limitations given the complexity and scale of urban life in a modern, industrial society. Among the problems he mentions are 'the uneven access which one has, as a researcher, to a range of areas of community life which are private or semi-private'; the difficulty in achieving more than limited and partial empirical coverage; 'the capacity of the (relatively) powerful to hinder one's attempts to examine their lives; and the ubiquity of more or less severe social conflict in many urban situations' (Jenkins 1993: 243–4). All of these difficulties have been evident, to a greater or lesser extent, in my own research.

I decided, therefore, to conduct interviews to supplement material collected through participant observation. As a first step, I mapped out the various groups and organizations involved with the Irish language (past and present) in an effort to avoid the pitfall of favouring one circle of Irish activists over another. I then conducted taped interviews with 82 people involved with the movement in a variety of different capacities, including full-time activists, Irish language learners and the parents of children in the Irish schools, taking what is essentially an oral history of each person's involvement with the language. The interviews varied widely, from length (from 20 minutes to almost three hours), to the articulateness and explicitness of the interviewee, to the amount of social contact we had before and after the interview.

I have also used archival material, particularly from newspapers and journals, to guide and inform the structure of interviews, and to complement ethnographic data. While it is important to be aware that newspapers are written by people with their own agendas and constraints, information obtained in this way can be quite useful, provided it is interpreted in a similar way to material collected from more conventional informants. Two local newspapers were particularly useful. The *Irish News* is a Northern Ireland daily with a Nationalist leaning which occasionally runs articles about the Irish language, especially local events, city council news and relevant government decisions. Since its inception in the 1970s the west Belfast weekly the *Andersonstown News* has carried articles and advertisements about Irish. This newspaper is particularly interesting, because it is edited and run by members of the Irish language community.

I have attempted to conceal the identities of most of my informants, primarily through the use of pseudonyms. When this is the case I use first names only, typed in capital letters. Where people's opinions are already part of the public domain, for example politicians' comments and articles written by journalists, I use the person's real name. In this case, both first and last name are written in normal type.

I quote interviews and articles at length throughout the book, avoiding paraphrasing as much as possible. Because discourse is the basis of my analysis, I feel quite conscious of the need not to take words out of people's mouths. In addition, I want to keep the context of what people say relatively intact. I hope the sources of my information and insights are transparent enough for you, the reader, to make your own judgements.

In the next chapter, I take a brief look at the history of the Irish language revival in Belfast and Northern Ireland. The main argument is laid out in Chapters 3–6. Chapter 3 describes how the three discourses are identified, including an historical analysis of each and a look at key phrases and concepts. In Chapters 4, 5 and 6, I provide examples of how each of the three discourses are used in turn, looking first at the professionals in the use of discourse, and then at the 'non-professionals'. Chapter 7 is divided into four case studies focused on government policy and the Irish language. The case studies provide examples of the different arenas in which the three discourses are manifest, and shows how they work in the complex reality of daily life. In Chapter 8, I compare the Irish language revival in Northern Ireland and the Republic of Ireland, discussing the similarities and contrasts between them. Chapter 9 is an attempt to draw broader comparisons between Northern Ireland and two other regions experiencing ethnic nationalist movements, Brittany and Quebec. In the final chapter, I summarize my findings and offer some conclusions about the politics of language in Northern Ireland today.

2 Language and Culture in Northern Ireland: the Background to the Irish Language Revival Movement

Before embarking on a study of nationalism and related phenomena such as ethnic revival movements, it is important to take note of the significant overlap between the ideologies of nationalism and the theories of the social scientists who study them. Social science inquiry and nationalist ideology grew out of the same social and historical contexts, and share many of the same concepts and assumptions about the world. Anthropologists in particular have in the past contributed to a view of the world as made up of discrete cultural groups, instead of emphasizing the fluidity of culture and the lack of discrete boundaries (Handler 1984, 1988).

Spencer (1990) underlines the political dimensions of anthropological representation by pointing out that our explications of politics and culture can confirm a community's own self-understandings and become incorporated into their own conceptions of society. The rhetoric of identity and nationalism dominates the discourses of the Irish language revival movement in Northern Ireland, and *Gaeilgeoirí* (Irish speakers and learners) hold an image of the Irish language revival which is rooted in social science exegesis. Giddens (1976) describes this as 'slippage'. As anthropologists, we reinterpret frames of meaning constructed by social actors in our own terms. Slippage occurs when the concepts constructed by anthropologists – or other social scientists – are appropriated by those whom they were originally created to analyse. Anthropological exegesis may end up influencing, or indeed becoming a part of, indigenous exegesis (Charsley 1987).

The first section of this chapter is intended to provide some background to the discussion. The brief history related below demonstrates some of the ways in which the Irish language and the revival are interpreted by local people, using categorizations they themselves use.

Histories of this sort serve the important purpose of description, but by using them I am in many ways simply reproducing the image created for public consumption by Irish language activists. Many of these representations will, however, be deconstructed in the chapters that follow.

An important belief held by many *Gaeilgeoirí* is that language is the single most important aspect of national identity. This belief has a powerful symbolic dimension, so much so that monoglot native English speakers often describe Irish as 'our own language'. The association between language and ethnic identity is well known, so these comments are not unusual in themselves. The similarity of the discourse, however, is actually glossing over a multitude of meanings.

Cohen (1985) argues that everything about a community, both conceptual and material, has a symbolic dimension. This symbolic dimension does not imply a consensus of sentiment; rather it provides people with 'something to think with … the means to make meaning' (Cohen 1985: 19). The symbols themselves are shared by all people who speak the same language or participate in the same behaviour in which they are used, but the meanings of these symbols are not shared, or at least not shared in their entirety. The concept expressed by the phrase 'our own language' in this context is highly symbolic, and this book is largely concerned with unpacking its meanings.

Until 20 years ago it is unlikely that so many people in Northern Ireland, with limited or no Irish, would have described the language in this fashion. Although in the past there were a few Irish language classes and events, learning to speak it was seen as a rather eccentric activity undertaken by a small minority of people. Most considered it to be a middle-class pursuit.[1] In less than two decades, Irish has come to be re-imagined as the language of the people, an important symbol of Irish identity in the North.

HISTORY AND THE IRISH LANGUAGE REVIVAL IN NORTHERN IRELAND

Brow writes that 'almost everywhere, it seems, the sense of belonging together is nourished by being cultivated in the fertile soil of the past' (1990: 2–3). This is as true in Northern Ireland as anywhere, and history is very important to modern day *Gaeilgeoirí* as a means of asserting their claim to the Irish language and an Irish identity. History, as a key form of knowledge, both reflects and affects the distribution and exercise of power. Competing versions of the past, therefore, are particularly important in the struggle for power.[2]

Gaeilgeoirí favour a version of history which says that Irish has always been a part of the geographical location which is now Northern Ireland. This idea is frequently expressed through the characterization of the Irish language revival movement as waxing and waning in one continuous flow, rather than starting, stopping and restarting in discontinuous spurts. They point out that the Irish language is usually ignored in 'official' versions of Northern Ireland's history, an omission which they believe has contributed to the language's decline and further marginalizes the position of Nationalists in the North.

Ó Donnaile (1997) provides a brief outline of the trajectory of the language's decline. He points out that until the seventeenth century, the Irish language was the primary means of communication for almost every group and class on the island. After the defeat at the Battle of Kinsale in 1601, Ireland lost much of its Irish-speaking nobility and the fortunes of the language began to change. English-speakers came to dominate in positions of power, first militarily, then politically, economically and finally socially. By 1800, no one seeking to improve or even maintain their social or economic position in society could do so without the English language (Ó Donnaile 1997: 196). The final stages of this linguistic shift happened during the nineteenth century, when English came to be viewed by the majority of people as the natural and essential medium of Irish society in all spheres of life.

Revivalism began first in the east, in areas where Irish had already been largely replaced by English. Revival activities have gone on sporadically in what is now Northern Ireland over the past two centuries.[3] Belfast in particular has been an important centre for Irish language activities. The Linenhall Library started a collection of books and manuscripts in Irish, the Harpers' Festival was held in the city and Irish was first taught in the Belfast Academy towards the end of the eighteenth century. The first printed periodical in Irish, *Bolg an tSolair*, was started in Belfast in 1795.

At the beginning of the nineteenth century Irish was still widely spoken in Counties Antrim and Down. As the population of Belfast grew, the number of Irish speakers in the city grew also, as people migrated from the countryside into the city. However, by the time of partition over one hundred years later, the number of Irish speakers in Northern Ireland had dwindled, and organic Irish-speaking communities had all but disappeared. A number of older Irish speakers had been scattered throughout four of the six counties of Northern Ireland, but they had all died by the middle of the century (Mac Póilin 1995: 9).

As Irish was coming to its final stages of decline as an ordinary means of communication, it became the object of some intellectual interest. There was a surge of academic and antiquarian interest in the Irish language in the 1830s and 1840s, but then a dip in revival activities until the end of the century. The founding of the Gaelic League in 1893 marked the beginning of a new phase of the revival. They had two primary (and rather optimistic) goals: the revival of Irish as a vernacular for the whole of the Irish people, and the creation of a new literature in Irish (Ó hAilín 1969). Their approach contrasted with the antiquarian-driven revival of earlier years. The turn of the century was the heyday of the League, with Irish language classes, Irish music and Irish dancing gaining in popularity.

The Irish language revival movement had mixed fortunes throughout the first half of the twentieth century. Interest was on the increase up to the formation of the Irish Free State and for some time after, but popular momentum was not maintained. There was a small, but vibrant period of revival activities in Belfast in the 1950s and early 1960s which was to have significant consequences for the language in later decades. During this period, 11 couples from the city who were involved with the Irish language movement met and married. They came together to house their young families on what was then the outskirts of west Belfast, forming the first urban neo-*Gaeltacht* (Irish-speaking area) in Ireland and later starting Northern Ireland's first Irish-medium primary school, *Bunscoil Phobal Feirste*. When interest in the language began to increase in the 1980s, the Shaws Road *Gaeltacht* became the foundation of the revival movement.[4]

For the 50-year period from partition to 1972, the Ulster Unionist Party ruled Northern Ireland's parliament at Stormont. The dominant ideological forces of Northern Irish society under this regime were inimical to the Irish language, and the state itself was self-consciously anti-Irish (Mac Póilin 1995: 10). Official policy reflected the attitude that Irish was a foreign language with no place in Northern Ireland. For example, Irish was banned from BBC Northern Ireland for 50 years, even though Scots Gaelic and Welsh programmes had been broadcast by the BBC since the 1920s (Andrews 1992: 25–57; Cathcart 1984). In the schools, a sustained effort was made for three decades to undermine the position of Irish in the education system. Today, Irish is treated like other modern languages such as German and French, but attempts have recently been made to undermine even this limited status (see Chapter 7, case study two).

An overall picture of the status of Irish in Northern Ireland is perhaps best obtained by examining educational policy over the past century, the area where the greatest efforts were focused for the better part of the revival movement. In 1904, Irish was recognized for the first time as a medium of schooling in areas where the majority of children spoke Irish as their home language. While this had effect in the whole of Ireland, by this time there were very few areas left in the six counties where a significant number of children spoke the language. The position of Irish in the educational framework of Northern Ireland remained relatively unchanged after the partition of the island in 1920. From that point on, though, any new regulations which were introduced were restrictive rather than encouraging.[5]

Throughout the 1920s efforts to improve the status of Irish in the schools were met with stalwart opposition. For example, during the mid-1920s *Comhaltas Uladh*, the northern branch of the Gaelic League, lobbied the British Ministry of Education for a more flexible attitude towards Irish. While *Comhaltas Uladh* sought to introduce Irish to classes below the third grade, the Ministry of Education actually restricted it further to grades five, six and seven in 1926. In 1933, all special grants for the teaching of Irish were terminated. At the time about 10,500 children were learning Irish in primary school, 14.11 per cent of children at Catholic schools, 5 per cent of the total primary population (Maguire 1991: 43).

Throughout the history of Northern Ireland, government policy has continued to oscillate between hostility and disregard, although more enlightened attitudes have been demonstrated on occasion since the fall of Stormont. For example, in 1974 the Department of Education issued a report which advocated second language teaching in general, and which acknowledged the particular attributes of Irish (Maguire 1991: 74). Unfortunately, none of this was reinforced in any concrete way through policy or planning initiatives.

The historical antipathy of the British authorities towards Irish in Ireland as a whole might be compared to former attitudes in Scotland towards Scots Gaelic, and in Wales towards Welsh.[6] However, the continued hostility towards Irish experienced in Northern Ireland since partition is in contrast to more recent progressive attitudes towards Scots Gaelic and Welsh. In Scotland, there has been significant progress in Gaelic-medium education, particularly since the 1980s.[7] In Wales, progress in promoting the Welsh language in education came much earlier. The Welsh Department of the Board of Education was formed in 1907, and the first official Welsh-medium school was established in Aberystwyth in 1939.[8]

In spite of official attitudes of indifference and antipathy, the Irish language has continued to find a niche in the North, and interest has been growing at a steady rate for the last few decades. Classes are organized wherever there is a group of interested people. There is an average of 50 Irish language classes for adults being held at any time of the year in west Belfast alone. Some are offered by further education institutions, but most of them are held in people's own homes, or on the premises of other organizations such as Gaelic Athletic Association (GAA) clubs, women's groups, community groups or Sinn Féin *cumainn*.[9]

Over the past two decades the Irish-medium schools have been the heart of the revival movement in west Belfast. The first all-Irish primary school, *Bunscoil Phobal Feirste* was established in 1971 to cater for the children of the Shaws Road *Gaeltacht*. Since then, five other primary schools have opened in Belfast alone (one in a Catholic area of north Belfast, one in south Belfast, and the rest in west Belfast). The first *Bunscoil* now has over 300 pupils. All of the Irish-medium schools were established without government support, relying on the donations of parents and the local people for funding. *Bunscoil Phobal Feirste* ran for 13 years without government recognition, and the second school, *Gaelscoil na bhFál*, for six. The third school, *Scoil na Fuiseoige*, is now officially associated with the *Bunscoil* on a temporary basis so that it, too, can obtain government support until it is large enough to gain recognition in its own right. *Bunscoil an tSleibhe Dhuibh* became government-funded in 1996 and *Bunscoil Bheann Mhadagáin* in 1997. The most recent school in Belfast, *Bunscoil an Droichead*, opened in 1996 with European funding.

There are an additional six *bunscoileanna* (primary schools) outside of Belfast. *Bunscoil Cholm Cille* in Derry opened in 1985, and was granted government funding in 1995. *Bunscoil an Iúr* in Newry opened in 1987, receiving government funding in 1997. *Bunscoil Luraigh* opened in Maghera in 1993, and continues to operate without government funds. *Bunscoil Uí Néill* in Coalisland and *Bunscoil Ard Mhacha* in Armagh both opened in 1995, the former without government funding and the latter as a satellite. *Bunscoil Dhál Riada* opened in 1996 and is to date unfunded. Four new *bunscoileanna* are scheduled to open in 1998 in Downpatrick, Derry, Portadown and Castlewellan. The schools will be discussed in more detail in section three of Chapter 7.

The secondary school sector is also growing. The first Irish medium secondary school, *Meánscoil Feirste*, opened in Belfast in 1991. The school received government funding in 1996. *Meánscoil Doire* opened in Derry in 1994. It was recently announced that the school will receive European funding in 1998 and state funding thereafter. There are also numerous Irish-medium nursery schools (*naoínraí*) which are preparing increasingly large numbers of children for entry into the primary schools. As of 1997 there were 1,247 children in Irish medium primary and secondary schools in Northern Ireland, along with approximately 700 children attending Irish medium nursery schools.[10]

There is more to the revival than the teaching of the language and the establishment of Irish-medium schools. The Irish language newspaper *Lá* is based in Belfast and distributed throughout Ireland. There is an Irish language cultural centre in west Belfast, *An Cultúrlann McAdam – Ó Fiaich,* which houses a bilingual café, Irish language bookstore, theatre and drama group, and is the venue for cultural events through Irish. Belfast's Shaws Road, which I mentioned earlier, houses the only urban neo-*Gaeltacht* in Ireland. The development of business and employment opportunities for Irish speakers has become a key focus of the revival in recent years, particularly as growing numbers of young people leave Irish-medium education. Belfast has an Irish language business development agency called *Forbairt Feirste* which offers classes through the medium of Irish and supports the establishment of businesses which operate primarily through Irish.

The largest 'community' of Irish speakers in Northern Ireland is in Belfast. It is a loose network of people who come into contact mainly because of their involvement with the Irish language. Even within this loose network, however, there are cross-cutting ties of friendship and of kinship, much of it centred in west Belfast. Friends often learn Irish together, and occasionally become fluent enough to switch from English to Irish as their primary means of communication. Siblings and cousins often have children at the same *naoínra* or *bunscoil*. At the core of this loose network is a dense network of fluent or nearly fluent speakers who relate to each other not just as Irish speakers, but as friends, neighbours, work colleagues, Irish language activists and in many cases, kin. For example, the children of a number of families on the Shaws Road are cousins, and many continue to be friends now that they are adults themselves. As more young couples meet and marry or establish households together, this dense core of Irish speakers may expand.

The status of the Irish language among the people of west Belfast, and among Nationalists in general, has changed. In the South, research

has shown that while the majority still believe the language is symbolically important, few believe it is worth the effort to learn and speak it
(see Chapter 8). This is in contrast to current views among many
Catholics in Northern Ireland today, where the ability to speak Irish
has become a sort of status symbol. People proudly tell others of their
efforts to learn the odd *cupla focal* (few words) in a local *bun rang*
(beginners' class). The degree of fluency achieved – or lack of it – does
not seem to detract from the value seen in making an effort.

PROTESTANTS AND THE IRISH LANGUAGE

The perceived link between politics, culture and linguistic loyalty which
prevails in Northern Ireland today places Irish firmly into the Nationalist cultural package. The language is seen as the preserve of Catholics,
a view widely held in both communities.[11] The historic roots of this
association lie in the political developments of the period between about
1885 and 1915. Before this time, Irish had a romantic and antiquarian
appeal, and was fashionable even among those who considered themselves British. There was no perceived conflict between an Irish cultural
identity and a British political identity, as there is today. What happened to change this is a complex story in itself.[12]
　　Irish had been the native language of a number of small Protestant
communities in the North, and was used by some Protestant clergy as
part of their missionary work (Blaney 1996). Protestant Unionists were
involved in the early revival of Irish in the mid-nineteenth century. At
the end of the century, however, the ideology of Republicanism was
spreading. In spite of the Gaelic League's claim to be apolitical and
its efforts to avoid party politics, the Nationalist implications of the
revival could not be overlooked. After the turn of the century, the Gaelic
League leaned more and more towards Nationalism.[13] At the same time,
it increased its association with the Catholic Church to encourage the
teaching of Irish in the schools. During this same period Unionism was
also undergoing a transformation, moving away from Irish Unionism
and towards a Unionism which rejected any form of Irish identity
(Mac Póilin 1997: 39).
　　The 1915 Annual General Meeting is symbolically important as the
juncture at which the Gaelic League was finally taken over by Republicans. From this point on, the association between Nationalism and
the Irish language was complete. An indication of the extent to which
this association had been naturalized was the League's continued

portrayal of itself as apolitical after 1915. The end result was 'an almost complete polarization of Unionist and Nationalist perspectives on the language' (Mac Póilin 1997: 44).

In recent years, there has been a renewal of interest in Irish among Protestants.[14] McCoy (1997) makes a distinction between Nationalist and Unionist Protestant learners of the language. Protestant Nationalist opinion on the language differs little from their Catholic counterparts. Protestant Unionists, on the other hand, face a whole host of difficulties when they decide to learn Irish. Some Unionists have ambivalent feelings about learning Irish because of its Nationalist associations, while others view the language through a 'Unionist cultural lens', redefining it in such a way that it becomes compatible with their political views and identity (McCoy 1997). It is a popular myth among Protestants and Catholics alike that Unionists who learn Irish will be converted to Nationalism, but this is not borne out by McCoy's study.

Not only are there issues of identity to overcome; there are practical difficulties as well. Many Protestants feel uncomfortable or even fearful of entering Catholic areas, yet this is where the majority of classes are held, especially at the advanced level. There is also a fear that people in their own areas might misconstrue their interest in the language and criticize or even physically harm them and their families. For working-class Protestants in particular, the association with Republicanism is a serious psychological block to learning Irish. In spite of a growing interest in the Irish language among Protestants, the great majority of those involved in the revival movement in Northern Ireland are Catholic and Nationalist.

THE CREATION AND RE-CREATION OF CULTURE AND IDENTITY

The representation of the revival movement presented by *Gaeilgeoirí* is, of course, only a fraction of the picture. The image portrayed is to a large extent a construction which disguises or leaves out certain intentions and strategies employed in the political manoeuvrings of the people involved. Beyond that still are the unintended consequences of their activities, one of which has been an impact on the ongoing reinterpretation and re-creation of identity which takes place in all societies as part of everyday experience.

Cohen points out that when a community presents itself to the outside world, it tends to simplify its message and its character down to the barest essentials (1982: 9). The phrase 'our own language' could be understood as an example of this phenomenon. However, nobody is making any great effort to hide the ideological differences within the movement. There are widely differing opinions as to the meaning of the Irish language movement, the best way to proceed with the revival, and the relationship of the language to politics.

By identifying and discussing the key discourses of the revival movement, I hope to accomplish two things: to illuminate the process of identity formation, and to show the way that different interests compete to have their particular version of meaning, belief and history accepted in whole or in the greatest possible part. This contest can have far-reaching consequences. The struggle to define and ascribe meaning has an impact on power relationships, and can influence key political processes, such as the issue of parity of esteem in the current peace process. In addition, it can influence the size and direction of government funding for arts and education, having an impact on the existence or non-existence of whole networks of schools and the education of potentially thousands of children. To succeed in having a particular view accepted as the most accurate or correct – or better yet, in having it seen as the only 'natural' way to perceive things – is to influence the very definition of Irish identity. The processes I am describing are at the very root of the interaction between politics, culture and identity.

For *Gaeilgeoirí*, Ireland can be fully and completely imagined only through the medium of Irish. Many believe that the Irish people cannot be truly Irish without their language.[15] Some go so far as to say that without it, the Irish would not be significantly different from the English.[16] No matter which way they frame their belief in the importance of the Irish language, the common goal of all *Gaeilgeoirí* is the survival of Irish as a living language. This is the core rationale given explicitly or implicitly as explanation for the actions they take.

However, the consequences of their actions on behalf of the language go beyond their expressed and intended goals. The activities of the revival and the process of proselytizing about the value of the Irish language has brought about a redefinition of what it means to be Irish. These new versions of Irishness alter previous meanings in subtle and not so subtle ways, at times self-consciously, and at times in ways of which most people are seemingly unaware. *Gaeilgeoirí* often push to revive traditions and values which they see as a part of their past. In their efforts to reclaim these things, they are actually engaged in a process of reinvention rather than simple revival. As M. E. Smith points out, 'all traditions of identity, even when claimed to be derived from an unalterable inventory of past facts, consist in large part of events altered in scale, sequentially rearranged, freshly understood, and even lately created' (1982: 135). I shall return to this point in later chapters.

Many *Gaeilgeoirí* are aware of a process of cultural change taking place, and few, if any, would argue that there is total continuity with the past. For example, an important issue of debate revolves around perceived changes in the language which are occurring in the main because of the degree of contact between Irish and English.[17] Mostly consisting of alterations and mistakes in grammar and syntax, these changes are generally seen as a negative development, although most agree that they are probably inevitable. In Belfast the incorporation into the language of *blas Bhéal Feirste*, or the Belfast accent, is usually seen as a more positive change. The Irish that people speak in Belfast is largely modelled on the dialect used in the *Rann na Feirste* region of western Donegal, but so long as correct pronunciation is used, a Belfast way of speaking is considered a good thing.

Greater status tends to be afforded to a person who has 'good Irish', rather than a person who speaks Irish with a very strong Belfast accent. '*Tá Gaeilge mhaith agat*' (You have good Irish) is a compliment often bestowed on promising learners. Generally speaking, 'good Irish' can be defined as Irish spoken with correct pronunciation and a rich vocabulary. For example, there are subtle differences in the Irish pronunciation of vowels and certain consonants, such as f, t, d, l and n, and considerable emphasis is placed on mastering these. Irish is also a very idiomatic language, and great pride is taken in knowing the correct way to phrase something. Direct borrowing of English ways of speaking is frowned upon. Dedicated Irish speakers will expose their newfound knowledge of a little-known idiom with obvious relish, waiting until the company and the moment is correct to let the phrase or sentence slip out, in order for it to get a proper reception.

On the other hand, people would laugh if someone from Belfast walked into the room using a genuine Donegal accent. It would sound 'funny' or just not right. McCoy (1991) notes that learners who visit the Rosguill *Gaeltacht* do not attempt to imitate the local accent. One student said that no one in Northern Ireland would understand him if he did. In the North, a distinction is made between *blas* (accent), *canúint* (dialect) and *foghraíocht* (pronunciation). To gain the highest prestige, a 'natural' northern accent needs to be combined with the Donegal dialect and correct Donegal Irish pronunciation. Most acknowledge that in order to do this, it is necessary to spend time studying Irish in the *Gaeltacht*.

However, even this most sacred of traditions, the yearly pilgrimage to Donegal, has been called into question by some. The notion that Belfast Irish is as good as, or even superior to, Donegal Irish has gained a small following. On a number of occasions I have heard people say that Belfast Irish is 'better' or more 'pure' than the Irish spoken in the *Gaeltacht*, which many feel is heavily 'contaminated' with English loan words and syntax. This view is not limited to Belfast residents – a native speaker from one of the strongest parts of the Donegal *Gaeltacht* once told me the same thing, though other native speakers hold precisely the opposite opinion. There is general acknowledgement that the process of revival brings change for better or for worse, although where you draw the line between acceptable changes and unacceptable ones is a matter of sometimes intense debate.

THE IRISH LANGUAGE MOVEMENT IN THE POLITICAL FIELD

Thompson describes the political field as 'the site *par excellence* in which agents seek to form and transform their visions of the world and thereby the world itself: it is the site *par excellence* in which words are actions and the symbolic character of power is at stake' (introduction to Bourdieu 1991: 26). As the following chapters reveal, the politics of the Irish language revival in west Belfast demonstrate this point clearly. The competing discourses of the revival movement not only reflect the differing ideologies and meanings associated with the language, they are the actual site of struggle to define what is at stake in the revival and to achieve the goals thereby defined.

At stake in all three discourses is the ultimate survival of the Irish language. Even what that means, however, is not agreed. In decolonizing discourse the ultimate vision is Patrick Pearse's dream of an Ireland not only free, but Gaelic as well – an Ireland free not only from British political and economic domination, but also from British cultural influence. Even if most would acknowledge that this vision is unachievable, it is considered an acceptable vision (or fantasy) to entertain. Many subscribers to cultural discourse would find this unacceptable or even offensive, since it seeks to replace English with Irish and rejects much of what is seen as part of the Irish or Northern Irish tradition. The cultural vision would tend to encompass the survival of Irish in those communities where it is already spoken, and an increase in the number of people able to speak it so that anyone with an interest may learn and enjoy it as part of their cultural heritage. The second version of cultural discourse would emphasize especially the intrinsic value of Irish as a language, and the terrible consequences to human culture and diversity if it was to be lost. At stake in rights discourse is the survival of an ethnic group identified first and foremost through their language, the loss of which is certainly preventable if the civil rights of Irish speakers were protected and the language positively promoted at an institutional level. There are innumerable variations on the above visions, just as there are innumerable combinations and permutations of the three discourses, but this skeletal outline of three visions of what is at stake in the revival of Irish helps to demonstrate the different bases from which these discourses flow.

All three discourses are permeated by two types of protest discourse commonly used in Northern Ireland. It could be argued that there are essentially two types of Nationalist political discourse since the civil rights movement. One portrays the Irish as a 'risen people', emphasizing their strengths, virtues and victories. The other is a kind of 'victimology', focusing on the oppression of the Irish people and their suffering at the hands of the enemy (usually the British). Both types of protest discourse have been drawn into the discourses of the Irish language revival movement, and especially into rights and decolonizing discourses.

Manoeuvring within this field are what might be considered, in Bourdieu's terminology, the professionals of the Irish language movement – fluent speakers who hold or are vying for positions of power. In the case of the revival in Belfast, there is no dominant hegemonic ideology as yet, so to hold a position of power is to have considerable influence over the very definition of the stakes of the game. Bourdieu sees the contest for power in this field as a competition 'for the monopoly of the right to speak and act in the name of some or all of the non-professionals' (Bourdieu 1991: 190). Important spokespersons for the movement compete, and occasionally join forces, to have their vision accepted by the 'non-professionals' – other Irish speakers or others with an interest in the status of the language, and in some cases the British government.

Joining the ranks of the professionals in the Irish language revival is relatively easy compared to other areas of the political field. Fluency in spoken Irish is the main criterion. Since teaching the language freely (and often for free) affords considerable symbolic capital to the teacher, the means to become fluent are readily available in places like west Belfast. Accumulating cultural and symbolic capital to enhance one's position in the movement is also relatively easy, requiring the devotion of a great deal of time more than anything else. Voluntary work on behalf of the language affords a large amount of symbolic capital to the volunteer, and is even considered a duty by some *Gaeilgeoirí*. Symbolic capital also comes from having good Irish; from demonstrating a high level of dedication to the language; from the use of non-language skills to promote or support the language, its speakers or the movement; and from raising children through Irish, or at least sending them to an Irish-medium school.

Cultural capital can be accumulated in two ways. The first is through a system of reward set up exclusively to promote the use of Irish, silver and gold *fáinní* (rings). Learners of the language can take an oral test, and upon passing are entitled to wear a *fáinne* indicating their level of ability in the language and their dedication to it. A silver *fáinne* indicates a very basic conversational ability, while a gold *fáinne* is meant to indicate fluency. Wearing a *fáinne* is supposed to indicate to others that you would prefer to speak Irish when you encounter another Irish speaker. It is intended to facilitate the use of Irish in situations where fellow Irish speakers may be unknown to each other, since the habit everywhere is to speak English unless it is known for certain that the other person can speak Irish. While fluent speakers consider the gold *fáinne* relatively easy to get and therefore not worth much, from the point of view of the learner it is an important symbol of fluency and provides a goal to work towards. In spite of the rather cavalier attitude taken by some fluent speakers towards the gold *fáinne*, it is worn by many on more formal occasions. The second way that cultural capital can be accumulated is through the education system in the form of GCSE and A-level qualifications, or a university degree in Irish.

By looking at the discourses used to talk about Irish, it is possible to examine deeper systems of meaning and belief among Irish speakers and learners. Based on what some of my informants have told me, and on my own observations, I have identified three main discourses used to talk about the Irish language in Northern Ireland.[18] I have given them the conceptual labels of decolonizing discourse, cultural discourse and rights discourse. It is possible to find professionals who exemplify each of the three discourses, each engaged in a competition both to enhance their own position and to form and promote their ideological vision of the Irish language revival. In most cases the professionals of the Irish language revival have a relatively high level of education. In some cases, individuals have returned to study or have gone to university as mature students in order to obtain a degree in Irish or a teaching diploma. There are also non-professionals, who perhaps have less of an input into the formation and transformation of the discourses, but are nevertheless involved in the process.

In Chapter 3, I shall describe each of the discourses and explore some issues related to the use of discourse. Although individuals often mix discourses to suit their own purposes, for the sake of clarity I shall focus first on talk which draws primarily from just one discourse. I will then look at how each of the three discourses is used in Chapters 4, 5 and 6. In Chapter 7, I shall present case studies which demonstrate how discourses can be used together in ordinary speech.

3 Identifying the Three Discourses

There is broad support for the Irish language among Nationalists, and a rather generalized feeling that it is an important part of Irish identity. In spite of this, the symbolic and practical meanings of Irish and the revival are by no means agreed. Different groups seek to advance their own interpretations of the importance and meaning of the language, while representatives of the British government also compete to neutralize the impact of this powerful symbol of identity. The contested nature of the language is reflected in different interpretations of events and institutions associated with Irish, and played out in the very discourse used to talk about the language, its revival, and its social, cultural and political role in Ireland today.

THE BALLOT BOX, THE ARMALITE, AND THE IRISH LANGUAGE: DECOLONIZING DISCOURSE

The title of this section is a play on the strategy articulated by Sinn Féin during the first half of the 1980s, that the struggle for Ireland's freedom would be won with an armalite in one hand and a ballot box in the other. In addition to the armed struggle and electoral politics, another aspect of the struggle as defined by Sinn Féin is cultural, as evidenced by the establishment of the Sinn Féin Cultural Department at the beginning of the 1980s. From its foundation, an important part of the work of the Cultural Department has had to do with the Irish language. Irish gained a very high profile during the hunger strike in 1981, partly because the first man to die, Bobby Sands, was an Irish speaker, and partly due to the increasingly widespread use of the Irish language to communicate among Republican prisoners in Long Kesh. Sinn Féin's involvement with the Irish language throughout the 1980s contributed a great deal to the current shape of decolonizing discourse, which is perhaps best typified by much of the rhetoric of Sinn Féin and a number of its prominent members.

At least since the split in the Gaelic League which culminated in the resignation of Douglas Hyde from his position as president in 1915, there has been an ideological division between those who made a strong association between the Irish language and the political independence of Ireland, and those who sought to keep politics outside of efforts to revive the language. Michael Collins is one Republican leader from the time of the Easter Rising who strongly associated the language with independence for Ireland. His words articulate the belief at the foundation of much of decolonizing discourse:

> We only succeeded after we had begun to get back our Irish ways; after we had made a serious effort to speak our own language; after we had striven again to govern ourselves. We can only keep out the enemy and all other enemies by completing that task ... The biggest task will be the restoration of the Irish language.
> (quoted in Ó Fiaich 1969: 111) [Quote 1]

This ideological battle has taken place largely in the field of discourse. The production, reproduction, contestation and transformation of different ideologies in the struggle for hegemony in the Irish language revival movement can be seen in some of the writings and speeches of the time. What I would now call decolonizing discourse is used in an article published under the title 'The Gaelic League and Politics' in the September 1913 issue of the journal *Irish Freedom*. It demonstrates the historical roots of this discourse and the manner in which it is expressed quite clearly.

> The work of the Gaelic League is to prevent the assimilation of the Irish nation by the English nation ... That work is as essentially anti-English as the work attempted by Fenianism or the Society of United Irishmen. ...
> The Irish language is a political weapon of the first importance against English encroachment.
> (quoted in Ó Huallacháin 1994: 66–7) [Quote 2]

The discourse in this quote bears some striking resemblances to much of the discourse examined below. There is more to this, however, than a simple continuity of discourse over time. Fairclough (1992) uses the term intertextuality to refer to relations between texts, both through history and contemporaneously. All texts are shaped by prior texts which people 'respond' to, and by the way people 'anticipate' subsequent texts. He goes on to say that 'The concept of intertextuality sees texts historically as transforming the past – existing conventions and prior texts – into the present' (Fairclough 1992: 85).

Texts are not only shaped by prior texts, they can transform prior texts by investing them with new meanings. They can also restructure existing discourses to generate new ones. The 'inherent intertextuality' of texts is an important aspect of hegemonic struggle (Fairclough 1992: 102). The struggle for ideological power is played out in part through discourse. The concept of intertextuality points to the productive capacity of texts, both written and spoken, to produce, contest and transform meaning.

In this sense, decolonizing discourse in its present form is not simply repeating the words of the past, such as those quoted above, but drawing upon them and transforming them into new configurations with new meanings suitable to the current social and political context. There is an illusion of continuity promoted by the obvious surface similarities in discourse, past and present, which is important in establishing both credibility and a sense of community and history, at least among those who subscribe to the ideologies expressed through and created by this discourse.

Particularly in the first half of the 1980s, decolonizing discourse was associated with quite an extreme ideology. Irish was literally seen as a weapon in the arsenal available to fight the British. A well-known statement demonstrates this position. A prominent member of Sinn Féin, who is also an Irish language activist, has been quoted as saying, 'Every word of Irish spoken is like another bullet being fired in the struggle for Irish freedom.' In the course of its development, decolonizing discourse seems to have been somewhat moderated. It would be relatively unusual, for example, to hear someone make such a statement today. While the most extreme versions of this discourse may be in retreat, the belief that the Irish language has an important political role and significance is still widespread, and this discourse is still fairly widely drawn upon.

One basic difference in orientation found in the three discourses is the way the relationship between the Irish language and politics is conceptualized. In decolonizing discourse, Irish is made an integral part of party politics in general and Republicanism in particular, identified as part of the process of decolonization. There is a strong naturalization of the connection with Nationalism, and a strong connection with the Republican struggle. The Irish language tends to be seen as inherently political.

Certain key words, concepts and arguments indicate the use of decolonizing discourse: 'resistance' or 'cultural resistance', 'oppression', Irish as a 'weapon', cultural 'struggle', particularly as part of a wider anticolonial struggle, and 'Republican', or a strong association made with Republican ideals or beliefs. Discourses of anti-imperialism, decolonization or political struggle are frequently used in association with the

Irish language. Connections are often explicitly made between a person's Nationalist political development and their interest in the language. Speaking and learning Irish are seen as political acts. Irish is also seen as a particularly powerful expression of national, and not simply ethnic, identity.

The following examples illustrate these points. When asked why she became involved with the Irish language, a young woman from north Belfast told me: 'I felt that with the struggle going on for Nationalists to free themselves, I felt that it was a good chance for me to play my part in the culture, more so than in the military.'[1] A Sinn Féin leaflet from the mid-1980s describes the situation regarding the language this way:

> Sinn Féin proclaimed loudly that the language question was political or that it was because of a political decision that Irish was taken from us in the first place. People must recognize that the anti-Irish campaign is interwoven with the British presence in Ireland. ... The language suffered after the English came and it will recover before they leave. We also have to accept that having the language back will help bring an end to the foreign rule in Ireland. As the Irish influence rises, the foreign influence decreases. [Quote 3]

DISENGAGING LANGUAGE FROM POLITICS: CULTURAL DISCOURSE

Cultural discourse stands in ideological opposition to decolonizing discourse. The clearest and most dominant feature of cultural discourse is the assertion that the Irish language and politics should be kept completely separate. The corollary is that the importance of the language lies in its beauty and cultural worth, not its political capital. What exactly is meant by 'politics', however, is not generally made explicit. Often the word 'political' is used as a synonym for 'Republican', or occasionally 'Nationalist'. When a person says the language should be kept apolitical, they are often making a veiled comment on the perceived relationship of the Irish language to Republicanism, usually casting it in an unfavourable light.

Another common implicit meaning of 'politics' is party politics, or more specifically, sectarian politics. In this case, the belief is that the language should not be used to further the ends of any one political party, or that Irish should be kept as far removed from sectarian politics as possible. In practice, though, this still usually refers to Republican politics, because Sinn Féin is by far the most vocal party on Irish language issues. Political acts in support of the Irish language, for example lobbying the government in support of Irish-medium education or campaigning for greater funding for the language, are not necessarily condemned and may even be condoned. Approval or disapproval of this type of political activity largely depends on the context and on who is doing the campaigning. Sinn Féin involvement might bring condemnation from some circles.

Like decolonizing discourse, cultural discourse has a relatively long history. Probably the best-known advocate of an apolitical view of the Irish language was Douglas Hyde, president of the Gaelic League from its inception in 1893 until his resignation (over the issue of politics and the language) in 1915. According to Hutchinson (1987), Hyde was a cultural nationalist embroiled in a classic confrontation with political nationalists. While cultural nationalists believe that '[O]nly by returning to their unique history and culture could Irish men and women realize their human potential and contribute to the wider European civilization', political nationalists believe that '[O]nly through the exercise of self-determination as citizens of an independent state could individuals find dignity' (Hutchinson 1987: 2). Hutchinson argues that the two forms of nationalism articulate different conceptions of the nation and have diverging political strategies, as Hyde found to his cost.

Hyde believed that for Irish to survive, it was essential to include people from all political persuasions in the revival movement. He tried to bring together all shades of Nationalist and Unionist behind the common cause of the Irish language. In a letter of introduction sent to America before Douglas Hyde's visit in 1905, the *Coiste Gnotha* (Executive Committee) of the Gaelic League wrote:

> The Gaelic League owes these great successes to the broad basis upon which it is founded. It recognizes in every Irishman a brother regardless of his religion or his politics. On its platform are found working side by side in a spirit of union and brotherly love – Catholic, Protestant, Dissenter, Nationalist, Unionist – and all are actuated by the same desire, to raise from the dust the Language, Music, Games, Traditions, Industries and Glory of Ireland.
>
> (O'Leary et al. 1905: 3) [Quote 4]

While on tour in the United States, Hyde adapted an older speech entitled 'The Necessity for De-Anglicising Ireland' (Ó Conaise 1986: 153–70) to his new audience. The notion of 'purifying' the Irish nation of English influence may sound crypto-fascist now, but at the time the idea of de-Anglicizing Ireland was hailed as the only alternative to either acceptance of the status quo, or a campaign of violence. Explaining his purpose to an audience in New York, he said:

I see that the papers say that this is the last grand struggle of the Irish race to preserve their language. Oh, ladies and gentlemen! It is ten times, it is a hundred times, it is a thousand times more far-reaching than that! It is the last possible life and death struggle of the Irish race to preserve not their own language but their national identity.
(Dunleavy and Dunleavy 1991: 266) [Quote 5]

To the contemporary eye there appears to be a contradiction here. The Gaelic League claims to unite both Nationalist and Unionist, Catholic and Protestant, yet it also claims to be out to preserve not just the Irish language, but the very identity of the Irish nation. The appeal, however, was to emotional rather than political ties to the idea of nation. What Hyde and the Gaelic League hoped to do was unite people of all political and religious persuasions under the shared identity of Irish men and women in support of their cultural heritage, the Irish language.

MacDonagh (1983) identifies two strains of Protestant Gaelicization which informed Hyde's vision of a non-sectarian Gaelic League. The Fergusonian strain (after the nineteenth-century political figure Samuel Ferguson) was not explicitly political, nor was it revolutionary in tone. Subscribers to the Fergusonian strain 'sought merely to break any "necessary" connection between Catholicism and Irish nationality and, conversely, any "necessary" connection between Irish Protestantism and subservience to or identification with British interests' (MacDonagh 1983: 111).

The second, Davisian strain (after the nineteenth-century political figure Thomas Davis) was not only explicitly political, it tended towards the chauvinistic and revolutionary as well. Davis's concepts of cultural separation and hostility towards things English was merged with Ferguson's notion that the Irish language was 'supra-factional and supra-sectarian' (MacDonagh 1983: 112), clearly the foundation of Hyde's insistence that political and religious issues be excluded from the revival movement. It was perhaps inevitable, however, that in any attempt to blend the two strains, the second would come to dominate. 'In practice one could not long preach de-Anglicization without slipping into anglophobia, or proclaim a cultural crusade without slipping into a political and constitutional one. ... The League inevitably manufactured separatists' (MacDonagh 1983: 112).

However much the political pressure in favour of Home Rule increased, and in spite of the clear political implications of the activities of the Gaelic League during this politically charged period, Hyde continued to insist that his work and the work of the League were purely cultural (Dunleavy and Dunleavy 1991: 11). Hyde, however, was a very complex man and his political beliefs can sometimes be difficult to sort out. As President of the Gaelic League he opposed physical force to promote the Nationalist cause, believing that far more could be accomplished through consensus. Yet Hyde wrote poetry under the pseudonym '*An Craoibhín*' in which he advocated the use of physical force (Dunleavy and Dunleavy 1991: 109).

This incongruity is probably a reflection of Hyde's own ambiguous feelings on political Nationalism (Mac Póilin 1997). MacDonagh suggests that while Hyde was realistic when it came to particulars, he was an unrealistic idealist in general (1983: 112). In any case, the pressure to make the Gaelic League overtly political increased during the period 1910–15. Still, Hyde believed that the League's policy of de-Anglicising Ireland was the best and most effective way to separate Ireland from England. He fervently believed that once Ireland began to think and act like a nation, the tide in favour of independence would be irresistible and might be achieved without the use of physical force (Dunleavy and Dunleavy 1991: 313; Ó Huallacháin 1994: 65). When Hyde felt that he could no longer keep the Gaelic League separate from the political maelstrom, he resigned from his position as president.

The apparent contradictions in Hyde's own political beliefs and in the politics of the Gaelic League help shed some light on the meanings of the words 'political' and 'apolitical' in the Irish language movement at the time. The association between the ideology of Nationalism and the Irish language had become so dominant that it was almost taken for granted as a 'natural' connection. In this context 'political' came to mean advocating physical force to achieve Nationalist ends, while 'apolitical' meant keeping the Irish language revival distanced from the advocates of violence. In spite of the insistence that Unionists were welcome in the movement, it was not long before Nationalism became an integral part of the Gaelic League. Most of its Protestant members eventually left the organization. The naturalization of Nationalism as part of the dominant ideology of the language revival meant that many felt they could no longer participate.

The powerful association between Irish Nationalism and the Irish language remains to this day, and it has once again become a serious issue of debate. This time, though, the meaning of 'political' is somewhat different.

'Politicizing the Irish language' can mean either associating it with Republicanism, or associating it with Nationalism in general, depending on one's perspective. In the effort to include Unionists, depoliticizing the language now often means disassociating it from Nationalism completely. The ambiguity of the meaning of 'political' and 'apolitical' can be a source of confusion, making the debate even more heated at the same time as it decreases the level of understanding between people. On the other hand, such ambiguity can also be beneficial, allowing people with different perspectives to find common ground, or at least the illusion of common ground.

Interestingly, Hyde is used by people of many different political views to justify their own stance. Hyde has been used by Nationalists and Unionists alike to suggest that the language revival movement has been hijacked by Republicans. He has been used by advocates of cultural discourse to prove that the Irish language is there for all the people of this island regardless of their political or religious persuasion, and used by Unionists to prove that Irish is a Republican language. The relationship between current texts and texts from this earlier period is clearly not a straightforward one, as many disparate meanings are read into the earlier debates about the significance of the Irish language to politics and Nationalism in Ireland.

In the ideology of cultural discourse, the Irish language must be kept strictly removed from party politics. The view of the relationship between politics and the language associated with cultural discourse is often strongly anti-Republican. The language ought to be kept wholly apolitical. Instead of naturalizing the relationship between Irish and Nationalism, this connection is challenged or denied, although some connection between romantic or cultural nationalism is implicit.

There are certain key words, concepts and arguments which indicate the use of cultural discourse: 'apolitical', 'non-political', 'depoliticize', 'beautiful language', 'heritage' and 'tradition', or 'cultural heritage' and 'cultural tradition' (as distinct from political heritage and traditions). Accusations that the language is being politicized, or attacks on specific individuals or groups for politicizing Irish, figure prominently. Anti-Republican discourse and the discourse of community relations are often associated with the language. A connection is frequently made between a person's interest in Irish and its inherent creativity, history, songs and literature. Speaking Irish is generally seen as a cultural activity, and it tends to be seen as an expression of ethnic or cultural identity (in contrast to the more dangerous and divisive political or nationalist expressions of identity).

I shall look in some detail at the more political use of cultural discourse in Chapter 5, but here are two examples of this discourse in its other, more romantic nationalist guise. A young housewife explained her interest in learning Irish: 'When I got into it, I realized that it is my language, it's our language, and I think it's a shame that we don't speak our own language. I enjoy speaking it. It's part of our culture.' A middle-aged teacher, whom I have called PROINSIAS, put it this way: 'I'd always promised myself to learn Irish and speak it, not through any sort of identity crisis, but because in it I find a certain inherent beauty and a different perspective for looking at the world.'

'YOU CAN'T HIJACK A LANGUAGE': RIGHTS DISCOURSE

In the previous two sections of this chapter, I introduced decolonizing and cultural discourses as constituting two sides of a debate about the relationship between politics and the Irish language. In this section, I will be looking at rights discourse, which is often used to side-step this debate and to open up new ideological avenues. There are two key, interconnected elements in this discourse which make it less straightforward than the other two.

The first element centres on efforts to break out of the confines of the political/apolitical dichotomy established by the first two discourses. In these discourses the terms of debate are more or less agreed – is Sinn Féin politicizing the language? Should politics be kept separate from the Irish language, or is the language an integral part of political struggle? In the third discourse, issues which lead into political/apolitical deadlock are side-stepped through a variety of different strategies, for example 'you can't hijack a language ...' or arguments favouring the 'multipoliticization' of Irish, as well as other techniques of avoidance.

The second element centres on efforts to broaden and reframe the debate over politics and the Irish language. In recent years this has been achieved primarily through the issue of rights for Irish speakers. Discourses of civil rights, human rights and minority rights have been adapted as a means of campaigning for the language and developing an ideology which challenges the confines of the dominant dichotomy.

There is a common accusation, made in some Irish language circles that Sinn Féin have 'hijacked' the language for their own political ends without genuine regard for the effect it might have on the language.

A person who favours cultural discourse is likely to agree with this statement, while someone who favours decolonizing discourse is likely to disagree. The most likely response of someone who favours rights discourse is to refute the idea that a language can be hijacked in the first place. As one of my interviewees exclaimed, 'I've got no time for people who criticize Sinn Féin for hijacking the language. What, can you put Irish in a little tin box, like *tiocfaidh ár lá*[2] or something?'

In a sense, people who say 'you can't hijack a language' are deliberately misunderstanding the accusation as a means of moving outside the restrictive framework of the debate. To address the accusation directly would mean becoming trapped in the political/apolitical dichotomy, so an alternative strategy of avoidance is used. The language as a symbol can, of course, be 'hijacked' in the sense that any symbol can be reinvested with new meanings. People who use this strategy choose in this context to deny this aspect of its symbolic significance.

The roots of rights discourse are not as historically deep as those of the other discourses. Evidence of decolonizing and cultural discourse can be found both at the turn of the century and in more recent debates over the relationship between politics and the Irish language. However, I have been unable to find evidence of a discourse similar to rights discourse preceding the current phase of the revival which roughly coincides with the start of the Troubles. The lack of evidence of rights discourse from earlier periods suggests that it has more recent origins. Certainly there have always been people who did not engage in the debate over politics and the Irish language, but silence seems to have been the main alternative available to them.

There are a number of possible explanations for the development of rights discourse. One is that it developed simply as a way of characterizing the Irish language revival movement and its history. In this view, the two extreme positions on the Irish language are portrayed as being in conflict, with the person doing the characterizing placed in a more moderate middle position. This explanation is inadequate, however, because it fails to account for the use of rights discourse in most contexts.

Another explanation is that people are attempting to break out of the older conventions of discourse about the Irish language. Inevitably, perhaps, the first two discourses have developed in close relationship with each other. Fairclough points out that 'discourse types tend to turn particular ways of drawing upon conventions and texts into routines, and to naturalize them' (1992: 85). The ideologies of cultural and decolonizing discourses have become crystallized into two opposing sides, and these two discourses carry with them an enormous amount of other ideological baggage. If a person draws too heavily or obviously from either discourse, it tends to imply that he or she agrees with the associated ideologies. When someone draws on decolonizing discourse, people tend to think they are Republican. When someone draws too heavily on cultural discourse, people tend to assume that they condemn Sinn Féin.

These first two discourses have congealed into a form that is heavily laden with meaning, creating a restrictive framework within which it is difficult to manoeuvre. Fairclough suggests that one way to deal with being in a problematic position in relation to existing discourse structures is to be creative, 'to put together familiar discourses in novel combinations as a means of finding new ways of doing things to replace the now problematic old ones' (1989: 171). Existing conventions may be adapted in new ways to suit the new circumstances, for example by drawing on certain discourses in situations which usually preclude their use, or by combining existing discourse conventions into new configurations. The inherent intertextuality of texts means that creativity is 'built in' as an option, since the process of reinterpreting previous texts and anticipating future texts is an intrinsic part of every speech act.

It is important to stress that this sort of creative process has resulted not only in the formation of rights discourse, but in the transformation of the first two discourses as well. The relationship between the three discourses is a dialectical one. Decolonizing and cultural discourses could be seen as thesis and antithesis, while rights discourse is to a certain extent a synthesis of these two, combined with other discourses common to Northern Irish politics. Rights discourse is part of the process of contesting the bifurcation created by decolonizing and cultural discourses. It combines elements of the first two, but both new and old elements are added – new, like the talk of Irish as a minority language in the context of Europe, and old, like the harking back to civil rights, the comparison with the status of other citizens in Britain, and the use of various Nationalist discourses. Rights discourse resists and challenges the older models of discourse, and they in turn must be adapted to deal with this newer discourse.

A third explanation for the growth and development of rights discourse is simply that there are now more *Gaeilgeoirí* than ever before, and rights discourse reflects a widening range of opinion found in a larger and more diverse group. These three explanations are not mutually exclusive, and I am inclined to believe that all three go some way towards explaining the development of rights discourse. Because the first and third explanations are relatively limited, the second explanation – that people are attempting to break out of older discourse conventions – is the most important.

It seems that in more recent years people began to see the existing conventions of the political/apolitical debate as too restrictive, and not representative of the way they were feeling about the Irish language and the political situation. Many people do see Irish as relevant to the political situation in Northern Ireland, but do not want to make an association between the language and Republicanism. This is problematic if the accepted conventions of discourse fix the language in either an apolitical position or juxtapose it with Republican ideologies.

This sort of alternative position is articulated by ANTÓIN. A man in his late fifties, ANTÓIN was among the original group of couples who conceived of and built the Shaws Road *Gaeltacht*.

> The whole Civil Rights era tended to pass us by, because we were more interested in our own projects and the cultural aspects, rather than one man one vote. We weren't involved but we were aware that they were going on. There were people with a political frame of mind, with nationalist politics or socialist politics, while you'd find in the Irish-speaking community, we were interested in Irish language affairs and weren't so much interested in party politics at all, or even in the broad political questions. The task we had set ourselves was so enormous that we wouldn't have had time to get involved in these things anyway. Nevertheless, when the Troubles broke out it did affect everyone, with burning outs, massive population shifts. And we had just moved into the new houses at the time, so that we were caught up in the whole thing. The response that we had to that as a group of Irish speakers was that we couldn't divorce ourselves from what was going on around us. When Bombay Street [in the lower Falls area of west Belfast] was burnt down, we decided that the best contribution we could make to alleviate the distress then was to help rebuild the street. Because we had some expertise, we decided to use that expertise to help rebuild when the City Council had decided not to rebuild and to use that area as a buffer zone between the two communities.
>
> ...
>
> We felt the Irish language had to become more than just a cultural pursuit, that it had to become involved in people's lives, it had to become involved in the well-being of the general community if it was to be taken seriously. Looking back on it, that was the attitude, but

as well as that it was the general feeling that we had to do something constructive to help a community that had come under attack and had been dealt a fairly sharp blow. People who didn't believe in a violent response to that were forced to examine how they were going to deal with this traumatic event in a non-violent way, and I'd say that the vast majority of Irish speakers wouldn't be interested in a violent response, so they picked a more constructive way to help the community. [Quote 6]

As just one example of how the relationship between Irish and the political situation can be conceived outside of Republican discourse, Quote 6 suggests the difficulties a person like ANTÓIN might have if he tried to express these views within the conventions of either decolonizing or cultural discourse. How do you suggest that the Troubles and your own beliefs as a Nationalist have something to do with your view of the importance and relevance of Irish within the restrictive framework of the first two discourses? Rights discourse has helped to broaden the debate to such an extent that alternative perspectives can be more easily developed and articulated, whether this is done through rights discourse (as is usually the case) or through the use of other discourses.

In the early part of the century Hyde himself tried, and eventually failed, to forge a path wide enough for the full spectrum of political opinion in Ireland to have a say, but the strength of the political/apolitical dichotomy prevailed in his day. Today, challenges to the dominant dichotomy have made it easier to express a view associating Irish with politics in the wider sense, without automatically being associated with Republicanism. Instead of being depoliticized, it could be said that the ideological associations made with the Irish language are being expanded and 'multipoliticized'.

With its emphasis on pragmatics and on the survival of the language, rights discourse is the most important medium of 'multipoliticization'. Indeed, it does tend to be used in a very political way. In terms of party politics, users of rights discourse often justify making Irish part of a party political agenda – in fact, they tend to encourage all parties to do so as a means of promoting Irish, and weakening the connection made between the language and Sinn Féin. In terms of the relationship between politics in general and the language, there is some naturalization of the connection to Nationalism, but there are also attempts to break this connection and widen the appeal of Irish. It is neither pro- nor anti-Republican, this particular issue being side-stepped and reframed as described above. Speaking Irish is seen as a right, a form of freedom of expression. In keeping with the notion that associations with the language ought to be broadened, individuals may see speaking Irish as an expression of national, ethnic, or cultural identity, or a combination of these.

Talk of civil rights for Irish speakers is commonly associated with this discourse, especially with reference to the funding of Irish schools and the right to use Irish when in contact with the state (for example on census forms, in court and in government offices). Comparisons are often made with the status of Welsh and Scots Gaelic as a way of asserting that the British government is discriminating against Irish speakers and, by implication, all Irish people in Northern Ireland. Connections are also made with the issue of minority rights in a European context. Rights discourse is particularly strong in calls for parity of esteem, and in efforts to use the Irish language as a sort of litmus test for equality in the current political negotiations. It resonates with Irish speakers and many non-Irish-speaking Nationalists alike, making it a prominent voice in current debates.

Rights discourse emphasizes Irish as a living language of everyday communication. All languages are considered to be means of expression, and it should be possible to express all things in all languages. This side-steps somewhat the issue of whether or not it is appropriate to use Irish in a political context or for political ends. Cultural discourse attempts to restrict the appropriate subject matter and ideological stance associated with the Irish language, while decolonizing discourse is limited by its strong association with Republicanism. Rights discourse, on the other hand, attempts to broaden the range of appropriate subject areas and ideological positions. If a person believes that the language should not be constrained in any way, then it should not be banned from the political arena, or indeed from any other arena. Often an analogy is made with English. If one can discuss both Republicanism and Unionism in English without implying that the language is the sole preserve of either group, then one can do the same in Irish.

Rights discourse is also signalled by particular key words, concepts and arguments: 'rights', 'civil rights' and 'human rights', 'you can't hijack a language', 'equality', 'parity of esteem', the responsibility of government to support minority cultures and uphold minority rights, and a denial that Irish can be wholly apolitical in the current sociopolitical context in Northern Ireland. Attempts are sometimes made to separate political allegiance from ethnic identity. And, importantly, the promotion of Irish is put above all other political and cultural considerations.

The following examples illustrate some of these characteristics. During a discussion of Sinn Féin's involvement with the Irish language, one man in his forties told me:

> I have a problem with people who *don't* run around and pro-mote the language. To people who say Sinn Féin has hijacked the language, I'd say go *you* and hijack the language. But I wouldn't even accept the charge that they have. I would urge people who do think so to go and try to beat them at their own game. [Quote 7]

During a discussion about the rights of minority language speakers and the responsibilities of government, another interviewee said:

> **C O'R**: Do you see any conflict in trying to get the British govern-ment to do things in support of Irish, when you say you believe they don't belong here in the first place?
> **Answer**: No, because we have to face the reality that we live under British rule whether we like it or not. If they left, then we'd have to face the same problems with an Irish administration. Whatever administration is there, it's there to provide us services. It owes us services because we pay for those services. The state claims that cultural diversity is a nice thing, but now they have to pay for it. They need to have a civil servant in every department that speaks Irish, and that costs money. [Quote 8]

Because rights discourse is somewhat more complex than decolonizing or cultural discourse, examples of it tend to be more diverse. For now, these two samples should suffice. I shall go into more detail and provide more examples of the use of rights discourse in Chapter 6.

CONCEPTUALIZING THE RELATIONSHIP BETWEEN DISCOURSES

It is possible to conceptualize the first two discourses as two ends of a continuum, ranging from the strongly politicized to the avowedly apolitical. Rights discourse, however, is a bit more problematic. If a continuum model is used, rights discourse becomes little more than a watered down or weaker version of decolonizing discourse, political in its outlook but perhaps not so extreme or dogmatic.

Decolonizing discourse and rights discourse do have much in common with each other. Both involve an overtly political stance towards the

Irish language in the sense that they acknowledge that it is appropriate to use the language in a political context, a position that contradicts that of cultural discourse. Both decolonizing and rights discourse tend to be placed in opposition to the status quo, while aspects of cultural discourse have become increasingly accepted as part of the status quo. Both rights and decolonizing discourse exist within a broadly Nationalist milieu. While decolonizing discourse would be heavily associated with Republicanism, rights discourse is more generally Nationalist and is more likely to be seen (by some people anyway) as at least partially separate from Nationalist politics. Although drawing heavily on the discourse of romantic nationalism, cultural discourse is often portrayed as being removed from Nationalism, or at least able to separate Nationalist politics from Irish language issues.

However, to view rights discourse as simply a diluted version of decolonizing discourse would be to underestimate its significance. It would not do justice to the different ideological underpinnings of each discourse, and it would seriously obscure differences perceived by the users of these discourses. Importantly, *Gaeilgeoirí* perceive the two as being different in their own models used to describe alternative perspectives on the language.

In addition, it is important to remember that the first two discourses developed at least in part in opposition to each other, crystallizing around the debates of the 1980s, while rights discourse developed at least in part as a means of contesting this bifurcation. This suggests that rights discourse is more than just a weaker version of decolonizing discourse. The linear model of a continuum with opposites at either pole does not adequately convey a sense of the dynamic process of innovation, adjustment, feedback and borrowing between discourses.

The different ideological underpinnings of decolonizing and rights discourses are important in distinguishing the two. While both are clearly nationalist in the most general sense of the word, and both are also Nationalist in the sense that this label is used in Northern Ireland, decolonizing discourse tends to have a strong Republican slant. Rights discourse, on the other hand, tends to range more widely from Republican to Nationalist, but in use it would rarely if ever be characterized as solely Republican.

Another important distinction between the two is decolonizing discourse's characterization of the Irish language revival as part of a wider, cohesive struggle against British oppression and the British presence in Ireland. While the revival of the language is seen as important in its own right, it is still placed firmly in the context of a specific form of resistance – Republicanism. Speaking or learning Irish makes you part of that resistance, seemingly whether you intend it to or not. This is in contrast to rights discourse, where Irish *is* the struggle; any other campaigns or political outcomes are generally seen as secondary. There are certain desirable political consequences which hinge on the status and survival of Irish, for example parity of esteem for Nationalists, but the struggle in support of the language is of primary importance. Certain political circumstances or actions might be seen as beneficial or even necessary to the survival of Irish – for some this might be some form of a united Ireland, for example, or the official recognition of Irish-medium schools – but the primary focus is on the language and its welfare regardless of the political context in which the struggle must be waged.

To put it another way, the essential difference between discourses is in the conceptualization of the relationship between the Irish language and politics, and between the language and Irish culture. In decolonizing discourse, Irish is nested firmly within party politics in general and Republicanism in particular. In cultural discourse, an attempt is made to remove Irish from party politics and to place it into the realm of culture, and occasionally into the politics of reconciliation. In rights discourse, politics in the general sense (as opposed to party politics) are nested within the struggle to revive Irish, which is seen as the primary objective and eclipses all other considerations in terms of importance.

4 Decolonizing Discourse

PROPAGANDISTS AND PROFESSIONALS

The politicians and political activists of Sinn Féin whom I shall discuss in the first part of this chapter are to a greater or lesser extent professionals in the use of discourse. They are in many ways more conscious of the process of discourse production than most others would be, since part of their job is to sway people's opinions. Undoubtedly they are familiar with the discourses associated with earlier Irish language and Nationalist movements, as well as the ideologies which informed and grew out of them. In some instances, they are consciously drawing upon these discourses, whether it is explicitly stated or not.

The first example of decolonizing discourse which I would like to examine is from a Sinn Féin booklet reporting on the findings of a one-day seminar for Irish language learners which took place in west Belfast in 1984. Part of this booklet was written by TOMÁS, Sinn Féin Cultural Officer at the time, and part by another Sinn Féin politician. Both parts contain relevant material, but I shall focus on the section written by TOMÁS in order to make a comparison with an interview I conducted with him almost ten years later, in November 1993.

Looking first at the context in which these texts were produced, the date of the booklet is significant for a number of reasons. First, the social and political context of 1984 was quite different from late 1993, when I spoke to TOMÁS in person. The Irish language movement has grown and developed considerably since 1984, and political developments over the years have changed the circumstances in which the discourses are used. Sinn Féin has also developed and changed as a party, both in its main political policies and in the Cultural Department, which takes responsibility for Irish language issues.

A second reason for the significance of the booklet's date has to do with TOMÁS himself. The interview I conducted with him in 1993 is different in many ways from what he writes in the booklet, even though much of it is drawn from the same discourse. It is possible that the newer and perhaps more fashionable rights discourse (which will be discussed in detail in Chapter 6) has influenced the tone of the interview I had with him. Another possibility is that knowledge of his audience influenced his use of discourse. Age may be another factor. TOMÁS had only recently left university in 1984, and was relatively new to an active role in Republican politics and the Irish language revival. He is now a relatively high-profile member of Sinn Féin. The experience of ten years is likely to have influenced TOMÁS's viewpoints, and therefore influenced his use of discourse in the interview.

Keeping these factors in mind, the following quote is a fairly conventional example of decolonizing discourse. It is taken from the opening essay in the booklet.

> Sinn Féin is pledged to resisting not only economical [*sic*] and political oppression but also the cultural and social controls imposed by the British and their allies on the Irish people. ... The actual form which cultural resistance in our communities should take is largely dependent on the resources available. However, it is our contention that each individual who masters the learning of the Irish language has made an important personal contribution towards the reconquest of Ireland.
>
> (Sinn Féin 1984: 2) [Quote 1]

This quote demonstrates the highly politicized view of the language which dominates this discourse, placing Irish firmly into the arsenal of cultural weapons to fight British oppression of the Irish people. Learning Irish becomes a political act, a 'contribution towards the reconquest of Ireland'. Irish culture is seen to be under threat from British control and oppression, and must be reclaimed in the same way that political and economic control must be recaptured from the British. The Irish language, as the most crucial symbol of Irish identity and culture, plays a key role in cultural resistance.

The idea that Irish is part of the struggle against the British is a frequent theme in decolonizing discourse. It is elaborated on by the second author in the same booklet.

> Make no mistake about it, either you speak Irish or you speak English. Every minute you are speaking English you are contributing to the sum total of English culture/language in this island. Every moment you speak Irish you are contributing to something that is distinctly ours.
>
> (Sinn Féin 1984: 4) [Quote 2]

Put this way, the inability or unwillingness to speak Irish can be seen as a betrayal of the Irish people and of the Republican cause. This passage seems to imply that it is impossible to say anything in Irish which does not in some small way support the struggle against the British. Conversely, it implies that whatever one says in English, no matter how well intentioned, in some way supports the British presence. The actual content of what is said seems to be largely irrelevant – it is the language in which you say it that counts. The logical consequences of this belief are quite far-reaching, and for a Republican might offer a compelling reason to learn the language or, if this is not possible, to ensure that one's children learn it. For those who are not Republicans, this can be a deeply disturbing assertion, because it attributes a particular political consequence to the act of speaking Irish with which they might not agree.

While each essay contained within the booklet is signed by an individual author, the booklet itself is produced and distributed by Sinn Féin. Strictly speaking, then, the content is not individually produced in a straightforward manner. In all likelihood it was written within the parameters of party policy on the Irish language. It is best viewed, therefore, as an individually produced text written to fit within collectively determined guidelines. This makes the text written by TOMÁS somewhat different from the interview to which I refer below. In terms of audience, the booklet is designed for collective consumption, while the interview material is meant to be consumed first by an individual (me), and then by an unknown collectivity outside the control of the speaker, when it is ultimately used for publication.

The quotes from the Sinn Féin booklet clearly draw upon historical texts, such as Quote 2, Chapter 3, although the authors of the booklet make no direct reference to any specific other text. Instead, the voice of the text producer is used on its own, without any clear indicator that another text or texts are being drawn upon. However, both the style and the ideational meaning of the Sinn Féin text, and the turn of the century Gaelic League text, are quite similar. Compare, for example, the following two quotes: 'The Irish language is a political weapon of the first importance against English encroachment' (*circa* 1913, quoted in O'Huallacháin 1994: 66–7) and 'each individual who masters the learning of the Irish language has made an important personal contribution to the reconquest of Ireland' (Sinn Féin 1984: 2).

Turning now to the 1993 interview with TOMÁS, I shall start by examining the autobiographical material which he supplied in the course of our conversation. He explained to me that he had no family history of interest in Irish. He describes his family as 'fairly well assimilated northern Catholics', supporting this by mentioning that his eldest brother has a British passport and went to an English university. His own interest in the Irish language, he says, was probably the result of a combination of school and particular teachers,[1] with the political situation being an added impetus. He goes on to say:

> It was a period of intense, almost open armed conflict at the time
> in Andersonstown [west Belfast], and we used to have IRA patrols
> on the streets ... So you had that, and a very oppressive and delib-
> erately punitive British army presence in the area, and you would
> be frequently stopped and messed about. All of that added up to an
> atmosphere where we were becoming politically aware, and becom-
> ing increasingly hostile to the British government. One of the ways
> we could strengthen our own Irishness in the face of this was to learn
> Irish. That's looking back, but I don't know if I took a conscious
> decision at the time. It's very hard to rationalize or explain all that
> looking back. [Quote 3]

While school influenced TOMÁS's interest in the language, his home
life did not. While not a very important point, it is interesting since
many people do first develop an interest in Irish in the home, either
from parents, older siblings or from a general atmosphere which is seen
as conducive to developing such an interest. Perhaps more significantly,
he sees his own political identity and awareness developing hand in
hand with his sense of Irishness and his interest in the Irish language.
Armed conflict and negative encounters with the British army are
directly linked to a nascent interest in Irish. Background information
like this suggests that the speaker might favour the use of decolonizing
discourse.

The connection between TOMÁS's involvement with Irish and
his developing political viewpoints is further elaborated later in the
interview.

> I got involved in Sinn Féin because during the hunger strike there
> were a lot of Irish speakers who were involved in the campaign *as*
> Irish speakers. After the hunger strike, some of those people gravi-
> tated towards Sinn Féin, joined Sinn Féin, and then within it set up
> an Irish section in the Cultural Department which was involved in
> Irish language issues, sort of lobbying around, and trying to develop
> a policy in relation to Irish culture. [Quote 4]

TOMÁS's interest in the Irish language developed along with political
and Republican activism. For him as for many others, politics and
Irish, and in some instances the language and Republicanism, are
intertwined in such a way that they cannot be fully separated, even if
this was to be desired (and for many, it is not).

Towards the start of the interview, TOMÁS was careful to play down the role of Sinn Féin and Republicans in the Irish language revival. His account of Sinn Féin's contribution tends to be more modest than it is later on. At the same time, it is possible to detect a sense of pride about the significance of that contribution.

I think you would find there was always a fairly steady line of Republicans who believed that Irish was an important part of Republicanism, just as there were always those who believe socialism was an important part of Republicanism. [Quote 5]

The sense of caution is most likely a reaction to the strong criticism which has been levelled at the party from some quarters of the Irish language movement for their over-politicization of the Irish language issue. A common accusation is that Sinn Féin uses the Irish language as a 'political football' to further its own aims, without regard for the damage it does to the reputation of the language itself and to other Irish speakers. Understandably, many who do not hold Republican views do not want to be associated with Sinn Féin just because they speak Irish or campaign for the language.

On the other hand, Sinn Féin generally do not attempt to claim full credit for the success of the movement or its many achievements. In spite of the fact that the great majority of Irish language activities have little or nothing to do with Sinn Féin, it is possible that someone unfamiliar with the Irish language movement might think otherwise from the impression that is sometimes given in the media. Ironically, the rather vocal and outspoken condemnations in the press of Sinn Féin's use of the Irish language has helped to contribute to their reputation as champions of the language. This strong reaction against Sinn Féin has not only affected the use of decolonizing discourse, it has had a powerful influence on the use and creation of cultural discourse, which I shall discuss in the next chapter.

TOMÁS is aware of the dynamics of the situation, and he does attempt to use the predictable negative reaction of Unionists (and others) to his and his party's benefit. For example, in reply to a question about how he became involved in Belfast City Council, TOMÁS responded by talking about representation for Irish speakers in local government and his party's commitment to this, saying:

We made a number of modest demands, and the council of course responded with a practical ban on the Irish language. And we have spent the last six years contesting that and embarrassing them, and proving that this is a bilingual city, that there are two languages here at least, and that the council policy that this is a Protestant council for a Protestant people and a British council for a British people isn't in agreement. [Quote 6]

Later in the interview, TOMÁS again emphasized the role of Republicanism in the Irish language revival, but this time more forcefully:

The reality is that the Irish-medium schools are packed with the children of Republicans, that many Republicans have made a conscious decision to learn Irish, especially in the 1980s, that you can't find an Irish language organization in the North which isn't being driven by Republicans or which Republicans aren't involved in and the place where Irish is strongest are the places where Republicanism is strongest. [Quote 7]

The change evident in the strength of the statement and the style of the discourse between this quote and Quote 5,[2] also about the role of Republicans in the revival of Irish, shows how context can affect discourse even within a relatively short space of time during the same conversation and within the same discourse. Quote 5 came directly after a measured statement about Sinn Féin's involvement in Belfast City Council (see Quote 6), a statement intended to outline briefly what TOMÁS sees as Sinn Féin's reasonable and 'modest' plan to promote Irish in the Council. Quote 7, however, followed a much more impassioned soliloquy about the association of politics with Irish, during which he uses an analogy with South American literacy campaigns to illustrate his point (see Quote 8 below), as well as an appeal to democratic and civil rights. In the course of this soliloquy, TOMÁS also makes a number of specific condemnations. While in Quote 6 about Belfast City Hall he refers to a rather generic 'them' as being the opposition, just before Quote 7 TOMÁS severely criticizes British rule in Ireland in general, and the Cultural Traditions Group in particular.

The following quote illustrates TOMÁS's analogy between Irish and literacy in the context of a discussion about politics and the Irish language:

I'd say there are three camps, those who don't worry about the connection between Irish and politics too much, those who are very against it, and those who believe it is every political party's duty to support it. I'd fall into the last camp, as would John Alderdice [an Alliance Party Councillor], who voted to have bilingual notepaper at the last Council meeting. It's a bit like literacy in South America. There's those who see no point, those who think that they should be taught to read and write, but that if they use it to write about politics, that would be communism. Then there's those who see it as a form of empowerment, and I think the analogy is quite good with the North. There are those who say you can speak the language, but you can't promote it in ways that, say, Sir Patrick Mayhew would find distasteful. There are those who say don't let them learn Irish at all, like Sammy Wilson, or let them learn Irish but it must be corralled, like taking money off *Glór na nGael* because that's not the type of Irish we wish to produce. Then there are those that say everyone should learn Irish, that you wouldn't be losing your English you'd only be gaining, and that if in learning Irish it educates you about the nature of British rule in Ireland, that the British shouldn't be here, and it increases your own sense of identity and self worth, so much the better. The bottom line is people are entitled to learn Irish, and you can't limit that or limit the people who have access to it, or try to say there are certain things you can't do with the language. ... You should be able to learn Irish as a basic democratic right, and once you've learned it you are entitled to do whatever you wish to do with the language. My position is even before you consider whose country this is, it's a very basic civil right to have an education in Irish. You should be able to deal with the government in Irish, you should be allowed to have access to radio and TV in Irish, and the petty restrictions on Irish should be lifted. [Quote 8]

The importance of the concept of intertextuality comes into play in the above three quotes. In Quote 8 TOMÁS engages with unspecified texts attributed to DUP councillor Sammy Wilson and British government representatives such as Sir Patrick Mayhew, as well as historical and contemporary leftist discourses on empowerment and oppression when referring to literacy and civil rights. His reference to Sammy Wilson probably springs from the latter's well-publicized, disparaging remarks about the Irish language.[3] Patrick Mayhew stands in as a symbol of all British government representatives and their attitudes towards the language. The direct association which TOMÁS makes between literacy and Irish implies a number of other associations which can be seen to reflect positively on Irish language campaigners in general, and TOMÁS and Sinn Féin in particular.

First, the association with literacy campaigns aligns the Irish language movement with struggles against institutionalized repression, and with anti-colonial and revolutionary movements in the Third World. The association suggests not only good Leftist credentials, but also assigns a certain status to Irish language campaigners, making them akin to those campaigning for basic civil and human rights in Latin America. In equating supporters of Irish with supporters of literacy, he is also juxtaposing in a most unflattering way opponents of Irish with opponents of literacy, and therefore with members of or apologists for repressive regimes. The analogy brings to mind some very powerful images, especially for someone who might be sympathetic to such struggles in Latin America.

The association between Irish and literacy also suggests an attempt to communicate the high level of importance and value placed on the Irish language. Irish is not just a symbol or a cultural artifact. It is an essential means of communication, and like literacy in a Latin American country under a dictatorship, it can be an avenue for liberation, growth and enlightenment on both a personal and collective level. TOMÁS himself talks directly about literacy as a form of empowerment, and by making this analogy implies that Irish can be too.

In Quote 7 above, TOMÁS engages with the debate about the appropriateness of associating Irish with Republican politics, indirectly criticizing those who detract from the involvement of Republicans and the contribution they have made. Quote 6 engages with comments and debate on the subject of Irish in Belfast City Council, an area where Sinn Féin has been accused of seeking to make political capital on the back of the language. TOMÁS also reworks the famous quote 'a Protestant Parliament for a Protestant people', which originally referred to Stormont, into a comment on the status of Irish in the North and on Belfast City Council.

Much has been made of Sinn Féin's politicization of the Irish language, so it is interesting to point out that in the course of the interview, when TOMÁS discusses politics and the Irish language, he implicitly suggests that other individuals and institutions do the same. He implies that the British government engages in the politics of Irish ('like taking money off *Glór na nGael*, because that's not the type of Irish we wish to produce' ... 'the petty restrictions on Irish should be lifted'), and special condemnation is reserved for the Cultural Traditions Group ('The cultural cringe people at Cultural Traditions see fit to give a £300 grant to the West Belfast Community Festival, but would give £6,000 to Ian Adamson,[4] whose books have been endorsed by the National Front, to go and write another one'). Politicians in Northern Ireland also come in for criticism ('There are those who say don't let them learn Irish at all, like Sammy Wilson'). Without explicitly saying so, the discourse that TOMÁS uses suggests that Sinn Féin are not the only ones who use Irish to achieve political ends.

While TOMÁS draws quite heavily on decolonizing discourse both in the interview and in his earlier piece of writing, other discourses are used as well. For example the comment 'everyone should learn Irish. You wouldn't be losing your English, you'd only be gaining' is more characteristic of cultural discourse. He also draws on the discourse of civil rights, which would be more commonly associated with rights discourse ('You should be able to learn Irish as a basic democratic right', 'it is a basic civil right to have an education in Irish. You should be able to deal with the government in Irish. You should be allowed to have access to radio and TV in Irish and the petty restrictions on Irish should be lifted'). TOMÁS also incorporates particular types of discourse which are commonly found when people talk about Irish, no matter which Irish language discourse they draw upon. For example he mentions the importance of language to identity ('If … it [learning Irish] increases your own sense of identity and self worth, so much the better').

THE NON-PROFESSIONALS

While the professional exponents of a discourse participate quite actively in the political field and have a significant impact on the meanings invested in discourses, ordinary people – the non-professionals – are also involved. They may or may not accept the versions created by the professionals, using discourses in a way that suits their own conceptions and beliefs about the world. Non-professionals interested in the Irish language revival movement actively engage with the texts produced by professionals like TOMÁS, interpreting them both directly and indirectly through their own speech.

As with TOMÁS, the hunger strikes had a profound impact on COLM, a school teacher in his thirties, who became involved with the language in the early 1980s.

> My way of challenging British rule in Ireland is being Irish, not just in games and music but with the language, which is sort of your first mode of national identity. I remember at the time of the hunger strike I saw it written on the wall, 'Everyone has their part to play'. At the time I was at the end of school, and one of the clubs was an Irish language club which was very relaxed and informal, just spoken

language and the teacher was very interested in the language. From there my interest started. [Quote 9]

The slogan he refers to is a paraphrase of a quote attributed to Bobby Sands.[5] The slogan still takes pride of place next to a massive mural of Sands on the side of the Sinn Féin offices on the Falls Road.[6] COLM goes on to say:

> At the time of the hunger strikes it was a political reaction with me, because Irish was the language I should be speaking and it's the least I could do for these men who were dying. I wanted to make it clear that I supported them standing up for their civil rights and human rights. If this hadn't happened I don't think that the Irish language would be as strong as it is today. [Quote 10]

Another formative experience came on a school trip to France. While on the metro he and a number of friends started to make fun of some punks who were sitting near them. They were very surprised when the punks turned around and told them off in perfect English, calling them 'English bastards'. He and his friends protested that they were not English, they were Irish. The punks asked if they were Irish, why were they speaking English, and a conversation on language ensued. COLM was impressed that the punks, who were actually Dutch, were fluent not only in Dutch and English but French as well. After explaining to them why they do not speak Irish in Ireland anymore, 'that's when I decided to come home and learn my own language'. Experiences abroad such as this seem to be a significant motivating factor for quite a number of people learning Irish.

Quite by chance, COLM met up with a family of prominent *Gaeilgeoirí*. They took him under their wing and taught him Irish on regular visits to their home. COLM is still close to this family, and expressed gratitude for the way they shared the Irish language with him. He sees it as a sign of their dedication and great love for the language that they were willing to spend time teaching him simply because he was interested. COLM, who works in a primary school which has no tradition of teaching or promoting Irish, now makes an effort to bring Irish into the classroom whenever he can.

COLM, like PÓL below, defends the association of Republicanism with the Irish language by saying that accusations against Sinn Féin are unfounded.

> People accuse Sinn Féin and people who are Nationalist minded of hijacking the language. No one hijacked it, it's theirs just like it's

anybody else's. The fact is that they were interested enough to do something about it. I don't like this yapping from people I see are using the language equally as a political football. It happens to be mainly Catholics who are connected with government circles, or some teachers who say Sinn Féin have put people off the language or that it's a Sinn Féin language. The ULTACH Trust are almost making the language a prostitute, selling it to some people yet keeping it from others with their money which they won't give to all organizations. ... As far as I'm concerned there's no one stopping anyone from learning it. That's only an excuse. [Quote 11]

While COLM and PÓL use the assertion that 'you can't hijack a language' to defend the association between Sinn Féin and the Irish language, others use the same assertion to side-step the issue of politics and the language altogether. This will be discussed in greater detail in Chapter 5.

PÓL is a teacher in his late thirties. He told me that he came from a Republican family with a GAA background who all had 'a wee bit of Irish', although it was not spoken in the home. He describes the school he attended as having 'an Irish background', with a favourable feeling towards the Irish language, Irish dancing and the GAA. He believes his love for Irish developed out of this background. Christianity, republican[7] politics, Gaelic sports and the Irish language are all still very important parts of his life. For him, all of these things are linked.[8]

Like TOMÁS, an interest in politics developed at the same time as an interest in the language. Time spent in *Gaeltacht* colleges, the experience of being a Catholic and of the arrival of British troops mingle together as important influences:

From about 13 or 14 going to the *Gaeltacht* made me think about using Irish all of the time, and the British soldiers came on the street about that time as well, so I started to read about Patrick Pearse and 1916 and developed republican ideas and Irish ideas. [Quote 12]

There was always that love for the Irish language from the beginning, as part of yourself, but then when the British came it was a bit of anti-Englishness and love for your country. There was oppression of Catholics by Protestants, and your own brothers and sisters not getting jobs because of their address or because they went to a Catholic school. It was a strong Catholic thing as well, the Catholic and the Irish thing were tied together. [Quote 13]

In the course of the interview, I asked PÓL if he was involved in activities related to the Irish language. He spoke about being involved in *An Cumann Gaelach* while he was attending the Queen's University of Belfast, and about teaching.

> After university I spent most of the time teaching voluntary. It was seen as wrong to teach Irish for money. What you got from the people of Donegal for free you shouldn't be making money for yourself from. I spent a long time teaching voluntary in places like *Cluain Ard* and in people's houses. ... There was the war going on as well and people giving up their time to fight, so if you weren't going to get involved militarily people would think you weren't doing anything. Being involved militarily was seen by some as the best thing you could do for your country, but others would say that teaching Irish was the best thing you could do. [Quote 14]

From this passage it is clear that PÓL is in broad agreement with much of the sentiments expressed in decolonizing discourse, and in the final sentence he draws quite clearly from this discourse. Most people involved with the Irish language would see nothing contentious in the first four sentences of this quote. They express widely held beliefs about the ethics of the movement and the role of the teacher in spreading the language. But for PÓL, there is another meaning associated with giving of your time and knowledge to teach Irish, and that is giving of your time to contribute to the Republican struggle.

Later in the interview, in the course of talking about *Cluain Ard*, PÓL touches on the issue of Republicanism and the language in a different way:

> People say that Irish has to be kept out of politics, but is English kept out of politics? Don't people say what they want in English? Why shouldn't they say what they want in Irish? It's this sacred cow sort of thing, you're only allowed to talk about Irish in Irish, don't talk about Republicanism, or if you are going to talk about anything in the world, don't talk about anything that's contentious .... This thing about Sinn Féin hijacking the language, how can anybody hijack a language? You speak a language and you say what you think. If more Republicans than anyone else speak Irish is that the Republicans' fault? But that's what they're trying to say. If I spoke French or German, it would be because I was interested in French or German. I speak Irish because I'm Irish, and that's a political statement. It's not an anti-English statement, it's an Irish statement.

I'm Irish and I want to speak my own language. I want to speak French and Spanish and German for different reasons, because I'd like to speak to Spanish people and German people in their own language. I want to speak Irish because it's mine, because it's the language of my country. And if that's hijacking a language, I don't know. You're supposed to say, 'I speak Irish but there's nothing political about it.' Of course it's political! Of course you want to speak your own language. ... Irish should be used for everything. If you can't promote what you believe in, what use is the language? A language is for saying your deepest feelings, isn't it? But if your deep feelings are Republican and you say it, and the same thing, if your deep feelings are Loyalist, why shouldn't you say it in Irish? [Quote 15]

I quote this passage at length because of the creative way in which PÓL combines decolonizing discourse with rights discourse to enhance his argument. He uses arguments that would be strongly associated with rights discourse, such as 'you can't hijack a language' and 'people should be able to express anything in a language' to rationalize and justify expressing a Republican viewpoint in Irish and using Irish in politics ('if you can't promote what you believe in, what use is the language?').

Once again, the concept of intertextuality contributes to our understanding of this passage. In this case PÓL is engaging in an ongoing debate about politics, Republicanism and the Irish language, taking the position that Irish is appropriately associated with politics. He argues against unspecified other texts which claim it is not by contextualizing the politicized aspects in talk more associated with rights discourse. He indirectly represents discourses from Republican thought, as well as rights and decolonizing discourses about the Irish language. This sort of mingling of discourses to achieve a desired end is probably more typical than the clear-cut use of one discourse or another, especially in the talk of non-professionals who would tend to be monitoring their speech far less.

CONCLUSION

Decolonizing discourse is historically deep, both ideologically and in the ways of talking which characterize it. There was a resurgence in its use in the 1980s, when Sinn Féin became more actively involved in the Irish language revival and began to reformulate the idea that anti-imperialist struggle should take place on three fronts – military, political and cultural. The high profile given by Sinn Féin both to the language and to this ideological construction of its meaning and importance stimulated the revival of the debate on the relationship between the Irish language and politics, this time with particular reference to the current sociopolitical situation in Northern Ireland.

Scott (1990) offers a way of understanding the relationship between ideology and discourse, and between dominant and alternative discourses, in his reworking of the Gramscian notion of ideological hegemony. He argues that it is often in the best interests of the weaker sections of society at least to appear to consent to their own domination. Existing power relations are reinforced in the public domain by participation in and engagement with dominant discourses, what Scott calls the 'public transcript'. It would be wrong, however, to assume that participation in this public performance means that people wholly accept the dominant order and are incapable of imagining an alternative. To understand fully the public performances of the dominant and subordinate groups, Scott argues, it is necessary to examine the 'hidden transcript' of both groups.

The hidden transcript is not shared or played out in the public domain, and it refers to the discourses of the weak and the powerful alike. While the public transcript requires that we wear a 'mask' while in the presence of the powerful (or in the presence of subordinates), the hidden transcript of the less powerful allows a critique of power 'spoken behind the backs of the dominant' (Scott 1990: 4). The more menacing the power, he says, the 'thicker the mask' the oppressed must wear. In some instances, however, the hidden transcript is made public, used in open defiance as a challenge to established power relations. Scott suggests that an examination of the hidden transcript and the circumstances in which it comes to the surface can help us to better understand power relations in society.

Decolonizing discourse appears to be in decline when compared with its heyday in the mid-1980s (see case study four, Chapter 7). In Scott's (1990) terms, it could be said that the discourse and its associated ideology have been largely submerged into the hidden transcript. The high profile of Sinn Féin activities in relation to the language helped to foster the impression that Irish was a 'Republican language', a state of affairs which was unsatisfactory to many and repugnant to some for ideological reasons, as well as dangerous in the violent context of pre-ceasefire Northern Irish politics. For these reasons, decolonizing discourse is not often used in the public transcript of the Irish language revival, although it still figures in some Republican discourse.

According to Scott, the hidden transcript is itself the result of power relations within a subordinate group, as it is articulated and practiced in offstage social sites (1990: 119). Even within the hidden transcript of Irish language activists, decolonizing discourse is not widespread because its articulation can be the cause of conflict. As the ideology constructed through decolonizing discourse becomes increasingly marginalized, the other two discourses are becoming more prominent. In the next chapter, I shall look at the other side of the debate as expressed through cultural discourse.

5 Cultural Discourse

Cultural discourse today is often used in an attempt to remove Irish from party politics, and to place it instead in the realm of culture, tradition and heritage, or occasionally in the realm of the politics of reconciliation. This discourse has two different aspects. First, it is used to criticize Republicans and discredit the use of Irish for certain political ends. Second, it is very commonly used when people are trying to express their reasons for learning Irish or having their children learn Irish.

In the first instance, to choose cultural discourse is to make a distinctly political statement about the appropriate relationship between Irish and politics. This version of cultural discourse is used by professionals and non-professionals alike, although for somewhat different purposes. Many non-professionals who hold this perspective disagree with Republicanism and do not wish to be associated with it simply because of their interest in the Irish language. Professionals might use it to show opposition to Sinn Féin, to enhance their own position or to obtain money from government-funded bodies which increasingly favour this type of discourse. Various government bodies have also adopted cultural discourse and have sought to promote it as the correct version of the meaning of the Irish language. It has been institutionalized in the discourse of the Cultural Traditions Group, and to a certain extent the ULTACH Trust,[1] both of which will be discussed in more detail later.

In 1989, the British government withdrew funding it had been providing for the west Belfast Irish language group *Glór na nGael*. In the same year, it funded the newly established ULTACH Trust and a number of other Irish language projects. It would seem that the British establishment has been attempting to reinforce the ideology associated with cultural discourse through the funding of 'acceptable' organizations, such as the ULTACH Trust (see discussion in section one, Chapter 7), and by penalizing organizations they see as overtly political or too Nationalist in outlook. *Glór na nGael* had a Sinn Féin member on its board of directors, and was perhaps vetted for this reason (see discussion in section two, Chapter 7).

The second way in which cultural discourse is used is in rhetoric about the intrinsic cultural value of Irish as a language. Reference is frequently made to the long history and exciting tradition of song and literature in the language, as well as to the beauty and poetic nature of Irish.[2] In one sense, this turns the old view of the Irish language on its head. Not long ago Irish was characterized as a language lacking any intellectual culture and too deficient to support a literary tradition. Essentially portrayed as the language of the ignorant, poorly educated, 'backward' peasant, many people were ashamed to admit that they could speak Irish.[3] The characterization of Irish found in the second version of cultural discourse is the antithesis of the negative stereotype.

This second version tends to be used by learners of Irish, as well as cultural nationalists who wish to distance themselves from the more aggressive and sometimes violent versions of Nationalism. It is also frequently used by people to help them articulate why they feel the language is important to them, while professionals often use this version of cultural discourse to further justify their ideological stance on the Irish language and politics.

THE MAKING OF A DOMINANT DISCOURSE

The Irish language has figured prominently in much of the discourse of Irish heritage, both in everyday speech and in 'official' quarters. Cultural discourse has been partly institutionalized under the auspices of 'heritage' through the Cultural Traditions Group, a sub-committee of the government-funded charity the Community Relations Council (CRC). The CRC is funded by the Central Community Relations Unit (CCRU), a part of the Department of Finance and Personnel. In this rather roundabout way, cultural discourse has been incorporated into state discourses. It is increasingly necessary to use cultural discourse in order to curry favour with major funding organizations, as well as local and national government. Considering, however, that the symbolic meaning and importance of the language is so deeply contested, it is not surprising that there is still a great deal of debate on the issue. The image and meaning attributed to the Irish language by government agencies is considered more or less acceptable by the Irish language community depending on with whom you speak.

Formally established in 1988, the Cultural Traditions Group (CTG) recently produced a booklet entitled *Giving Voices* to review its development and accomplishments over the period 1990–4. In the Chairman's Report, Professor Ronald Buchanan explains the rationale behind the organization:

Every society is a mosaic of many different groups, based on class or ethnic background, religion, education, gender and generation.

Culture contributes to this diversity, for it represents knowledge and belief inherited from the past ... Culture in this sense exerts a powerful influence on the way we think and live, and cultural differences between groups and people can be a potent source of division and conflict – especially when used to bolster political groupings and the exercise of power. Conversely, cultural diversity can be a source of richness, a stimulus to new ideas and new approaches to community life. It is this latter concept that we have tried to nurture, in the belief that cultural differences can become a source of strength, rather than weakness.

(Cultural Traditions Group 1994: 3) [Quote 1]

The Irish language has been an important part of the CTG's work from the beginning, so much so that the Irish word '*dúchas*'[4] has been incorporated into its official logo and a sister organization, the ULTACH Trust, was set up to deal specifically with the language. 'From the outset,' the booklet states, 'the new committee realised that it had to pass what was called the "green litmus test" – finding a credible policy on the Irish language' (CTG 1994: 6).

The place of the Irish language within the organization is described by Dr Maurice Hayes, chairman of the CTG in 1990–3:

The main object [of the Cultural Traditions Group] is to promote discussion and debate about the validity of the various cultural traditions in Northern Ireland in a constructive and non-confrontational atmosphere. One shorthand was to help Protestants to contemplate the Irish language without necessarily feeling offended by it, or for Catholics to look on Orange processions without feeling intimidated. Of course this rather begs the question that some Orange processions are indeed intended to assert a claim to territory, or to superiority, and sometimes to intimidate, and *some manifestations of the Irish language are precisely employed in order to cause as much offence as possible to Unionists.*

(CTG 1994: 9, emphasis added) [Quote 2]

In Hayes's view, the Irish language can be viewed as a kind of 'shorthand' for Catholic or Nationalist culture, and presented to Unionists as a non-threatening manifestation of that culture. This is not entirely consistent with another view expressed by CTG, where Irish is portrayed as belonging collectively to both Catholics and Protestants. The problem is indicative of two conflicting versions of cultural traditions discourse. Hayes is drawing on the 'two traditions' version, while the latter view is from 'common heritage' discourse (McCoy 1996). This ambiguity in cultural traditions discourse gives it a certain flexibility which not only helps to widen its appeal, but makes it more resistant to attack.[5] Either version of cultural traditions discourse – or both – can be drawn upon depending on the context.

The final sentence of Quote 2 implicitly accuses at least some people of using the Irish language in an unacceptably political manner. The CTG makes a clear effort to place the Irish language firmly in the realm of culture and to 'release it from misunderstanding and prejudice, not use it as mere graffiti to exclude, confuse or taunt others' (CTG 1994: 6) – in other words, to depoliticize the language.

The idea to establish an independent trust to promote the wider use of Irish came out of the 'Varieties of Irishness' conference organized by the CTG in 1989.[6] The conference concluded that 'the language had unfortunately become associated with Republicanism in the eyes of many Protestants, which was a distortion of its real cultural significance' (CTG 1994: 24). The following year, the issue of the Irish language was again discussed at the 'Varieties of Britishness' conference (Crozier 1990a). A seminar on law and administration concluded that 'statutory or financial impediments to the use of Irish should be removed to enable those who wished to use it to do so more freely', while a seminar on educational issues said that 'Irish had suffered from being seen in a politicised context which alienated those who wanted to retain their Britishness' (CTG 1994: 24–5). According to the booklet *Giving Voices*, the CTG was 'quickly persuaded of *the need to confer a new legitimacy on its use* and the study of its origins and dialects, including its relationship to the Ulster-Scots tradition' (CTG 1994: 25, emphasis added). Here, 'to confer a new legitimacy' can be read as a euphemism for depoliticizing the language, or disassociating it from Republicanism.

To this end, *Iontaobhas ULTACH*/ULTACH Trust was formed in 1989, opening an office in Belfast city centre in 1990. In April 1991, the British government agreed to contribute £250,000 to the Trust's capital fund, ensuring long-term viability and allowing the Trust to generate an independent income. The priority of the ULTACH Trust is 'to make [Irish] classes available in areas in which people from the Protestant community will not feel threatened and to help create an environment in which they can comfortably learn and use the language' (CTG 1994: 25). In practice, this has sometimes been difficult to achieve. There is a great demand for funding and support for Irish language activities from people in the Catholic community who are already involved with the language, while on the Protestant side efforts are still being made to generate interest in Irish. This means that the Trust still funds a greater proportion of projects from the Catholic community, at the same time as it is working hard to implement its cross-community ideal.

Through the establishment of the Cultural Traditions Group and the ULTACH Trust, particular interpretations of the meaning and importance of the Irish language have become incorporated into the discourse of the state. This has profoundly affected the development of efforts to revive the Irish language in a number of ways. For the first time an organization has been set up by the British government with a remit exclusively devoted to the Irish language. The significance of Irish has been officially recognized, although in a particular way which sometimes attempts to dissociate the language from Nationalist identity. Perhaps even more importantly, one discourse of the Irish language has been given the official 'stamp of approval' and is now being used as the blueprint for further developments in relation to Irish. Effectively this means that other discourses are placed outside of circles of power, in opposition to the dominant discourse. Cultural discourse has become part of the public transcript of the more powerful.

APOLITICISM AS A POLITICAL STANCE

Of course, the apolitical claims of organizations like the Cultural Traditions Group are not taken at face value by everyone concerned. People and organizations who favour decolonizing or rights discourse are not inclined to accept a situation which casts them in a less than favourable light. In a situation where the equation 'political equals bad' has come to predominate, three basic strategies can be taken to combat the status quo. First, it is often pointed out that the use and promotion of cultural discourse is anything but apolitical in practice. This is reinforced easily enough with examples of the political use of this discourse, particularly with reference to the 'vilification' of Sinn Féin. Second, an attempt can be made to suggest that the connection between the Irish language and an Irish or Nationalist identity is a 'natural' one, usually by the use of historical references which connect the two, and occasionally by pointing out that Protestants/Unionists for the most part have no interest in the language. Finally, the use of decolonizing discourse and rights discourse continually challenges the representations created by cultural discourse.

Gaeilgeoirí are not the only ones to contest the apolitical nature of the discourse of the Cultural Traditions Group. English (1994) argues that according equal respect to both cultural traditions in Northern Ireland amounts to giving support to political aspirations and instincts as well. According to English, the 'equal legitimacy thesis' – the 'two traditions' theory which asserts that the Nationalist and Unionist traditions are equally legitimate – exposes the position adopted by the state as dangerously incoherent. 'The important point here is that – predictably, if not inevitably – attitudes toward parity of *cultural* esteem have *political* implications' (English 1994: 98, emphasis in original).

PROPAGANDISTS AND PROFESSIONALS

Cultural discourse frequently appears in the texts of professionals who hold widely differing points of view both on the Irish language and on the political situation in Northern Ireland. It has become increasingly important to be able to claim a sort of 'moral high ground' by stressing the apolitical orientation of one's own or one's organization's views and activities. An example might demonstrate how compelling the need to appear apolitical can be. An article appeared in the *Andersonstown News* (12 October 1991) entitled 'Irish paper to sue DUP man?'. Excerpts from the text of the article tell the story:

> The Belfast Irish language daily newspaper, *Lá*, is taking legal advice about remarks made by DUP Councillor Gregory Campbell at a recent meeting of Derry City Council. Mr. Campbell accused the paper of having a pro-Republican editorial policy and employing people with Republican views. ... He also attacked the paper for employing Mr. MacCormac [a former Republican prisoner] under a Northern Ireland Office scheme for parolees.
>
> Mr. Gearóid Ó Cairealláin, the Editor of *Lá*, has challenged Mr. Campbell to substantiate his claim of republican bias or withdraw his remarks. ... 'Our editorials have consistently put forward a peaceful solution to our political problems and have frequently taken a strong stand against violent action no matter where it comes from. This is a policy we will continue to pursue and for Mr. Campbell to suggest otherwise is wrong. As far as I know Mr. Campbell can't read any Irish and I would suggest that whoever is supplying him with his information is having him on.' ... 'We suspect that

Mr. Campbell's outburst has more to do with his dislike for the Irish language than it has to do with *Lá*'s so-called political bias.' [Quote 3]

To be accused of politicizing the Irish language can be considered slanderous, at least in some circumstances. The accusation of political (Republican) bias is damaging enough that the editor of *Lá* felt it necessary to threaten legal action against Councillor Campbell, although to the best of my knowledge no such action was taken. That a public accusation such as this is considered to be damaging to the newspaper in question is evidence of the power of cultural discourse.

In this exchange, both Campbell and Ó Cairealláin engage with past and present texts about the Irish language and Republicanism. Campbell draws on well-rehearsed condemnations, common in Northern Irish politics, of any kind of association with Republicanism. Ó Cairealláin, rather than entering into that debate directly by denying the accusation, draws on different discourses. He makes an appeal to apoliticism, and backs this up by suggesting that Campbell is unable to read the newspaper in any case and has been misinformed. The ideal of the objectivity of the press seems to be implied as a subtext. Ó Cairealláin concludes by suggesting that Campbell is biased against the language, an accusation which is loaded with political implications from a century of discourse on the relationship between the Irish language, Nationalism, Unionism and identity.

Both the accusation of political bias and the rejection of the claim take place in the public arena, designed for a wide audience. When the audience is this broad, it is generally prudent to use the broadly acceptable cultural discourse as much as possible. Ó Cairealláin chooses to assert that his editorial policy has taken a stand in support of peace and against violence, instead of defending the paper in some other way. For example, he might have decided to emphasize the broad spectrum of opinion expressed in *Lá*, representing not only Republican ideologies but also a cultural or apolitical point of view, and many other positions as well. In the terms of the current debate, however, where cultural discourse dominates official circles and decolonizing discourse is considered by many to be illegitimate, he decided to focus on the apolitical angle.

In a more recent opinion piece in the *Sunday Times* (10 October 1993), Seán Ó Cearnaigh articulately expresses the first version of cultural discourse, using it to condemn Sinn Féin and Republicanism. Ó Cearnaigh is a columnist for the Irish language newspaper *Lá*, and a member of the executive of the Peace Train committee and Families Against Intimidation and Terror (FAIT).

The danger to the language now comes not from British government's attempts to suppress it but from nationalist and republican efforts to harness it to a narrow sectarian agenda. If they have their way they will push the language into a political ghetto, cutting it off from the wellsprings of popular goodwill which it must have if it is to flourish as a living part of our heritage. ...

It is in these same [Catholic working-class] areas that Sinn Féin has its grassroots support, and the party has been moving in to claim the Irish language movement for as long as the Troubles have blighted the lives of people. Republicans are at pains to identify with the language movement, and some Sinn Féin spokesmen try to give the impression that their party has a monopoly on Irish, and that language speakers are natural supporters of their policy. ...

This situation presents the leadership of the revival movement with a dilemma. On the one hand, it claims the movement is non-political and non-sectarian, and seeks Protestant/Unionist involvement in its activities, while on the other it allows itself to become identified with militant republicanism. ...

Because of its ambiguous attitude to Sinn Féin, violence and Ulster Unionism, the Irish language movement in Ulster remains entrenched in a Catholic ghetto, unable adequately to address the wider world. Even in these days of official approval and generous government assistance, it fails to relate to the real world. The only contribution Proinsias Mac Aonghusa, its [the Gaelic League's] president, made to Irish politics in recent times was to call for the election of Gerry Adams in West Belfast. This, and the failure of the movement to identify with the peace movement, is a cause for concern to many democrats who are committed to the language. ... [Quote 4]

In this passage Ó Cearnaigh echoes some of the common themes found in the more political version of cultural discourse, including the equation of 'politics' with 'Republicanism', and a strong condemnation of Sinn Féin and its policy on the language. The worry expressed about associating the Irish language with politics is not a broad one. An association with the peace movement, according to Ó Cearnaigh, would be a good thing.

Ó Cearnaigh gives us a hint as to whom his article is directed in the last sentence of Quote 4, where he refers to 'democrats who are committed to the language'. He is contrasting himself and his assumed audience with the leaders of the Irish language movement, whom he perceives as being unduly sympathetic to Republicanism. In this way he reinforces the representation of the Irish language revival movement as being divided into two camps, apolitical/democratic/peaceful and politicized/Republican/willing to work with terrorists. The article is published in a major newspaper rather than a journal focused solely on Irish language issues, so it has to be assumed that there is a wider audience outside of Irish language circles. This audience is catered for in sections of the article that give some basic descriptions and background history to the current situation (not cited above). They are presented with a representation of the Irish language revival movement as divided into opposite poles, and are encouraged implicitly to sympathize with the ideology of cultural discourse.

As a journalist, Ó Cearnaigh is a professional articulator of ideas and ideologies. He is a columnist both for *Lá* and *The Sunday Times*, so he is especially practised at presenting his own points of view. His position on the executive of FAIT also tells us something about his politics. FAIT is a significant voice in the peace movement, and the organization is strongly anti-Republican. As one of the 'more interested and more articulate', Ó Cearnaigh is in a position to make a significant creative contribution to the meaning of Irish as a symbol, and to influence the direction of cultural development in this respect.

The text is interesting on a number of other points as well. Ó Cearnaigh tends to portray the Irish language revival movement (or its leadership, at least) as a monolithic group, when in reality there is little consensus on most issues within the movement. He portrays the apolitical versus political/Republican issue in black and white terms which do not reflect the complexity of the relationship between politics and the Irish language. Ó Cearnaigh's depiction of west Belfast as a 'ghetto' where the Irish language 'remains entrenched' is an unflattering one, which is at odds with the self-perception of resident *Gaeilgeoirí*, who see themselves as succeeding against the odds in increasing the language's appeal and popularity. The assertion that west Belfast is not part of 'the real world' is unlikely to be accepted by the majority west Belfast *Gaeilgeoirí* either. While many of my informants have expressed a desire to see the language expand beyond the confines of Catholic west Belfast, few if any would agree that their efforts do not engage with the 'wider world' at all. At the same time, Ó Cearnaigh's reservations about Sinn Féin's involvement in the movement and its motivations for an interest in the Irish language would ring true with a significant section of the Irish-speaking community.

Other users of cultural discourse are more subtle. In a speech entitled 'The Background to the Irish Language Revival in Northern Ireland', spokesperson for the ULTACH Trust Aodán Mac Póilin expressed his view on the relationship between political ideology and the Irish language revival:

I believe that political nationalism often provides the impetus for involvement in the language movement. It is, however, frequently satisfied with promoting the language as an emblematic cultural marker – street names, the *cupla focal*, Irish as a subject within the school curriculum. I would like to draw a distinction between impetus and momentum. Impetus signifies the original stimulus for involvement or support, momentum involves the commitment needed to develop a viable speech community. The actual momentum of the Irish language movement derives from a quite different source, which often transcends political considerations. The failure of a movement dominated by the Catholic Church and political nationalism to create a valid, self-sustaining organic speech community, and the perception that those forces have sometimes used the language for extra-linguistic ends, has driven many language enthusiasts into a position which is effectively apolitical.

(Mac Póilin 1994a) [Quote 5]

In this formulation, the advocates of a politicized view of the language as expressed through decolonizing discourse make a largely symbolic contribution, and are for the most part unsuccessful in terms of reviving the language. Instead of a moral stance against the politicization of the Irish language, Mac Póilin is here making a practical critique which presents the cultural stance as the more viable choice for those who are genuine in their interest in reviving the language.

The widespread use of cultural discourse can and does gloss over very different opinions on the best way to promote the language and to ensure its survival. For some, an 'apolitical' ideological stance on Irish means focusing strictly on its cultural aspects, while for others it means disengaging Irish from Nationalist politics. In some cases, though, cultural discourse can be used to justify greater political involvement on behalf of the language, for example in this *Andersonstown News* editorial (15 March 1980).

Tá sí á labhairt i mBéal Feirste agus sa cheantar thart air chomh fada siar agus a théann an chéad tuairisc staire nó traidisiúin, gan trácht ar an chéad mhearchuimhne. Bhí sí á labhairt ag baill gach aicme creidimh agus díchreidimh agus gach aicme polaitiúil. ...

Ainneoin sin, tá sí gan aitheantas a thabhairt dí ag gach sort údaráis. Ó thaobh lucht oideachais de, is ábhar eile scoile í (bímis buíoch ar a shon sin féin). Ó thaobh na bpolaiteoirí de (na Poblachtaigh san áireamh) níl sí ann.

It [Irish] has been spoken in Belfast and the surrounding district as far back as the first historical accounts or traditions go. It was spoken by members of every type of religion and no religion and every political class. ...

In spite of that, every sort of authority has failed to give it recognition. On the one hand, to the education authorities it is just another school subject (let's be thankful for that at least). On the other hand to the politicians (including the Republicans) it does not exist.

(my translation) [Quote 6]

According to this editorial, in order for Irish speakers to obtain recognition, the Irish language must be brought out into the public domain as much as possible, including both politics and the media. The demand for recognition by the authorities is justified in the first paragraph in Quote 6 by an appeal to its long history in the city and the claim that it is the common heritage of all regardless of religious belief or political view. In other words, cultural discourse is used to justify greater political intervention on behalf of the Irish language. Written in Irish by an anonymous author in the form of an editorial for a relatively small local newspaper, the audience is somewhat limited. It is clearly directed at Irish speakers in west Belfast. It is interesting to note as well that this editorial, calling for greater involvement on the part of politicians and other public figures, was written before the 1981 Republican hunger strike, which was the watershed for increased Republican and Sinn Féin involvement in the revival movement during this period.

Perhaps the best known of Irish language organizations commonly associated with cultural discourse is *Cumann Chluain Ard*. Originally founded as a branch of the Gaelic League in 1936 or 1937 (there seems to be some disagreement as to the exact date), *Cluain Ard* organizes classes in Irish year round, and is the venue for many Irish language activities, especially ceilidhs, concerts and evening events which require the availability of a licensed bar. There is reputed to have been a major split over the issue of politics and the Irish language in the 1950s. The result of the split was, first of all, an Irish-only policy which meant that groups which conducted their activities through the medium of English could no longer use the hall, and second, the taking of an avowedly apolitical stance, both of which remain in place to this day.

In the case of *Cluain Ard*, the definition of 'apolitical' is closer to that used in the early years of the Gaelic League. The organization has a clearly Nationalist ethos, but it actively distances itself from party and sectarian politics. The *Cumann* does not engage in campaigns to win recognition or support from the British government, being more inclined (in the past, at least) to take the Irish government to task for its policies on the *Gaeltacht*. In the present political climate, they prefer to go quietly about their work of teaching Irish and providing a strictly Irish-only space.

The 'Nationalist but apolitical ethos' is perhaps best described by PADRAIG, an Irish language stalwart and key figure in *Cumann Chluain Ard* for a number of decades. A man in his late fifties with a professional career, he describes *Cluain Ard*'s policy in this way:

> PADRAIG: Our idea is very simple, that the Irish language is the language of the land, and that it is so many thousands of years old and that it should be preserved as our national identity. ... Everyone is welcome to it and politics are something else and religion is something else. Does that surprise you?
> C O'R: Well, isn't it difficult to actually keep those things separate?
> PADRAIG: It is very difficult, but it must be done, because at the moment it seems that people who, political parties who push the Irish language for political gain are not doing the language any service. Because, I mean, there was somebody who said that every word of Irish spoken was another bullet, or something, that's nonsense! ... It's very very difficult to separate them but it can be done and it's done in here [*Cluain Ard*], hopefully. [Quote 7]

As the discussion progressed, I asked PADRAIG to clarify what 'politics' meant. The distinction he made was essentially between politics in the broad sense of public action, and in the narrow sense of political parties and sectarian politics found in Northern Ireland. On the subject of political parties, he said:

> I suspect all political parties. This is our problem with the Irish language, the Irish language has too many friends. ... The problem is that the SDLP doesn't do enough to promote the Irish language, and the other parties don't do enough of it, and Sinn Féin do just enough to get people thinking that they are the pro-Irish party.

But you could not become president of Sinn Féin and not speak English. The Irish language is not essential for a president or any sort of member of Sinn Féin. English is essential. [Quote 8]

Although PADRAIG asserts that Protestants and Unionists are welcome in *Cluain Ard*, as in the early days of the Gaelic League the connection between Irish and Irish Nationalism is taken for granted:

C O'R: I wanted to ask you a question about that old pamphlet[7] you gave me. It mentions Nationalism, and says that Nationalism is the natural corollary of the Irish language.
PADRAIG: Yes.
C O'R: Is it the same now?
PADRAIG: Yes. This country could never ever have its freedom of any sort without the Irish language. It's impossible to have it.
C O'R: Doesn't that contradict the no politics policy?
PADRAIG: No, because politics in that sense, we are not trying in any way to revise the political system. What we're saying is that this country cannot be independent, cannot be a nation, this island, this people, without their language. Now that's not right or left, or saying that Ireland should be partitioned or have four provincial governments or whatever. But what it does say is very simple, the Irish language *is* Irish Nationalism, and without it Irish Nationalism doesn't exist. That's really the point that was being made there. Pearse is the one that people usually quote, 'not free merely but Gaelic as well, not Gaelic merely but free as well'. ... They are not two things. If you look at Ireland today, the Irish language is being choked out by the English language. Right? So, I mean, if it doesn't retain this, then the whole nation's gone. It may as well be like Yorkshire or somewhere. It's not politics as such. [Quote 9]

PADRAIG engages with historical texts on the importance of the Irish language to the Irish nation, most vividly from early Gaelic League literature and discourses of romantic nationalism, investing them with meanings relevant to the current political situation as he sees it, and to the policy of *Cluain Ard*. He also engages with more contemporary discourses on politics and the Irish language, favouring cultural discourse but blending it with reworked versions of different nationalist discourses.

PADRAIG is not a politician or journalist, and generally avoids the public spotlight. Nevertheless, he exerts a strong influence over one of the most important Irish language organizations in Belfast, an organization which over the years has had a profound influence on the formulation and articulation of the ideologies of many other Irish language organizations throughout Northern Ireland, and in some instances the island as a whole. The version of cultural discourse formulated in *Cluain Ard* and refined by people like PADRAIG has had a powerful effect on much of the discourse of *Gaeilgeoirí* in west Belfast, and has strongly influenced the development of rights discourse as well.

THE NON-PROFESSIONALS

For those who do not make a living on the public stage of the Irish language revival, cultural discourse is commonly used to explain why they have taken an interest in the Irish language. Its beauty, its creative capacity, its long and illustrious history, its lyrical songs and unique literature, all are called upon to offer some explanation as to why Irish means so much to them. Whether or not Nationalism or politics plays a part, most people talk about the inherent beauty and cultural worth of the language when seeking to explain or describe their interest.

For some, the more political version of cultural discourse affords an opportunity to express opposition to Sinn Féin or Republicanism without having to come right out and say so. Again, the word 'political' can in some instances be seen as code for 'Republican', so that expressing the belief that politics and Irish ought to be kept separate, or that political parties should not use the Irish language as a 'political football', becomes a statement against the Republican stand on the language. Others are not so squeamish, coming out openly against Sinn Féin policies on Irish. It is not uncommon for the party to be accused of 'jumping on the bandwagon', 'hijacking the Irish language' or taking credit for the hard work of others in the movement.

While it is easy to make generalizations like this, in reality there are almost as many variations of cultural discourse as there are individuals who use it, although some ways of using the discourse are more novel than others. All users of this discourse are engaging with the versions articulated by the professionals as well as the versions of fellow non-professionals. The first of the following examples would be fairly conventional, while the last three are more novel for a variety of reasons.

MAIRE is a worker in an Irish nursery school. A woman in her thirties, she did not learn any Irish at school as it was not available in the schools she attended. She became involved with the language through friends and her husband, who speaks Irish. When I asked her why she decided to get involved with the Irish language, she said:

> Because when I thought about it, it was my language and it was part of my culture and I was deprived of that. Every other country has its own language. I got angry at that, so I promised myself from then on that I was going to push until I learned it. Listening to my husband speaking in Gaelic, I think it's a far, far richer language. You can say things many different ways, and they're all beautiful ways of saying it. You can only say things one way in English. ... It's a beautiful language, but it's difficult, the grammar and all. [Quote 10]

MAIRE does not engage with the debate concerning politics and the language. Even though she expresses anger at being deprived of her language and culture, she does not speculate as to who is responsible for that deprivation. Her discourse remains firmly in the realm of the cultural.

PROINSIAS is a school teacher in his forties. He identifies himself as '100 per cent working-class', but concedes that he has moved into the growing Catholic middle class in terms of lifestyle and income. He describes his upbringing as 'apolitical', although he became involved in the civil rights movement of the late 1960s. His family had 'no interest in Irish whatsoever'.

> I'd always promised myself to learn Irish and speak it, not through any sort of identity crisis, but because in it I find a certain inherent beauty and a different perspective for looking at the world. I find this more and more as I study it. In any language a mindset is built into it, a way of looking at the world, and this is used in their vocabulary and their grammar, and their poetry and music. That would be peculiar to any language, including English.
>
> . . .
>
> I think my interest [in the Irish language] is purely aesthetic. It's not a political thing. I'd be reluctant to say I learned Irish because I'm Irish. I'd say I am a person who's lost my whole culture, but sees certain indications of what it was, what it could be, and it's like an interest in art or religion – I want to study it, I want to be able to converse in it. I want to know it to be a better person in myself. And there's almost a slight mystical thing there, something in the collective unconscious, the archetypes in Irish people, deep mind sets that the

language can express for you. There are echoes in the unconscious memory of your past, your ancestors, past generations.

. . .

I am encouraged by people who do know the language and their attempts to keep it apolitical and to try and encourage everyone on the island to develop the language. A lot of people have moved away from any kind of republicanism because they feel it threatens the language. I know people who know the language well, but are not involved because they think the Provies[8] have hijacked it, people who could do a lot for the language. I agree that you can't hijack a language, but you can use it as a political football, and some do. [Quote 11]

The first paragraph of Quote 11 is typical of the second version of cultural discourse, focusing on the language's 'inherent beauty'. PROINSIAS also articulates a popular folk version of the Sapir–Whorf hypothesis, the belief that a language shapes a person's world-view. In the second paragraph, he draws on discourses of personal development and psychology. The idea of a collective unconscious which the Irish language helps a person to tap into, while less widely held, is still commented upon by a significant number of people. In the final paragraph, PROINSIAS switches to the first version of cultural discourse, although he is careful to qualify what he says by adding, 'I agree that you can't hijack a language', a phrase more typical of rights discourse. While aware of the political significance of the language for some people, PROINSIAS takes care to emphasize that this is not the case for him. He is clearly responding to unspecified texts on politics and the language, and anticipating the response his words might arouse in others.

There is an increasing number of young people in the North who have grown up speaking the Irish language. While their numbers are still relatively small, there is every indication that growing up as part of the new generation of native speakers has had a profound impact on how the language is viewed. It is too soon to make any definitive conclusions on the matter, but excerpts from an interview with DÓNAL, a young man in his twenties, give some insights into the views of at least one of this new generation. DÓNAL is now a teacher. A majority of his family life was, and continues to be, through the medium of Irish.

I never really got active in the Irish movement. I just kind of carried on what I was doing. ... I suppose if you're brought up with the language it's put to the side as part of your consciousness. [Quote 12]

Since both he and his spouse speak Irish, he plans to bring his children up with Irish, 'because you have to put yourself on one side of the fence or another'.

> Denying them Irish would be a difficult thing to do, since both parents would have it. Its part of our legacy, our education. ... It's like asking your grandparents what was in Royal Avenue before they built Castle Court [shopping centre]. It's a difficult thing to describe. ... Knowing your language is like knowing who your grandparents were. It gives you that sort of perspective. You don't need to know Irish to communicate; I think it's always going to be a cultural thing. It's like teaching your kids what certain flowers are for a nature walk – city kids don't need to know that, but it may be of benefit and an enriching experience. That's the same with the Irish language. Knowing what their relatives spoke and what they called things gives them an insight, like that a train was called a 'black pig', and a bicycle an 'iron steed'. It's knowledge, and it's part of the process of rationalizing our environment. If it helps in that, gives them some sort of information, then it's good. As far as communicating goes, they could do that in English. [Quote 13]

In many ways this passage is typical of cultural discourse. DÓNAL clearly views the Irish language as a cultural rather than a political issue. He relates Irish to a sense of place and of belonging, and makes a link with past generations. What is different about his narrative is the way it ties in specifically with his own experience. He establishes a sense of place by referring to specific location in Belfast (Royal Avenue, in the city centre), and a modern building (Castle Court shopping centre). Usually references to place are more generalized, often referring to natural features, such as the Black Mountain to the west of Belfast, or to a rural past. DÓNAL's narrative is lacking in references to the countryside except as a contrast to city life, his own experience. He does not refer generally to the language that his ancestors spoke, as is more typical when this sort of comment is made, but specifically to the language of his (or his children's) grandparents. This is perhaps unsurprising, considering that Irish has been part of his life since birth, rather than adopted or rediscovered as part of his heritage later in life.

After a brief pause at the end of the above quote, the discussion turned to the issue of identity:

> **C O'R**: A lot of people relate the language to their sense of identity. Does that mean anything to you?

DÓNAL: No, not really. I'm an Irish Nationalist, in that sense, but we live in a global economy and GATT means more than *Conradh na Gaeilge* [the Gaelic League]. In terms of political power the Irish language doesn't mean anything, identity and so on doesn't mean a hell of a lot. ...
The idea about identity, I don't know, you really need to ask someone who identity means a hell of a lot to. The idea of identity is very important if you are drawing boundaries. As an Irish Nationalist, I would draw boundaries in certain areas. I would say that the border is completely contrived, although the 'bible belt' would be as different from south Armagh or west Belfast as South Carolina is from Los Angeles. Where do you draw boundaries? Do you say that Ballymena and north Antrim should be a state of its own, like Luxembourg or something? ... The only time it really becomes important to me is when people say to me, as they have done, 'you're not Irish'. If you're into having an identity, the Irish language has got to come as number one in importance. For me, I'm just interested in what happened before me and what will happen after. I think it's important to have Irish, to have Channel 4, to wear the colour blue, to have seen a certain film like *Rebel Without a Cause*, or to hear the Beatles. If you put it on a scale, I'd say it's definitely one of the most important, more important than Irish music, more important than Irish art or cuisine. It's more important than any of the elements that you would say are the Irish contribution to world culture. [Quote 14]

A friend once lamented that in order to survive, the Irish language needs fanatics, people who would dedicate their entire lives to the language. Paradoxically, he says, the existence of fanatics is a strong indication that a language is in serious decline. Fanatics can never just accept Irish as a language like any other, because if they did they may as well just speak the dominant language and leave Irish to its fate. Ironically, by their very existence, fanatics prevent the language from becoming a normal, natural means of communication, which is, in the end, the key to any language's survival. According to my friend, the mission of the fanatic is to stir up enough passion in people that they will learn the language and pass it on as a native language to their children. Eventually, though, the passion must subside to the point that Irish becomes just another ordinary part of life, but one that is no longer under threat. It is a tall order, but perhaps my friend would be heartened by the words of 'ordinary' young people like DÓNAL, for whom Irish is simply another part of culture and daily life, albeit an important part.

BRIAIN presents an interesting contrast to the other examples of cultural discourse above. A working-class man in his late thirties, he might best be described as a Republican who favours cultural discourse. No one in his family ever spoke Irish, and he only studied it briefly in school. In the late 1970s he went to jail for a political offence, and it was there that his interest was sparked.

> Everybody was learning Irish, so I tried to learn it. I tried for a year, but it was the 'blanket protest'[9] at the time. You were in your cell 24 hours a day, and you had to write your lessons on the wall. A couple of guys in the wing who had Irish would have shouted it out. ... In jail, I was there for a political reason, and I didn't even know my own language. That was the main reason I wanted to learn it. I was supposed to be in for political crimes, and I hadn't a clue about my own language. [Quote 15]

Although his political views were instrumental in introducing him to the language, he draws heavily from cultural discourse:

> The Irish language is for anyone, Catholic or Protestant. It's for anybody and everybody to learn and speak it. Some people say that the Republican movement is capitalizing on the language, and if they were I would think it was wrong. At times I think they are. Definitely at times they push it as if it was their language, although it is their language, like it was theirs and theirs alone. I don't think that's right. You get maybe [X], now I like that fellow and he's done a lot for the language, but he'll get in the paper shouting about the language. Now maybe other people have been shouting about it for 20 years, but because it's him that's saying it, it's getting the publicity and he's getting the press. So Protestants think that it's all Sinn Féin promoting the language, and they think, I don't want nothing to do with that. ... You can't blame Sinn Féin at the same time, because they have to promote what they think is right, too. I would separate the language completely from politics, if possible, but it's difficult to do, because you need political pressure to get TV programmes in Irish, to get money for different schemes in Irish, you need political pressure for to do that, but if Sinn Féin do that, people are going to look at it as a Sinn Féin thing. I don't think political parties should have anything to do with it, if possible. ...

C O'R: How does that reconcile with your own personal political beliefs?

BRIAIN: I wouldn't put it in with my political beliefs. ... Being in jail made me think, if you're in here, what are you in here for? You're in here fighting for Ireland, and you can't even speak your own language. That made me want to learn the Irish language, but I wouldn't really connect it – then I would have connected it politically, but not now. I just do it for my own personal reasons. I want to be able to speak my own language, there's nothing political about it.

C O'R: What changed your mind from the way you used to think about it to the way you think about it now?

BRIAIN: Listening to different people talk. I've always voted for Sinn Féin, but say I voted SDLP or Alliance, it wouldn't change my thoughts on the Irish language. My goal in life is to be able to talk to anybody and get into a conversation in Gaelic. I don't associate it with the political now at all. I don't know what's changed my mind, but I don't associate it with the political. [Quote 16]

In this text, BRIAIN enters into a dialogue with both decolonizing and cultural texts, comparing them with his own experiences. He acknowledges the critique of Republican involvement in the language made by users of cultural discourse, and agrees that it is most probably correct. At the same time, he walks an ideological tightrope by conceding the legitimacy of the Republican point of view on the matter as well. In the end, personally and in spite of his political views, he agrees with the ideological assertion that the language and politics, especially party politics, ought to be kept as separate as possible. In the third paragraph of Quote 16, he seems to be making a distinction similar to that made by Mac Póilin (in Quote 5) between impetus and momentum. If the impetus for learning Irish for BRIAIN was his Republican politics, the momentum necessary for maintaining and developing his interest meant that eventually, the language became disconnected from politics in his mind.

CONCLUSION

Like decolonizing discourse, cultural discourse is historically deep. Different versions of it figure prominently in institutions such as *Cumann Chluain Ard* from the 1950s to the present day. It has also had a wide appeal for many individuals in the revival movement, and has been a prominent discourse for many decades. When decolonizing discourse came to the fore in the 1980s, cultural discourse did as well, as public debates raged about the appropriate relationship between politics and the Irish language. In the context of intense political conflict in the North and controversy about Irish, the terms of debate became quite narrow during this period, with the great majority of arguments being made from these two discourses.

In contrast to decolonizing discourse, cultural discourse appears to be gaining in status and has been institutionalized to a certain degree, for example in the discourse of the Cultural Traditions Group. It is increasingly part of the public 'mask' which must be worn in dealings with the powerful – the British government and many funding agencies. Cultural discourse is dominant in the public transcript of the government when dealing with Irish language organizations, as well as the public transcript of many individuals and Irish language organizations in certain contexts. This institutionalization has no doubt increased the legitimacy afforded to the ideologies associated with cultural discourse, and has helped to counteract the perception held by some people that Irish is a Republican language. In the next chapter, I shall examine rights discourse, which exists to some extent outside the terms of debate between decolonizing and cultural discourses.

6 Rights Discourse

PROPAGANDISTS AND PROFESSIONALS

Rights discourse figures prominently in the campaigns to obtain funding for Irish-medium schools and for official government recognition of the language. The Irish language activists whom I shall discuss in this section are also professionals in the use of discourse. In their positions as spokespersons for the Irish language, they are more conscious of the process of discourse production than most. Like their counterparts who favour either decolonizing or cultural discourse, their job is to sway people's opinions, and they actively engage in the struggle for hegemony in the political field.

CAOIMHÍN is a secondary school teacher who began his career in English-medium education. He was involved in the establishment of *Meánscoil Feirste*, and is now a teacher at the school. He told me that he remembers attending Irish classes throughout his childhood, starting at five or six, up until he went to university. 'My whole life could be traced out in a series of going to Irish classes', he told me, though he cannot now remember what his original motivation was. For CAOIMHÍN the connection between culture, politics and identity is a complex one:

The language is central to culture, and the culture and the language are central to a sense of identity. In the North, in the Nationalist community in particular, or people who would call themselves Irish anyway, people have been refused the opportunity to express that sense of Irishness through the political way they live their lives, through government structures. There's no way in which an input into how our society is structured could be made, or has been made, that takes recognition of our sense of Irishness. People have therefore had to create their own avenues for doing this. ...

Language has a connection with this place from which we come, to put it vaguely. Where the political aspect comes in is how you view this place from which we come. Language is not directly connected to any political philosophy – people from a Protestant or Unionist tradition could get the same sense of connection to their people, our people, people who have lived here for generations and came before them – the townlands, the hills, that connection could be made for them. The politics comes in in how you view that.

85

If you view this piece of land as part of Britain, you could view this us-ness in that context, so I don't think there's a direct connection [between Irish and a particular political philosophy]. But the Nationalists have tended to make that connection more readily, and to see it as more important, and therefore it has become more an aspect of Irish Nationalism. Supposing Ireland was still under British rule, people could get in touch with their Irishness in the context of being part of Britain. The language leads to an ethnic identity, and a political identity could be connected, but it's not necessarily so. A Welsh speaker could be a Tory or a Labour voter and still have that sense of Welshness and that connection. One does not necessarily predetermine the other. This is an extreme situation here, but looking at Wales again, it is possible to change your political identity without changing your ethnic identity. It could be seen to be less deeply ingrained. In this situation, because of the depth of political identity, it seems to have been a bigger problem, and particularly historically you get how the Gaelic revival has fed into the national revolution, and that's an aspect of it at the political level, that's creating a political identity. [Quote 1]

CAOIMHÍN makes a strong connection between politics, identity and the Irish language, yet he emphasizes that the language is not necessarily connected to any one political philosophy, a point of view which he highlights by the comparison he makes with Wales. This is in contrast to decolonizing discourse, in which Irish is seen in connection with Republican ideology, and cultural discourse, in which there is a desire to see a complete break between politics and the Irish language. Looking at intertextuality, he is implicitly responding to the political/apolitical debate in this text. When he denies a connection between Irish and a particular political philosophy, he is referring to the widespread connection between Republicanism and the language which is made by supporters and opponents of decolonizing discourse alike. A denial of the ideology associated with cultural discourse is implicit in the connection he makes between the political situation in the North, identity and Irish. He anticipates a certain response from both the decolonizing and cultural camps, which he endeavours to answer by careful construction of discourse.

In Quote 6, Chapter 3, ANTÓIN talks about the involvement of Irish speakers with the wider community of west Belfast at the start of the Troubles. Here, he talks about the 1980s and the increasing involvement of Sinn Féin in the Irish language movement.

I don't think that Sinn Féin gave Irish a high profile, but that the reaction to Sinn Féin trying to promote the language gave it a high profile. That's why people have the idea that Sinn Féin tried to hijack the language, when that was not the case. There was never a very high proportion of people involved in Sinn Féin who were interested in the Irish language. The more effective members of Sinn Féin like [X] and [Y] were generally interested in promoting it because they were involved in the Irish language before they got involved in Sinn Féin. ... But nevertheless the influence of Irish speakers in Sinn Féin has been limited. ... It's sort of politically correct in Sinn Féin to be connected with the Irish language, but I'd say in 90 per cent of the cases that's all it is.

. . .

There was a certain political agenda there all right, because there was a change in philosophy within the Republican movement, especially when they entered into the political sphere. The image of fighting a war and killing people is very negative, especially for a political party, so they had to latch onto ideas that were more positive and the Irish language just happened to be one of them. Nevertheless, it had an effect, in the sense that the profile of the Irish language was raised, be it negative or positive. You know the old saying that no publicity is bad publicity. No matter what way they were thinking about it, at least people were thinking about the Irish language and that was a plus all right.

. . .

Because certain individuals in Sinn Féin started to promote the Irish language, you had the SDLP and possibly Unionists coming out and saying, oh, they're trying to hijack the Irish language and use the Irish language to their own political purpose. I'd say that the very fact that they came out and attacked Sinn Féin on that, they created the image that Sinn Féin actually had control of the Irish language movement which it never had in any way. It always has been apolitical, in party political terms, since I was involved in it. [Quote 2]

In the first two paragraphs of Quote 2, ANTÓIN answers some of the common criticisms of Sinn Féin made both in the past and contemporaneously. While he maintains that Sinn Féin did not hijack the language, he also asserts the belief that most people in the party are not truly interested in the language. He does not deny the political connection made by the party between their political philosophy and the Irish language, seeing it as a logical connection under the circumstances, but neither does he support it. From what he says in Quote 6, Chapter 3, it is possible to surmise that he himself, like 'the vast majority of Irish speakers', opposes the violent political means of Republicanism. Instead of criticizing Sinn Féin for making the connection between their ideology and Irish, he blames those who criticize Sinn Féin for bringing that political connection to the fore themselves. The final sentence in the third paragraph indicates which definition he applies to the term 'apolitical'. Unlike many users of cultural discourse, ANTÓIN limits the idea of 'political' to political party associations, not to Nationalist associations in general.

MARCUS works for the Irish language newspaper *Lá*, also writing columns on occasion for other papers. Before getting involved with *Lá*, he was unemployed. He studied Irish in school and enjoyed it, but did not do well on his A-level examination and lost interest. No one in his family speaks Irish. He became involved in the Irish language in 1981 after running into a friend at a hunger strike march. The friend invited him to attend classes at *Cluain Ard*, and he has been involved with the language ever since.

In my last year at [primary school] I did *Buntus Cainte*, and I remember thinking 'I like the sound of this', and that attracted me to it even though I was only ten. At 17 or 18 it tied in with the political element. I found out that there was a political element to being Irish, and that this was another element of that, the cultural element is another element of your Irishness, another element of your not-Britishness. That tied in with whatever Nationalist attitudes I had at the time and still have. I never know which of those elements is dominant: the love of the language which I felt at the time I left school, or the fact that it's also a political and cultural expression of non-Englishness and Irishness. I think the element that dominates might be the love of languages, but I don't think in an area like this that you can isolate that fact from the political situation and that it has a relevance to the political situation. The love of the language is very dominant, but the other element is not small either and was always there. Once I became involved in the political situation, the Irish language fitted in like a piece of the jigsaw. [Quote 3]

Quote 3 is interesting because MARCUS sees the ideologies of both cultural and decolonizing discourse personified in himself and his own feelings about the Irish language. Unable to select one of these ostensibly conflicting perspectives as the dominant one, he embraces both. MARCUS strongly favours rights discourse, perhaps because it is easier to accommodate the full range of his feelings and beliefs about the language in that discourse.

MARCUS feels strongly that the Irish language is a political issue, but not necessarily in the way it is formulated in decolonizing discourse. It is a political issue, he believes, because the state makes it so.

> **C O'R**: What do you think about that, the debate about the Irish language and politics being kept separate?
> **MARCUS**: I think that's a load of rubbish. The Irish language can't be separated from politics any more than any aspect of your life can be separated from politics. It's impossible to separate normal everyday activities from politics, least of all ones which involve speech. If the Irish language is to survive it has to have state intervention, it has to have active community participation. ... If you want to register your child's name in Irish and the state tells you you can't, who's making a political issue of it? Are you making a political issue of it, or is the state telling you, this is a political issue, this is a political football, it's too hot for us to handle and we're denying you this right. ... The state refuses to give grant aid to Irish-language schools which it gives to English-language schools, that brings me into conflict with the state. I don't want to be in conflict with the state necessarily, but that makes me a participant in a conflict with the state. [Quote 4]

On the relation of the Irish language to politics and political parties, MARCUS says:

> There has always been an Irish language movement in Belfast, and it has always been motivated by one thing, the Irish language. The fact that many people in that movement had political backgrounds has nothing to do with it. At the end of the day, that is the way that the thing has developed historically, but they didn't try to be exclusive of anybody. Just the opposite, they made an effort to attract Protestants and Catholics, and the large element who practise no religion and are hostile to the practice of religion. Sinn Féin are a party and they have a political agenda. If they decide to push the Irish language as part of that agenda, I have no problem with that. At times we've had to talk to Sinn Féin and say that we don't think this is the best way and in the long run this could do damage to the

language, and make our views known. They're a political party and they can accept it or not, same as the SDLP can with approaches we make. ... The thing is, you can't isolate Irish from the political scene. It is part of the political scene. But it has to try as much as possible not to be seen as a party political thing. That's the problem. The problem is there's a Sinn Féin phobia on. There are people that as soon as Sinn Féin puts anything on the table about the Irish language, they say that's associating Irish with the armed struggle. Coming from the community I come from, that's not how I see it. I see it that these people as much as anybody else are entitled to use the Irish language, to promote the Irish language. They have a party political angle which I wouldn't have, but I'm not in their party. As regards to our own political angle, we're not promoting a party political angle. Sinn Féin didn't set up the *Bunscoil* or the *Gaeltacht* community on the Shaws Road. Sinn Féin didn't set up the *Cultúrlann*, Sinn Féin didn't set up *Lá*. Sinn Féin had nothing whatever to do with any of these initiatives which are much more long-term and have solidified the community. Now, you could look and you could say, Sinn Féin did that and Sinn Féin did that, but you could also say that the SDLP did a little bit there, and people with no political association did most of the things. ... At times, a political party can have an agenda which dovetails with ours, but we have a non-political agenda. If you had three political parties supporting the Irish language, Sinn Féin would only be one among many. As it is, the other political parties shy away from it and give Sinn Féin the spotlight, which is what Sinn Féin wants. [Quote 5]

I reproduce this part of the interview with MARCUS at length because it is an especially good example of rights discourse. In Quote 5 alone, MARCUS expresses many of the primary ideological under-pinnings of this discourse. While he sees Irish as an inherent part of the political scene which cannot be detached from the political context of the North, he asserts that the main motivation for the activities of the revival movement is and always has been the survival of the language itself. He has no problem with Sinn Féin promoting Irish, but is critical of them at the same time. He emphasizes that Irish should not be viewed or presented as a party political issue, and he makes an effort to distinguish between politics in the general sense and party politics. He appears to have no difficulty with the association between Nationalism and the Irish language, and does not even raise it as an important issue. For MARCUS, the association between Nationalism and the Irish language has been naturalized to a large extent.

THE NON-PROFESSIONALS

People who do not make a living out of manipulating discourse also make use of rights discourse in a critical capacity. PROINSIAS, a teacher in his late forties who was introduced in Chapter 5, moved freely between cultural and rights discourse during the interview I conducted with him, as he did in conversation on other occasions. He admires the thinking behind cultural discourse and the people who work to keep the language apolitical (see Quote 11, Chapter 5). However, he has a background of involvement with the civil rights movement, and has quite an interest in Northern Irish politics which seems to incline him towards rights discourse in some instances.

C O'R: What do you mean by 'attempting to keep the language apolitical'?

PROINSIAS: There are those who have stood back from the language because they see the Provies as hijacking it with phrases like *tiocfaidh ár lá* ['our day will come'] and *beidh bua orainn* ['victory will be ours'], that this is going to put off Protestants who are interested in learning the language. But on the other hand, it's been used as a political football by extreme Loyalists who regard it as a mickey mouse language and anything Irish as anti-Unionist. There are people in Sinn Féin who think that to learn Irish is going to make them a better Republican, and I think that's wrong. There are people who think that if you learn Irish it will make you less of a Unionist and that's wrong too. I'm inclined to agree that any language transcends politics, that it does not belong to any one political grouping but to a people and a culture. It's just indicative of this state that people would use something like that there to score political points. It may sound a wee bit contradictory here, but you can't avoid being political about a language in another sense, because it was political and economic decisions which helped to downgrade it and destroy it in the first place, it was part of a colonizing process, the plantations. They're all political moves and you have to accept that these things destroyed not only the development of a nation but a language.

To be honest I don't know where I stand here myself. The people I know who feel it should be apolitical believe that certain organizations have hampered the growth of the language and made it impossible for it to develop properly and have kept everyone from wishing to learn it. I believe this is a valid point, because there are people who will not learn it because so and so is learning it, or so and so is learning it for political reasons.

. . .

Ultimately I'm not sure who's responsible, but responsibility for funding and resources lies with the state, and if they neglect their responsibilities, they're culpable for adding to the downgrading of the language. I would apply culpability to both governments in Ireland. Stormont discouraged the language and under direct rule the government has been a very reluctant contributor. Everything they've added in the form of resources had to be fought for. [Quote 6]

As soon as PROINSIAS gives his interpretation of cultural ideology at the beginning of Quote 6, he goes on to say that, 'on the other hand', Unionists also politicize the language. This perspective could be indicative of either decolonizing or rights discourse, but in this case, the acceptance of criticisms of Sinn Féin and his assertion that language transcends party politics indicates rights discourse. Looking at the Irish language as political 'in another sense', aside from the use of 'political' to mean 'Republican', is also characteristic of rights discourse. In the final two sentences of the first paragraph, he seems to slip into decolonizing discourse as well. In the second paragraph, PROINSIAS agrees that those who advocate a cultural point of view have a point, which is in keeping with much of what he said during the interview (see discussion in Chapter 5). However, in the third paragraph he switches to a discussion on the responsibility of the state to support the language, perhaps picking up on the final point in the first paragraph about the effect of colonization on the Irish language. In a rather roundabout way, he is conceding the opposite point as well, that those who bring Irish into the political arena in order to push the state for funding and support for the language also have a point.

PROINSIAS relies on rights discourse to help him express his sometimes ambiguous feelings about the relationship between politics and the Irish language. He clearly favours much of the ideology espoused and created by cultural discourse, but at the same time, this is not enough. Decolonizing discourse stands in direct ideological opposition to cultural discourse, so drawing on decolonizing discourse to express his political points of view is not satisfactory. Instead, rights discourse gives him an avenue to talk about his political thoughts on the language in a way which suits his beliefs. A creative balancing act between cultural discourse and rights discourse allows him to express the ambiguity which he feels as well.

In everyday speech, it is perhaps more common for people to draw on a variety of discourses rather than just one at a time. An examination of a section of the interview with DEIRDRE, a nurse in her late thirties, demonstrates this. DEIRDRE learned a small amount of Irish in primary school, but had a negative experience with Irish in secondary school. DEIRDRE's father had learned to speak Irish and had a very positive attitude to it, but never taught it to the children. When she asked him about this later, he told her that he thought it was more important for the mother to have Irish and teach it to the children. She told me that her father did use bits of Irish in the house, for example when asking them to do simple tasks, or calling his jumper a *geansaí.*

DEIRDRE strongly believes that Irish and politics are two separate things, yet at the same time she feels that language is intimately connected to identity and nationality. 'To me the language shouldn't be affected by politics, but I suppose it is in some ways here, where it shouldn't be.' She expressed amazement that 'people who are supposed to know how to speak English' cannot distinguish between three different words, Irish, religion and politics. But because language is part of a person's cultural identity, it inevitably becomes a part of their national identity in the context of Northern Ireland:

It's the unique thing about each country, something you can bring with you and always have. It unites people as one nationality. Language in Ireland is associated with the political thing. If you go to France, it wouldn't be. This is the thing about the British being in Ireland, it's drummed into us by the Brits. It's going to take a long time to get over. Negative attitudes need to be overcome, like the association with politics, or people saying what use is it to you?

. . .

In my own mind, you could have the best Irish and be a Unionist. To me language and politics are different, but maybe it's like the religion and politics thing, where subconsciously you talk about the Protestants and the Catholics instead of Unionists and Nationalists, which is not necessarily the same thing. Same with the language. [Quote 7]

Following Frazer and Cameron (1989), the seeming contradictions in what she says are explicable at least in part by examining the discourses she draws on. In the first two sentences of Quote 7, she takes from the discourse of romantic nationalism, which is founded on an ideology that equates the boundaries of a nation with language. In the third and fourth sentences she switches to a discourse associated with talk about the Troubles, where the political situation in Ireland is considered to be in some ways unique and without comparison elsewhere in the world. In the fifth sentence, she seems to be blaming the British for the political association, a belief that suggests a certain affiliation with decolonizing discourse. In the final sentence of the first paragraph, DEIRDRE switches to cultural discourse, labelling the association of politics with the Irish language as a 'negative attitude'. The second paragraph, on the other hand, is more like rights discourse, reiterating that political aspirations and the Irish language are two separate matters that often become convoluted in the context of Northern Ireland, just like religion and politics. The apparent ambiguities in her stance on the Irish language and politics comes in part from combining different discourses which are informed by widely differing ideologies, and in part from her own possibly ambiguous feelings about the issue.

IAIN comes from a working-class Protestant background, and his parents have a British identity. In spite of his upbringing, he is very proud of his Irish identity, and traces the change back to a period spent in London.

I went to London to work at 16, and there were people from all sorts of backgrounds, including people from the South [of Ireland], Greeks, Australians, Jews, from other parts of England. It was an education for me. I was there until I was 20. As an east Belfast Protestant, I was shocked and offended to be called 'Paddy', but I eventually got used to it. As you work with people the old barriers break down. When I came back to Belfast and was living in east Belfast, I would have had very different interests, and I was very interested in Irish folk music and it was a very up and coming thing then. In London I had worked organizing folk nights at a club, with world famous acts and the best of folk singers. But then when I came back to Belfast this wasn't happening in east Belfast, but it was happening in west Belfast, so I started socializing in west Belfast. When the civil rights campaign started, I got very involved in People's Democracy. So I tended to be mixing with Catholics. [Quote 8]

IAIN's parents had no interest in Irish, and there was no Irish taught in the state schools which he attended. His first encounter with Irish came when a friend invited him to *Cluain Ard*. The main reason he went along, he says, is because there was a late bar on that night. His first words of Irish were how to order a pint of Guinness and a pint of Harp. He was 'astounded' to find they were not allowed to speak English, but he enjoyed listening to the traditional music which was playing that evening. Although it was a good experience, it did not inspire him to learn the language. He became involved with the Irish language a number of years later after his first child was born, when he and his wife had to decide on a school. They decided on the *Bunscoil* because his wife had connections to the Irish language, and because they did not want their daughter to attend a religious school. He says it is very important to him that his children have a strong Irish identity and understand Irish history and the Irish language.

IAIN started to learn Irish to help his daughter at school. When she surpassed his abilities at Primary 2 (as usually happens), he continued to learn but could no longer help her with her school work. Learning Irish was an important experience in the development of his sense of identity, and helped him make sense of some experiences in his youth:

> When I began to learn Irish I became very, very angry that I had been deprived of this, of not having learned these things at school. It's great when you can read things in Irish, like the old poetry and all. I'm annoyed at the whole bloody system that told me I was British. I don't feel British. I suppose going to Britain at sixteen and being treated like a foreigner, which I was, had something to do with it. ... I never really felt British when I was a kid, maybe because my parents were politically aware. Because they were involved with the Labour Party, they would have been excluded from things in the community. If you weren't a member of a Unionist party you were suspect. I remember not being invited to a street party for the Queen's coronation because they assumed my parents weren't loyal because of their politics. [Quote 9]

IAIN has a different perspective on the issue of politics and the Irish language, formed by his own relatively unique experiences.

> Everything is political, and when people learn their language and learn they can be independent and can stand up and feel confident in themselves, that has to do with your political identity, because

the croppies are not going to lie down again. I think the more that people are speaking the language, the stronger they feel in their identity. I haven't really thought about this thing. If people could have a bilingual society that would be a brilliant thing, and I think it does tie in with the political thing. It'll forward the demand for independence from the British. I think even with Protestants like myself, it changes them, it breaks down the bigotry. I've come across a lot of Protestants who are starting to learn the language. Some of it comes from a wrong attitude, from people who are rewriting history to justify the existence of the Six Counties,[1] and I find that a wee bit bizarre. The Loyalist identity, the culture, it doesn't exist really at all. There's so much Irish culture, it's such an amazing thing, having been geographically separate from Europe, and the culture is very strong, but this doesn't exist with the Six County Loyalists. All they can do is beat a big drum and say 'I hate Fenians'.[2] That's what it comes down to. There aren't any good Orange songs, they're all so filled with bigotry and hate, it's incredible. [Quote 10]

In this passage, IAIN uses a very broad definition of 'political', both in his assertion that 'everything is political' and in his reference to the political motivations of Protestants learning the language. He does not use 'political' in the narrower sense of 'Republican' in this quote, although he seems to use this definition as well in Quote 11 below. IAIN makes a strong association between the language and political identity, a characteristic of decolonizing discourse. When he says that a bilingual society would further the demand for independence from Britain, he is also drawing on decolonizing discourse. In the next quote, however, IAIN uses both decolonizing and rights discourse.

When it comes to the parties and the Irish language, if you write a letter to the SDLP to ask them to support you, they'll write back and say certainly, but they won't send you any money. But if you write to Sinn Féin to ask them, they'd organize something to raise some money like a big bunch of them hiking up a hill and getting sponsorship, or the prisoners running around the yard or something. They would be more involved, and why not? Sinn Féin deserve all credit for their participation in the language, for the money they've given the schools and the infant schools, and the support they've given. Any language group that I'm involved in, politics is irrelevant, you're not going to stop someone becoming involved because they're in Sinn Féin. It's their contribution to the group that's important. I've worked with people who I have profound political disagreements with, but it doesn't matter because the language is for everyone. The more people that come to the language the better. Irish is the right of everybody, but at the same time I would find it hard to imagine sitting down and teaching an RUC man Irish, although I know people who wouldn't see anything wrong with it and would do it.

C O'R: Why wouldn't you teach an RUC man Irish?

I've known of kids who've talked in Irish when the house is being raided, even though they don't really speak it, just repeating a prayer or something to each other, to freak out the RUC and the British. If they knew it you wouldn't be able to talk about them, they could understand. I don't know, you've put me on the spot by asking why I wouldn't teach them, it seems the obvious thing. I guess it's that they've accepted a different culture, I don't think they have the right to both worlds. They have to make a choice. If you're Irish and living in Ireland, and you decide that you want to accept your identity that's fair enough, but if you're saying you're not Irish, you're British, and you want to learn Irish, I can't see how you'd justify it in your head.[3] Irish Catholics don't have a choice. I had a choice, and I made the choice to go forward through the Irish culture and the Irish identity. It's a big step to take, because I can never live in east Belfast again, I've made my bed and I have to lie in it. I don't think you can just, I can't understand why there are some Unionist politicians who want to learn Irish, and while they may seem liberal, to my mind they are just as bigoted as the other politicians and Loyalists. I can't see how they reconcile it. They do it through a whole complicated thing that I don't think is based on anything strong, like rewriting things, or picking things out and saying we are all Cruthins.[4] It's nonsense. People can learn Irish in the same way as you would learn French or German, and that's okay, and maybe that's where these Unionists are coming from. To me it's not just learning Irish, it's becoming part of the whole culture. It's a different thing to say you are learning Irish and I am Irish. It's not like learning German. There's a lot more to the revival, it's the whole culture that's tied in with it, literature, music, dancing, everything. It's like the difference between learning to speak Irish at an English school, or learning Irish at an Irish-medium school where it's not just a subject. It's part of my reason for involvement. I want to see all that other stuff kept going as

well. We're trying to reclaim our culture rather than the culture
that's been imposed on us. It's different when you're trying to
learn a language that the English tried to destroy completely, and
almost did. [Quote 11]

The first paragraph of Quote 11, where IAIN defends Sinn Féin's
involvement with the Irish language, is typical of rights discourse. He
is not defending Sinn Féin's policies so much as their right to participate, whether he personally agrees with their politics or not. The
precise meaning of 'politics' is not clear in this passage. When he says
'politics is irrelevant', he could be using the word in the narrower
sense of 'Republican' because of the context (talking about Sinn Féin),
or he could be using the same, broader definition used previously in
the discussion.

At the end of the first paragraph, he qualifies what he is saying by
adding that he could not imagine teaching Irish to an RUC man. His
reply to my inquiry, while admittedly an on-the-spot formulation, gives
an interesting insight into one aspect of how IAIN, and others as well,
view the Irish language. If members of the RUC knew Irish, its status as
'our language' might be diminished. It would lose part of its power to
mystify, and its position as a sort of 'secret' language used by insiders
and those who are 'in the know' would be subverted. Not only is it fun
and potentially useful to be able to say things that the RUC and British
army cannot understand, it affords the speaker, and Irish speakers as a
whole, a certain amount of symbolic capital. The inability of most
Protestants, and the RUC in particular, to speak Irish, combined
perhaps with their lack of desire to know it, sets up a dichotomy – us
versus them, Irish versus British. IAIN does not believe people should
have access to 'both worlds', and the Irish language is a key point of
access. As a language that the English tried to destroy, the defenders of
English hegemony should not have the privilege of knowing it.

PROINSIAS and IAIN both use rights discourse in combination
with another discourse, but in contrasting ways. PROINSIAS combines
rights discourse with cultural discourse to accommodate his ambiguous
feelings about the relationship between politics, culture and the Irish
language. IAIN, on the other hand, combines decolonizing discourse
with rights discourse, creating a more politically charged feel and indicating a strong sympathy with Republicanism. All of the non-professionals
quoted here combine discourses to construct and communicate their own
individual versions of the relevance of the Irish language to identity,
Irish culture, and the politics of the North.

CONCLUSION

Decolonizing and cultural discourses are so well rehearsed that certain familiar phrases and formulations are heavily encoded with meaning which do not need elaborate explanation. When a person says, 'I believe that the Irish language ought to be kept separate from politics', they are making a statement with profound implications about their beliefs with regards to Republican involvement in the Irish language movement, and the importance and meaning of the language to Irish identity. In contrast, rights discourse is not so heavily encoded and tends to require more explanation. This is, of course, part of its appeal, because it leaves more space for interpretation.

Rights discourse is at least as widely used as cultural discourse, although it is less institutionalized. In spite of this, or perhaps in some ways because of it, the ideology of rights discourse has a high level of legitimacy not enjoyed by decolonizing discourse. As the dominant oppositional voice in campaigns to obtain recognition and funding for the Irish language from the British government, it is part of the public transcript of the Irish language revival movement. Although part of the public transcript, it is for the most part not accepted by those who hold positions of authority, particularly in the government. As such, it is frequently ignored, or responded to with reference to cultural discourse.

This can be clearly seen in a correspondence which took place between Secretary of State Patrick Mayhew and ten prominent Irish language campaigners representing different Irish language groups in Northern Ireland. In response to a letter requesting that the Secretary of State help to promote a bilingual policy in Northern Ireland, Simon Rogers, writing on Mayhew's behalf, argues that the government

> seeks to respect the special importance of Irish, encourage interest in it and appreciation of it, and highlight its contribution to the cultural heritage of the whole community. The Government is anxious to remove structural barriers to the use of the language by those who wish to do so.
>
> (Rogers 1995, correspondence with Ó Muilleoir et al.) [Quote 12]

Interestingly, this is very similar to a section of the CTG's booklet *Giving Voices* which states that 'statutory or financial impediments to the use of Irish should be removed to enable those who wished to use it to do so more freely' (CTG 1994: 24–5). After drawing on cultural discourse in this section, Rogers draws on rights discourse (heavily used by the letter writers) when he argues that the government's current policy with regards to the Irish language does indeed reflect 'parity of esteem between the cultural traditions of the two main sections of the community' (Rogers 1995, correspondence with Ó Muilleoir et al.). He concludes by warning:

> The aggressive politicization of the language ... could make it a highly divisive issue. I hope that you and the other signatories of your letter would share the Government's desire to avoid that happening.
> (Rogers 1995, correspondence with Ó Muilleoir et al.) [Quote 13]

The Irish language activists reply by using rights discourse once again, even though it had little effect in the first letter which sparked off the correspondence:

> Your statement that Irish already enjoys 'a parity of esteem' in the North worries us as it shows a failure on your part to recognize the gross discrimination by your government against the Irish language. ... There is a world of difference, of course, between this policy and the status Irish enjoys in the South, or indeed the status Welsh enjoys in Wales or Scottish Gaelic in Scotland. Yet you insist that this shameful situation 'reflects a parity of esteem between the cultural traditions of the two main sections of the community'. We find it difficult to understand how such an [*sic*] statement can be defended when your government spends £171.48 per head on the promotion of Gaelic in Scotland but just £8.99 per head on the promotion of Irish in the North of Ireland. ... We hope now that these discriminatory policies are a thing of the past and that the Irish speaker in the North of Ireland will be given the same rights as the Irish speaker in the South of Ireland, or, indeed, the same rights as the Welsh speaker in Wales or the Gaelic speaker in Scotland.
> (Ó Muilleoir et al. 1995: correspondence with Rogers on behalf of the Secretary of State) [Quote 14]

In its position as an oppositional discourse, rights discourse pervades campaigns for status and funding for the language. The consequences of this will become more apparent in Chapter 7.

TEXT PRODUCER, AUDIENCE AND CONTEXT

Before moving on to the case studies, I want to pause to consider the importance of text producer, audience and context on the production of discourse. Choice of discourse, and the various ways in which they are used, are part of a dynamic and creative process which is affected by numerous variables, including perceived audience, situational context and the goals, social position and characteristics of the person speaking. Looking at extracts of decolonizing discourse as an example, I would like to briefly examine how these variables come into play.

Paine (1981) notes the importance of audience to the construction of political rhetoric. The task of rhetoricians is to see that the experiences and interests of the audience are reflected in their words, in order to persuade the audience to believe or act in the interests of the speaker, or those whom the speaker represents. In the *Learning Irish* booklet examined in Chapter 4, the second author writes:

> The process of decolonization will have stopped half way if, the day we succeed in driving the English from our shores, what is left behind is an Irish people possessed of the language, culture and values of the English.
>
> (Sinn Féin 1984: 6) [Quote 15]

As with all of the passages, the audience which the author intends to address is an important influence on the discourse used. The 'we' in this passage unites readers and writer into one group, Republicans and more than likely, Sinn Féin supporters. The assumption of shared beliefs implicit in this 'we' means that a great deal can be left as 'understood' between reader and writer (or between speakers, as the case may be). The writer can be quite sure that the reader will be able to 'fill in' the appropriate 'blanks' from their pool of shared knowledge. For example, it is assumed that all present agree that a 'process of decolonization' is indeed desirable and necessary, and that there is at least broad agreement on what that process might entail. A reader who is not a Republican might find this phrase problematic, lacking the same pool of knowledge which the writer assumes he and his audience share. Having a sympathetic audience with a certain amount of shared background means that the writer need not worry too much about misunderstandings. If the audience was sceptical or even hostile, such implicit assumptions might be fertile ground for misunderstandings or criticism.[5]

In the case of the interview with TOMÁS, there are two audiences – me, in the immediate context of the interview, and the wider audience of those who would eventually read what I wrote based on that interview. In the first case, while TOMÁS could assume that I was probably sympathetic to the revival of Irish because I was learning to speak it and frequented Irish language events, he could not be certain about my background or political beliefs. Who would actually be reading the final product was also uncertain. Possible audiences might include other *Gaeilgeoirí*, various academics, those sympathetic to Irish and those unsympathetic, perhaps even government representatives. This meant that TOMÁS could not be sure of his audience, and therefore had to be more careful about assumptions of shared knowledge and the possibility of leaving himself (and the Irish language in general) open to misinterpretation, criticism or hostility.

In the case of both the booklet and the interview, TOMÁS's personal beliefs about the Irish language and the political situation in Ireland, among other things, influence his choice of discourse. In this particular case, because TOMÁS is a public figure and because he was quite open about some aspects of his personal beliefs in the interview, it is almost self-evident that his Republican beliefs, his political aspirations and certain experiences in his past are an important part of the pool of knowledge which informs his choice of discourse. In other instances, a person's individual beliefs might be more difficult to ascertain. In some of the other examples cited in Chapters 5 and 6, people were less forthcoming about their beliefs and their past experiences. In these cases, it is more difficult to see the connection between background and choice of discourse.

Fairclough (1992) warns of the dangers involved in overemphasizing the construction of the social through discourse, without taking enough account of the social determination of discourse. The relationship between social structure and discourse is best viewed as a dialectical one. To paraphrase Giddens (1984) and Barth (1987), it is fair to assume that there is a real world out there, but people construct their representations of that world in their own minds. This is done in large part through the process of talk and writing – through discourse. The deeper social reality of the world in which people find themselves shapes the use of discourse, but at the same time people have the power to influence and change that world through discourse. To quote Fairclough, 'the discursive constitution of society does not emanate from a free play of ideas in people's heads but from a social practice which is firmly rooted in and oriented to real, material social structures' (1992: 66).

Thus TOMÁS's social position exerts an influence on his use of discourse – male, mid-thirties, university-educated, a Belfast City Councillor, member of Sinn Féin and a journalist by profession. His two occupations suggest a person fairly skilled in communicating, able to manipulate situations to his advantage in at least some circumstances, and possessing a certain amount of political savvy. One would expect that TOMÁS is aware of his role in the power games of the various spheres of politics in which he is involved, from City Hall to Irish language circles, and is able to participate and attempt to manoeuvre to advantage his own interests. The social position of the others quoted in this book likewise influences their use of discourse.

A final consideration is the relationship of an individual such as TOMÁS to the creative process of cultural construction. By focusing right down to the individual person as we do when looking at discourse, it can be all too easy to lose sight of the collectivity. On the other hand, a close look at the role of the individual can yield important insights, as Barth (1987) shows in his examination of the role of the ritual leader in Ok cosmology. In many ways, Irish language 'professionals' such as TOMÁS play a role similar to that of the ritual leader in Ok society.

In the foreword to Barth's book, Goody reminds us that culture is always 'in the making', which suggests that the 'the distinction between the social and the personal, the cultural and the individual' is blurred rather than crisply defined (1987: viii). Barth argues that to understand any social process, individual as well as group activity must be taken into account. He goes on to demonstrate that in Ok society, individual creativity is channelled in such a way that collective rites and symbols are profoundly affected. In their capacity as spokespersons and leaders, professionals in the Irish language revival movement, like a ritual leader among the Ok, work with the cultural material available to clarify, harmonize and rework the meaning of important symbols.

Barth argues that 'when the products of such work are incorporated in public rituals and assimilated by the audiences, the result is an ordering and elaboration of the fans of connotations that characterize sacred symbols' (1987: 38). Through this process, culture develops and changes in different directions. However, what Cohen (1994) calls the 'managers of meaning' – artists, politicians, advertisers and preachers – can only lead us to the meanings they wish to communicate. They cannot impose those meanings. If their interpretations do not resonate, they will not be adopted. Our own interpretations may be variations on the themes produced by the managers of meaning, but it is through our own variations that we make sense of the world.

Wherever symbols and conceptions carry unresolved ambiguities and contradictions, there will be the focus of intellectual and symbolic work. It is in such areas that the 'creative visions of the more interested and more articulate' will have the most effect in reshaping meaning and concepts (Barth 1987: 79). The Irish language in Northern Ireland is in just such a position today, and the more interested and the more articulate, like TOMÁS, Ó Cearnaigh and CAOIMHÍN are making their mark. In Chapter 7, I shall delve further into the complexities of how these discourses are used through the examination of four detailed case studies.

7 The Discourses in Practice: Four Case Studies

There is a certain danger in laying out these three discourses in an orderly fashion as I have in the last four chapters, because it might imply that these are static categories which can be ascribed to particular individuals or groups with predictable regularity. All of the discourses are fluid to a greater or lesser extent. It is also important to emphasize that they are not exclusively associated with specific individuals or groups, although certain individuals or groups may eventually be seen as representative of a particular discourse. While many people tend to favour one discourse over the others, most people draw creatively on two or even all three discourses, shifting and combining them to suit their purposes and needs at the time. The context in which a person is speaking, as well as the person's own background and individual history, influence choice and use of discourse.

In the last four chapters, I have outlined three discourses and looked at some of the factors which influence them. In this chapter, I shall show how these discourses work in the complex reality of daily life by looking at four examples of different arenas in which the three discourses are manifest. All four case studies focus on different aspects of the relationship between the Irish language revival movement and various branches of the government, both at the local and UK level. While the establishment of the ULTACH Trust in 1989 was perceived by some to be a concession by the British government to the language movement, within a year the Northern Ireland Office (NIO) had removed funding from the west Belfast group *Glór na nGael*. Soon after the successful campaign to restore funding to *Glór na nGael*, the Irish language revival movement launched a new campaign to obtain grant aid for the new Irish-medium secondary school *Meánscoil Feirste*. The ambiguous reception given to the establishment of the new Trust, and the campaigns to have funding restored to *Glór na nGael* and granted t]o *Meánscoil Feirste*, suggest an inconsistent and piecemeal approach on behalf of the British government towards the Irish language, as well as revealing the conflicting ideologies of the revival movement itself. In the final section of this chapter, I shall look at the long-running campaign against legislation prohibiting street signs in Irish, and the efforts launched to erect these signs over the years in spite of the law.

SYMBOLIC CONFLICT

Harrison's (1992, 1995) work on ritual and symbolic conflict can offer important insights into these case studies. He argues that ritual constitutes a special class of intellectual property which can be compared with the concept of property found in gift economies. In a gift economy goods are personified, symbolizing their owners' identities, rather than being objectified as in a commodity mode of exchange (Harrison 1992: 234). If the Irish language is conceptualized in Harrison's terms as a kind of intellectual property, we obtain a different perspective on the struggle to impute and interpret its meaning. It becomes more than just a symbol of Irish identity, merely standing for or representing a certain type of Irishness – it becomes the symbolic personification of the Irish people, and the struggle to put forward the definitive meaning of the language becomes a part of the struggle to define what it means to be an Irish person in Northern Ireland today. The politics of the Irish language revival movement involves a struggle over the control of Irish as a collective symbol, and over 'the very right to employ this symbolism in the first place' (Harrison 1992: 236).

The staging of rituals and ceremonies is more than simply an expression of a sense of unity and collective identity. It is also a manifestation of the current state of power relations within a group (Harrison 1992). The campaigns of the Irish language revival movement can be understood in some ways to be political rituals, the playing out of which display the struggle for power between different groups and organizations within the movement, and between the movement and the British government.

Harrison (1995) has suggested that 'symbolic conflict' can take four different forms – valuation contests, proprietary contests, innovation contests and expansionary contests – reflecting the four different ways in which a political symbol can be used. All of these different strategies are, in essence, part of the competition for symbolic capital. Harrison argues that 'political symbols are to symbolic capital what money is to economic capital' (1995: 16). Political symbols have four characteristics which correspond to the four ways in which it is possible to accumulate symbolic capital: they are property, they are status markers, their possession confers legitimacy as well as certain rights and prerogatives, and they are invested with their owner's sense of self.

In a valuation contest, 'the issue at stake is the ranking of symbols' (Harrison 1995: 2). He points out that ethnic and nationalist movements offer numerous examples of valuation contests, and that 'political theatre' such as marches and demonstrations are pervaded by valuation contests. The linking of the Irish language with the notion of parity of esteem for Nationalists could be seen as part of a valuation contest seeking to increase the ranking of the Irish language as a symbol of Irish identity in Northern Ireland.

What Harrison calls proprietary contests are also key to understanding the Irish language revival movement. Groups, he says, often claim proprietary rights in their symbols. Any dispute over these rights, over ownership or control of an important collective symbol, is a proprietary contest. The need to establish legitimacy can lead to struggle to reinvest the same collective symbolic form with different meanings (Harrison 1992: 236). Clearly, there is a struggle within the Nationalist community in Northern Ireland – and to some extent between Nationalists, Unionists and the British government – for proprietary rights in the Irish language.

A key feature of innovation contests is the creation of symbolism. Processes of innovation can involve, on the one hand, the competitive elaboration of an existing symbolic form, and on the other, the creation of new categories of symbols. The fourth type of symbolic conflict is the expansionary contest, where one group attempts to displace another group's symbols of identity with its own. Harrison identifies expansionary contests as the exact opposite of innovation contests, because in an expansionary contest the symbolic inventories of a group may be partly or totally destroyed (1995: 9). For example, some Unionists seem to fear that the granting of recognition to the Irish language in Northern Ireland threatens the replacement of their own British cultural symbols with Irish ones.[1]

As I shall argue in the case studies which follow, Harrison's ideal types of the valuation contest and the proprietary contest are of particular relevance to an understanding of the Irish language revival movement in west Belfast.

CASE STUDY ONE:
WHICH DISCOURSE? THE ESTABLISHMENT OF
THE ULTACH TRUST

The ULTACH Trust was founded in 1989, a year after the Cultural Traditions Group (CTG), specifically to deal with the Irish language. The same set of seminars which resulted in the establishment of the CTG laid the groundwork for the ULTACH Trust. When it became clear that money would be made available to support the Irish language, but only through the community relations budget, the Trust was established so that control of the funding would be in the hands of Irish speakers. In 1990 a capital fund was set up with a grant of £500,000 from the European Union, £250,000 from the Community Relations Council, £100,000 from the International Fund for Ireland and £20,000 from Gael-Linn. The capital fund was set up to ensure long-term viability should annual funding be reduced or discontinued in the future. The interest from the capital fund, combined with additional money provided by the Community Relations Council and *Roinn na Gaeltachta*, goes towards providing grants to interested Irish language groups. The annual grant giving capacity of the Trust is now over £100,000 per year (ULTACH Trust 1994: 5).

Many Irish language activists, particularly in west Belfast, perceive the ULTACH Trust as advocates of an 'apolitical' view of the Irish language. The presence of Unionist politicians on the Board of Trustees; the special efforts made to attract, or at least to not alienate, Unionists; the criticism made of Nationalists and Republicans who, in the perception of the Trust, are using the language for their own political gains; and the type of discourse favoured by the Trust, suggest to many that the Trust is promoting the depoliticization of the Irish language. The result has been a considerable amount of suspicion on the part of some *Gaeilgeoirí*, and even outright hostility amongst a minority.

Critics of the ULTACH Trust can be loosely grouped into two camps, those who are suspicious of the very rationale behind the founding of the organization (usually, but not always, Republicans), and those who welcome the founding of the Trust, but believe that it is flawed in some way. Such was the intensity of the criticism in the year after its founding that its director, Aodán Mac Póilin, complained that a campaign was being waged against the Trust. The Irish language newspaper *Lá* reported him as saying, '*Tá mise tinn tuirseach ag tógáil miodóga amach as mo dhroim*' ('I am sick and tired of taking daggers out of my back')[2] (25 October 1990).

Members of Sinn Féin have expressed grave doubts about the motivations for the founding of the ULTACH Trust, drawing almost entirely on decolonizing discourse in their criticisms. They suggest it is a government front, designed to regulate the Irish language revival by keeping control of its funding. Sinn Féin councillor and Irish language activist Máirtín Ó Muilleoir calls Mac Póilin '*fear an NIO*' – the Northern Ireland Office (NIO) man – in numerous articles on the Trust (for example, *Lá*, 14 June 1990: 3). In another article, he accuses the government of having a deliberate policy designed to portray the Irish revival movement as sectarian, so that they could blame the decline of Irish on its association with Nationalism rather than on their own policies. He suggests that this is the reason why funding for Irish has been tied to the Community, Relations budget, rather than being treated separately as are Welsh and Scots Gaelic (*Lá*, 5 August 1993).

Derry Sinn Féin councillor Gearóid Ó hEára writes that having failed in their policy to oppress the Irish language, the British government needed a more clever policy '*na Paddies a choinneáil faoi smacht*' ('to subjugate the Paddies'), and that the ULTACH Trust is part of that policy (*Lá*, 5 August 1993: 14). The Republican newspaper *An Phoblacht* (20 February 1992) accuses the NIO of trying to buy off the Irish language vote by setting up the Community Relations Council and the ULTACH Trust, while at the same time cutting funding for *Glór na nGael*. Republicans have also complained that there is no Sinn Féin or even SDLP representative on the Board of Trustees.

These fears and accusations have been echoed by others as well. One prominent *Gaeilgeoir* also suggested to me that the ULTACH Trust is part of government efforts to control where the money goes in the Irish language revival movement. She described west Belfast as a bottle with its neck to the government.

When it was blocked people got on fine, but now that they've stuck a teat on it and feed down a trickle of milk, people become dependent on it, and when it's withdrawn we're fucked, because people won't be willing or able to do for themselves any more. [Quote 1]

The fear that people will become too dependent on government support and lose the self-help ethic is a common concern. Some believe the best solution is to dissolve the ULTACH Trust and create an independent Irish language funding body with more power and a larger budget. Mac Póilin, however, believes that much of this criticism has more to do with a desire to get rid of the ULTACH Trust than it does with a genuine fear of government dependency.

Criticisms from other quarters have focused on perceived flaws in the organization, but tend to be somewhat milder in tone. An editorial in the *Andersonstown News* (6 April 1991) gives a 'warm welcome' to an increase in funding for the Trust, but suggests that more money should be channelled into projects in west Belfast, where the bulk of language revival activities and organizations are located. Three years later, in a regular Irish language column, it was suggested that the ULTACH Trust's money would be better spent on the Irish-medium schools, since they are the heart of the movement and lacked government funding (*Andersonstown News*, 21 May 1994).[3]

Aside from disagreements on how the Trust's money should be spent, the most common criticisms are that the Board of Trustees is unbalanced or not representative on the Nationalist side, and that they, too, use the Irish language for political ends. An article in Irish in the *Andersonstown News* (25 January 1992) focused on the latter point, although it is careful to temper its criticism by congratulating the Trust on its many accomplishments. The author softens the blow by suggesting that it would be dishonest not to raise the issue of problems which he or she sees with the Trust. The article then goes on to say that the first annual report of the Trust seems to side with the NIO on the issue of politicizing the language, because it says that some Irish language groups are alienating Unionists by making it part of a Nationalist political agenda. The article claims that this is inaccurate and insulting to Irish speakers, and asks for an explanation. It would be more fair, the article suggests, also to criticize the British government for using Irish as part of their efforts to entice Nationalists away from Sinn Féin.

A more recent article written by Gearóid Ó Cairealláin, the current president of the Gaelic League, takes up both points mentioned previously, addressing the issue of the Board of Trustees being unbalanced as well as the politicization of the language (*Andersonstown News*, 11 March 1995: 24). Ó Cairealláin perceives a gap between the ULTACH Trust and the public, caused in part by their political stance. He, too, criticizes the Trust for adopting the same stance as the NIO in opposition to Sinn Féin, suggesting that some members of the party are the most die-hard, diligent *Gaeilgeoirí* in the North.[4] He argues that if there are Unionist politicians on the Board of Trustees, it is only right that a Sinn Féin representative should also be on the Board. The representativeness of ULTACH's Board of Trustees is one of the key criticisms of the organization, and the one that is the most disturbing to many Irish speakers. In its efforts to attract Unionist support for the Irish language, some argue that the Trust is being unjust towards Nationalists who are genuinely dedicated to the language.

A look at the ULTACH Trust's own materials gives a picture of how the organization portrays itself. The first annual report of the ULTACH Trust was published in 1991. Under the heading 'Cross-Community Initiatives', the Trust explains its emphasis on the

Protestant community:

> There appears to be an increase in interest in Irish among people from Protestant or unionist backgrounds ... However, it would be unwise to overestimate this trend, as the entire area is fraught with difficulties. Many unionists see Irish as being alien to their own tradition, and are deeply hostile to and distrustful of the language movement, which many of them see as having an essentially political agenda. The Trust's cross-community work is, and will be for some time, in the very delicate area of trying to overcome deep-seated prejudices. ...
>
> While nationalism is a perfectly legitimate motive for wishing to keep the Irish language alive, there are, of course, other alternative motives. There is no necessary conflict in an Irish-language student or enthusiast also being a unionist in politics. However, at present, the vast majority of language enthusiasts are nationalists, and, unfortunately, many of those nationalists fail to recognize that there can be any other rationale for involvement in the language movement. As a result, they often, despite themselves, make it difficult for interested unionists to learn the language. ...
>
> The main problem relates to the issue of political identity, largely because those who claim that the language is equally the heritage of nationalists and unionists have not always fully worked out the implications of this principle. This problem arises from the fact that the cultural commitment of many Irish-speakers is inseparable from their political allegiance. Again, it should be emphasized that this is a perfectly justifiable ideological position: however, it is often accompanied by an assumption that unionists interested in Irish culture are well on the way to becoming nationalists. ... This unconscious ethnocentricity, rooted in an unresolved conflict between principles which claim to be non-political, and assumptions which are essentially political in their implications, is deeply ingrained in the Irish language movement.
>
> (ULTACH Trust 1991: 8–10) [Quote 2]

I have quoted this section of the first report at length to illustrate the effort made to achieve a careful balance between support for attracting Unionists to the language (without offending distrustful Unionists), and criticism of Nationalist attitudes (without alienating what the report admits is the majority in the revival movement). The report asserts that a Nationalist position in relation to the language is legitimate, but at the same time it sees this as worrisome because such a position contains an element of unconscious ethnocentricity. This position has contributed to bad feelings on the part of some Nationalists, as is evidenced by the comments mentioned above.

Mac Póilin himself is not unaware of the dilemma. He argues that for many, inclusive rhetoric about the language carries a different ideological subtext, one that in actuality excludes Unionists. The Trust tries to make such inclusive rhetoric a reality, but this is not a simple task. As Mac Póilin sees it, the problem lies in the weakness of Irish among the Unionist population. This weakness means that the Trust must take positive action to promote Irish to Protestants. At the same time, the Trust is supposed to promote Irish throughout Northern Ireland to Unionists and Nationalists alike. While they must try to get Unionists involved in the language, Mac Póilin emphasizes that the Trust has no right to undermine Nationalist perceptions of the language. This dilemma has led Mac Póilin to seek an alternative to the political/apolitical dichotomy, which he attempts to do through the creative use of discourse.

The ideology formulated in Quote 2 above is similar to rights discourse in that it confirms the legitimacy of the association between the Irish language and Nationalism, and it contains assertions that the language belongs to everybody, Nationalist or Unionist. It differs from most examples of rights discourse, however, in its criticisms of the position of some Nationalists and in the special care taken to appear balanced and fair for the benefit of Unionists. The first report does contain a sprinkling of cultural discourse as well:

> Not all Irish-language activists are well-meaning, and, for a highly vocal minority, the language is an integral part of a political programme. Sometimes it is in the interests of these groups to encourage unionist alienation from the language, and to identify Irish ever more closely with the nationalist community.
>
> (ULTACH Trust 1991: 10) [Quote 3]

In the ULTACH Trust's Second Report, published in 1994, the emphasis on increasing the language's cross-community appeal is reiterated. It indicates a greater emphasis on Irish language education, from Irish-medium schools and Irish as a school subject, to adult learning and the development of teaching materials. The new emphasis on funding Irish-medium schools was due in part to the development of the capital fund, which gave the Trust greater freedom in the allocation of grants. The Second Report also seeks to define the Trust's philosophy more closely with regards to its cross-community emphasis.

The Trust has endeavoured to present the language and culture to the Protestant and unionist community in a way that will not be perceived as threatening their political identity. This process is sometimes described as the depoliticisation of the language: however, it is often more a process of creating the conditions through which Irish will become acceptable and accessible within all political traditions.

(ULTACH Trust 1994: 15) [Quote 4]

This is in keeping with Mac Póilin's idea that the language needs to be multipoliticized, rather than depoliticized. Still, the notion persists among many west Belfast *Gaeilgeoirí* that the Trust, amongst others, are attempting to depoliticize the language, and that this amounts to a threat to their own perceptions of the meaning of the Irish language and importance of Irish culture to their ethnic and political identities, since 'depoliticize' is often used as shorthand for denying the validity of a Nationalist or Republican perspective on the language.

A number of factors contribute to the persistence of the perception that the ULTACH Trust favours the ideology of depoliticization which is generally associated with cultural discourse. The 'hands-off' policy towards Sinn Féin and the Trust's association with the Central Community Relations Unit (CCRU) fosters suspicion among some Nationalist *Gaeilgeoirí*, as demonstrated in the above discussion of attitudes towards the Trust. The relationship with the Cultural Traditions Group, strongly associated with cultural discourse and the community relations ethos, tends to colour perceptions of the Trust as well. The perception of open and eager support for Protestant interest in the language, combined with a perceived lack of support for language initiatives and organizations in Catholic areas, also fuels suspicions. Taken together, these particular perceptions give some people the general impression that the Trust favours the ideology of cultural discourse, in spite of what is explicitly stated in official reports.

The controversy and misunderstandings which surrounded the founding of the ULTACH Trust can be better understood if one looks at different factions of the Irish language revival movement as being involved in a proprietary contest. Republicans and some Nationalists fear that the British government is attempting to appropriate the Irish language as a symbol for their own ends, and that the ULTACH Trust is a part of that strategy. They are also contesting the entitlement of the Trust to distribute funds, arguing that other people should be part of the Board of Trustees, or that another organization entirely should have control over the distribution of government funding. From the

Trust's perspective, Nationalists have successfully appropriated the language already. The Trust, then, sees itself as attempting to appropriate Irish for all the people of Northern Ireland, Nationalist and Unionist. Alongside the strategy of appropriation, it could also be said that the ULTACH Trust is using a valuation strategy, since its ultimate goal is to increase the status of the Irish language in Northern Ireland as a whole. The British government, finally, fears the symbolic appropriation of the Irish language by Republicans, and is seeking the best method to subvert this.

CASE STUDY TWO:
IRISH UNDER ATTACK? THE *GLÓR NA NGAEL*
CONTROVERSY

Glór na nGael is the name of an annual all-Ireland competition to reward the community that has done the most to promote Irish in everyday life, a sort of Irish language 'tidy towns' competition. As early as the mid-1970s, the Andersonstown area of west Belfast entered the competition. In 1982, the west Belfast committee of *Glór na nGael* was formed as an umbrella group for Irish language organizations to coordinate and facilitate entry into the competition, and to help promote the Irish language in Belfast. West Belfast was awarded a number of the more minor prizes every year starting in 1982, and in 1986, 1990 and 1996 west Belfast won the most prestigious prize, the *Glór na nGael* trophy for the overall best area.

From its founding until its funding was withdrawn in 1990, west Belfast *Glór na nGael* was involved in numerous activities. Initially the focus was on rights for Irish speakers, and the group was prominent in the bilingual street signs campaign of the 1980s as well as campaigns to increase the status of Irish in English-medium schools, and for funding for Irish-medium schools. Over the years, *Glór na nGael* has shifted its emphasis from campaigning to providing services for Irish speakers and learners. It holds Irish language classes in its own premises and provides instructors for classes held by other organizations, including classes and seminars in 'neutral' venues like the Ulster People's College, designed to attract both Protestants and Catholics. *Glór* also provides support and teachers for the Irish-medium nursery schools movement, the organization's primary focus at the time funding was withdrawn.

In the months before the withdrawal of funding, there seemed little indication of the difficulties to come. The announcement that west Belfast had once again won first prize in the *Glór na nGael* competition came in March 1990. That same month, an editorial in the *Andersonstown News* (31 March 1990) congratulated west Belfast *Glór na nGael* for the work they had done to 'bridge the gap' between Protestants and Catholics through the Irish language. At this stage, *Glór na nGael* had 20 Action for Community Employment (ACE) workers, most of whom worked in Irish medium nursery schools throughout the city. The money provided by the government to support these ACE workers constituted the bulk of the organization's funding, and allowed them to become involved in the community on a much wider scale than would have been possible with solely voluntary workers (although they did have a number of volunteers as well).

On 25 August 1990, without warning, the west Belfast office of *Glór na nGael* received a letter from the Northern Ireland Office stating that their funding under the ACE scheme had been withdrawn. No explanation was offered in the brief letter, but reference was made to a 1985 statement made by then Secretary of State Douglas Hurd, in which he said that funds would not be made available to groups when that funding would 'have the effect of improving the standing and furthering the aims of a paramilitary organization, whether directly or indirectly'. *Glór na nGael* was not the first community group to lose funding under the new policy of 'political vetting' – among others, the Twinbrook Tenants and Community Association (west Belfast), Conway Mill (west Belfast), the Mac Airt Centre (the Short Strand area of east Belfast), Dove House (Derry) and the Glencairn Community Association (Protestant west Belfast) all had their funding withdrawn over the period of time since the Hurd declaration.

Ironically, permission to hold a fundraising collection in Belfast city centre was granted by the Royal Ulster Constabulary (RUC) the same day that *Glór na nGael's* ACE funding was withdrawn. In spite of the NIO decision, *Glór* was allowed to proceed with the scheduled collections. Many commentators mentioned this seeming contradiction as an example of the injustice of the NIO's decision – if the RUC saw nothing wrong with allowing *Glór na nGael* to collect money in the streets of Belfast, how could they NIO justify their decision?

The withdrawal of *Glór na nGael's* funding was immediately interpreted by west Belfast *Gaeilgeoirí* as an attack on the Irish language and on west Belfast as a whole. Many people were clearly shocked by the actions of the British government, coming as it did on the heels of the announcement that the government would be funding the newly established ULTACH Trust. One article in the *Andersonstown News* (1 September 1990) listed a number of well-known and respected public figures who had recently sung the praises of *Glór na nGael* – including Minister for the *Gaeltacht* Pat 'The Cope' Ó Gallchóir, Bishop Cathal Daly and Cardinal Tomás Ó Fiaich – as if to prove that the accusations against the organization were unfounded.

Seven of Belfast's eight Irish nursery schools, catering for approximately 140 children, were affected by the NIO cut in funding to *Glór na nGael*. None of the nurseries was receiving government funding of their own, so the loss of their *Glór na nGael* ACE workers was a severe blow. The schools were maintained through a variety of different fundraising drives, but the lack of ACE workers took its toll.

Within weeks of *Glór* receiving the news, a campaign to restore funding was launched, starting with a picket on the Training and Employment Agency which had paid the wages of the ACE workers, and a letter writing campaign to then Secretary of State for Northern Ireland, Peter Brooke. *Glór na nGael's* ACE workers had been members of NUPE, the National Union of Public Employees, and the Union also put their weight behind the campaign. *Glór* is also a member of NICVA, the Northern Ireland Council for Voluntary Action, which protested against the policy of political vetting and came out in support of the organization. The committee of the Shaws Road nursery school accused Brooke of 'an attack on our culture and language', and the Trustees of the ULTACH Trust took the unusual step of writing to Brooke asking him to reconsider his decision (*Andersonstown News*, 15 September 1990).

Speaking at a conference on censorship, the editor of *Lá*, Gearóid Ó Caireálláin, said 'Since the government withdrew funding from *Glór na nGael* there has been an increased awareness of how political vetting and censorship is used to control people's lives and culture' (*Andersonstown News*, 20 October 1990). A hard-hitting editorial in the same paper strongly criticized the policy of political vetting as an attempt by the British to 'divide and conquer':

> *Glór na nGael* was targeted because the Stormont mandarins decided it didn't fit into the greater scheme of things. Unlike most other groups receiving community aid it was neither church-orientated nor middle of the road. ...
>
> Without the nationalist community the political vetting policy is in tatters. We are being asked to act as our own worst enemy – turning our backs on our neighbours because the Government decrees

that they are unacceptable and unclean. We are to serve as a vetting body, screening our own community. Thus we can appear on the radio as long as we agree to the censorship of our neighbours. We can receive grant-aid for community projects as long as we agree to use government buzzwords and adopt as Gospel government policy. ...

(*Andersonstown News*, 27 October 1990) [Quote 5]

The final sentence appears to be a veiled reference to the ULTACH Trust and the new government policy on the Irish language. 'Government buzzwords' seems to be a reference to certain aspects of what I have called cultural discourse, particularly the version used by the Cultural Traditions Group, which has become increasingly important to the acquisition of funds for Irish language groups (see discussion in Chapter 5).

The accusation that the British government was using the Irish language to further its own ends was repeated in another editorial almost six months later. Commenting on an increase in funding for the ULTACH Trust, the editorial snipes:

Certainly Brian Mawhinney's patronizing claim yesterday that the money is designed to take the Irish language out of politics will be the cause of much mirth in the *Glór na nGael* offices. But then the parents of the eight nursery schools, run by *Glór na nGael* and denied funding since August last, know all about the Minister's determination to keep politics and the language separate – all politics that is except his own.

(*Andersonstown News*, 6 April 1991) [Quote 6]

Clearly, resentment over the treatment of *Glór na nGael* reinforced some people's suspicions about the ULTACH Trust and increased mistrust of NIO motivations in funding the Irish language.

After a few months, the campaign to have funding restored was stepped up. A case of maladministration was taken up with the Northern Ireland Ombudsman, a petition to Peter Brooke was started, the *Dáil*[5] was lobbied and *Glór na nGael* offered to publish its accounts for all to see. Messages of support came in from many different quarters, from Labour's shadow Northern Ireland Secretary Kevin McNamara to Boston Mayor Ray Flynn. In December 1990, SDLP deputy leader Seamus Mallon tabled over 20 parliamentary questions on the issue. The British government, however, remained silent throughout the 18-month campaign to regain funding, declining to comment when inquiries were made by journalists and refusing to give further details as to why funding was withdrawn.

An appeal for a review of the decision was made soon after the withdrawal of funding, but it was dismissed by the NIO without comment in October 1990. When *Glór na nGael* tried to gain access to documents regarding the NIO's decision to withdraw funding, their request was blocked by the issuing of a public immunity certificate. They then sought a judicial review in an effort to gain access to the documents, arguing that they could not defend themselves if they were not allowed to know the precise allegations that were being made against them. However, in a decision released in March 1991, the court decided against the case. In the end, *Glór na nGael* was never allowed access to any documents regarding their case, and no evidence was ever presented against them to support the allegations of paramilitary links.

Rumours, however, were rife. Some people believed that *Glór* was vetted because a prominent Irish language activist, who is also a Sinn Féin councillor, was a member of the committee until a few months before funding was withdrawn. To counter this, it has been argued that this person was a founding member of the organization and active with the group since 1982, so why was ACE funding granted in the first place? Besides, since this person had left the committee before funding was withdrawn, why was *Glór na nGael's* appeal of the decision denied when the government must surely have been aware of this fact? If the involvement of people with Republican sympathies was the problem, again, Republicans had been involved in the founding of the organization. Rather than reflecting any strong Republican sympathies in the Irish language movement, some people have suggested that this is because Republicans are relatively 'thick on the ground' in west Belfast, so you are bound to find people with Republican sympathies in almost any type of group or organization, from tenants' associations to church groups.

About the only evidence that could be mustered in support of the government's allegations against *Glór na nGael* came after funding had already been withdrawn. A former ACE worker with *Glór na nGael* who was once on the committee was later arrested and charged with paramilitary-related offences. Not surprisingly, perhaps, this incident was downplayed and was not widely reported by the Nationalist press. Labour's Kevin McNamara pointed out at the time that 'had all employers lost funding when staff were charged with criminal offences the whole economy would grind to a halt, including the security forces' (*Irish News*, 28 March 1992). More importantly, perhaps, this person was not on the committee of *Glór* when funding was withdrawn, nor at the time of his arrest. None of the speculation about the alleged paramilitary links attributed to the committee of *Glór na nGael* seemed to offer a satisfactory explanation for the withdrawal of funding. For west Belfast *Gaeilgeoirí* who were familiar with the organization and friendly with the members of the committee, there was no logic and certainly no truth in the accusations.

Alternative explanations for the denial of funding were suggested by some of the more conspiratorially minded. Perhaps the NIO was less interested in alleged paramilitary links and more concerned with the threat that the Irish language movement posed to the British government. A series of high-profile campaigns about the status of the Irish language in schools and funding for the burgeoning Irish-medium education movement were embarrassing for the government, which was trying to promote a new image of equal respect for the 'two traditions' in Northern Ireland. According to this line of thought, the ULTACH Trust was established to prove the government's credentials in supporting the Irish language, and funding was removed from the less domesticated *Glór na nGael* to help bring the movement under control. Others saw it as a personal vendetta on the part of the former Minister for Education Brian Mawhinney, who was attacked by *Glór na nGael* for his education proposals which would have reduced the status of the Irish language in secondary schools.

As the high-profile campaign continued and gained increasing support at home and abroad, rumours surfaced that there were splits in the civil service over the decision to cut *Glór na nGael's* funding. Some people believe that those who made the decision behind the scenes were surely reprimanded for underestimating its consequences. The RUC continued to grant permission to *Glór* to make street collections during the period of the ban, perhaps indicating conflicting intelligence between the RUC and NIO sources. The sustained questioning and publicity was clearly becoming embarrassing for the NIO. The *Irish News* reported that a 'reliable source' told them that certain people were 'rapped hard over the knuckles because it was felt they had drastically underestimated the ensuing controversy' (28 March 1992).

There were also splits in the ranks of the Irish language movement itself over the decision and the subsequent campaign to restore funding. One commentator suggested that *Glór na nGael* give up the campaign and continue their work without funding (*Andersonstown News*, 15 September 1990). Gearóid Ó Cairealláin, the editor of *Lá*, wrote an article saying that *Glór* should put an end to their campaign and disband the organization, arguing that it was a lost cause and that it would be better for west Belfast *Gaeilgeoirí* to try another strategy. He suggests forming another umbrella group to cater for all the Irish-medium schools throughout Belfast, believing that the money taken away from *Glór na nGael* might then be retained for the Irish language movement, but coming through another organization (*Lá*, 22 November 1990).

One of *Glór na nGael's* chief organizers, Diarmaid Ó Breasláin, responded in an article published two weeks later (*Lá*, 4 December 1990), arguing that first and foremost, giving up the campaign would be letting down all those who had supported their fight against political vetting both in the Irish language movement and outside it. If a new organization was established, as Ó Cairealláin suggested, what would stop the government from taking the funding away again? How could any such organization ever take a stand against the government if they were constantly afraid of losing their funding? Ó Breasláin also points out that *Glór* is involved in other work aside from nursery education which would suffer if the organization folded. Finally, he argues that giving up the campaign would be tantamount to admitting that the government was right to cut the funding in the first place.

Lá's editorial policy is nothing if not provocative, and the issue of *Glór na nGael's* funding is no exception. As far as this particular issue is concerned, it has also been a rather inconsistent policy. An editorial from 17 May 1991 is supportive of *Glór na nGael* and calls on the government to restore the organization's funding. Yet the call to end the campaign was repeated in an editorial some months later (*Lá*, 31 July 1991). It has been suggested that this debate might be a reflection of a certain amount of competition between *Glór na nGael* and the newly established *Cultúrlann*, which Ó Cairealláin played a large part in organizing. Both operate as umbrella organizations for the Irish language, and when the *Cultúrlann* first came into being in 1991 there was no clear division of labour between the two. Some of the arguments against continuing the campaign also reveal a fear of a growing dependence on government funding which might damage the autonomy of the revival movement.

Regardless of the motivations behind the debate, the interesting thing is that it was carried out entirely in Irish. To the best of my knowledge, no such critical consideration of the issues was undertaken in public in English. The use of Irish in this case effectively kept the potentially divisive debate 'private' and out of the public domain. Had it been in English, it would have been available for all to see and might have exposed divisions within the movement which *Gaeilgeoirí* under-standably prefer to kept behind closed doors. According to Harrison (1992), the right to take part in internal disputes is an 'insider's right', not open to people who are not members of the group. As this case demonstrates, the privilege of participation can be protected by the use of the Irish language, which effectively excludes all but the closest of insiders.

Whatever the reasons behind the NIO's decision to withdraw funding from *Glór na nGael*, it seriously heightened hostility towards the British government on the part of the Irish language movement, as well as fuelling suspicions of the ULTACH Trust. There was resentment at what was perceived by many to be an effort to rein in and control the movement, first through the manipulation of funding, and second by efforts to promote an 'acceptable' stance on the role of the Irish language in Northern Ireland. Increasingly, it seemed, there was an official line to toe when dealing with government agencies and fund-ing bodies with regards to Irish. A certain discourse had to be used, particular 'buzzwords' employed, to get grants and official approval. The conciliatory 'feel good' language of cultural discourse has become increasingly favoured, although even this does not guarantee support as will be seen in the discussion of *Meánscoil Feirste*'s campaign below. There was also resentment at what was perceived by some to be an effort to force the community to police itself and marginalize Repub-licans. In the Irish language movement, as with many other community groups, this would mean shunning a number of important activists and in some cases, personal friends and colleagues.

The *Glór na nGael* controversy highlights a number of important issues. It clearly demonstrates the often antagonistic relationship which exists between large sections of the Irish language revival movement and the British government. It is also revealing in terms of *Glór na nGael's* place in the revival movement in west Belfast. For the most part, the movement closed ranks behind *Glór*, as did NUPE, NICVA and civil rights organizations such as the Centre for Research and Documentation (CRD) and the Committee on the Administration of Justice (CAJ).[6] However, it also revealed some dissension, particularly on the issue of to what extent the Irish language movement should rely on, or become dependent upon, government funding.

The controversy also provides a glimpse into the struggle to define the meaning and importance of the Irish language to Irish identity and Nationalist political aspirations. *Glór na nGael* used confrontational tactics in its campaigns to increase the profile of Irish and defend the status of the language in education. Although this was combined with seminars, Irish courses, publishing projects and more moderate politics as well, it was the confrontational aspects of their work which drew the attention of the NIO. As a grassroots organization in west Belfast, it became associated with Nationalist politics, even though *Glór na nGael* made some of the first concerted efforts since the Troubles started to provide neutral access to Irish language classes in Belfast. In spite of these efforts, *Glór na nGael* did not conform to the more conciliatory two traditions/common heritage image which the British government wished to promote. In order for the Irish language to fit into the community relations project, its strongly Nationalist and Republican image had to be shed, or at least neutralized. The establishment of the ULTACH Trust and the acceptance of the CTG's interpretations of the significance of the Irish language were part of that project, as is the strategic use of funding to support groups and organizations that fit the desired image and ideology.

Further light can be shed on the *Glór na nGael* episode by viewing it in terms of Harrison's second type of symbolic conflict. As with the controversy over the ULTACH Trust, it seems likely that the British government feared a successful appropriation of the Irish language by the Republican movement and hoped to undermine this trend. *Glór na nGael* fought back, not only by denying the Republican connection implied by the withdrawal of funding under the Hurd declaration, but by asserting their own proprietary right to the Irish language on behalf of the people of west Belfast.

Parkin's (1984) point about the power of discourse lying partly in the ability to name or label is also relevant here. The British government had the power to label *Glór na nGael* as an organization with paramilitary links. It also had the power to deny *Glór* the right to contest that label directly by refusing to offer any evidence they may have had for public scrutiny. In the same way that Republicans are often objectified in the political discourse of Northern Ireland, *Glór na nGael* activists, and by association many Irish language activists in general, were objectified and placed outside the bounds of legitimacy.

The British government policy of vetting 'undesirable' community organizations was officially shelved in 1995, but not before it had a profound effect on the Irish language revival movement. *Glór na nGael* regained its ACE funding in March 1992 after 18 months of campaigning. No explanation was offered, other than the suggestion made by Peter Brooke that circumstances had 'changed significantly', a suggestion which *Glór na nGael* denies, since the membership of the committee and the work of the organization had not changed since funding was withdrawn in 1990.

During the period of the campaign to restore funding, perhaps due in part to the *Glór na nGael* controversy, the ideology associated with cultural discourse made significant headway. It has become increasingly necessary and desirable to use this discourse, especially when dealing with government bodies, funding agencies and those 'outside' of the revival movement. At the same time, other discourses are still used in different situational contexts, and rights discourse still figures prominently in many current campaigns, particularly the campaign to obtain funding for *Meánscoil Feirste*.

CASE STUDY THREE:
THE CAMPAIGN FOR *MEÁNSCOIL FEIRSTE*

The first Irish medium primary school in Northern Ireland was established in 1971 by the founders of the Shaws Road community. Originally intended to provide for their own Irish-speaking children, *Bunscoil Phobal Feirste* ('Belfast Community Primary School') was opened to children from English-speaking families in 1978. To prepare children without a background in Irish for learning in an Irish-speaking environment, they were required to attend two years of nursery school before entering primary school. The first three classes to enter the nursery were quite small, consisting of six pupils in 1978, five in 1979, and six in 1980. After the first group started primary school in 1980, however, numbers entering Primary One more than tripled to 20 in 1981, rising to 28 in 1982, 37 in 1983, and 60 in 1984 (Maguire 1991: 77). By the late 1980s numbers had peaked, with entering classes ranging in size from just over 50 up to 70 pupils (Maguire 1991: 77). No longer able to accommodate the number of children wishing to transfer from Irish nursery schools to the *Bunscoil*, it became clear that another primary school would have to be opened.

The call for a second Irish-medium primary school first went out in 1986, and *Gaelscoil na bhFál* ('Irish School of the Hedgerow') opened its doors in 1987. This school also experienced phenomenal growth, and within a few years plans for other schools were under way. The third school, *Scoil na Fuiseoige* ('School of the Lark'), was opened in 1992 on the premises of the Irish-medium nursery school in Twinbrook on the outskirts of west Belfast. This was followed by three more Irish-medium primary schools in Belfast alone, opening in 1993, 1994 and 1996. There are now six primary schools outside of Belfast as well. Northern Ireland's first Irish-medium secondary school, *Meánscoil Feirste* ('Belfast Secondary School'), opened in 1991 to cater for the growing number of children who had received their primary education through the medium of Irish. A second *meánscoil* opened in Derry in 1994.

All of the Irish-medium schools in Belfast are located in areas of poverty and high unemployment, areas which have suffered disproportionately from the violence of the Troubles. In spite of this, all of the schools have managed to open and operate for years on shoestring budgets with no government funding, surviving on donations from local people and the occasional foreign sponsor. The struggle to meet the criteria set by the Department of Education for funding can go on for years (see Appendix II for a discussion of DENI funding criteria). Each school has had to devise its own strategy for survival, but all have learned from the difficult experience of the first school, *Bunscoil Phobail Feirste.*

The experience of the parents who established the Shaws Road *Bunscoil* reveals the Stormont government in their more hostile aspect. There were discussions as early as 1965 with the Ministry of Education about the parents' desire to set up a school, but responses were not favourable. They were warned that the endeavour was of dubious legality, and that

> it is the Ministry's view that instruction given entirely through the medium of Gaelic would not constitute ... efficient and suitable instruction ... (paragraph (c) of section 66(1) of the Education Act) for the pupils of an Independent School. A complaint would therefore be served by the Ministry. (Letter from Mr Benn, Permanent Secretary of the Ministry of Education, to the secretary of *'Teaghlaigh'*, 29 November 1965).
>
> (Maguire 1991: 78) [Quote 7]

The relationship between the Department of Education and the Shaws Road parents changed little after the fall of Stormont in 1972. Negotiations by letter were ongoing throughout this period. In April 1976 they applied to register the *Bunscoil* as an Independent School, but temporary recognition on this basis was all they were able to achieve. By this stage relations between the parents and the Department of Education were acrimonious, to say the least. By 1978, they had applied for voluntary maintained status which would have entitled the school to financial help from the government. In April 1979 they were finally allowed to register fully as an Independent School, but maintained status was denied. In 1982 the school received another in a long string of favourable reports by inspectors, yet maintained status was again denied. The following two years saw the final process of negotiation for maintained status, which included a large amount of stonewalling on the part of the Department of Education. Finally, in 1984, maintained status was granted after 13 years of campaigning.

Subsequent campaigns for recognition have run into similar difficulties with the Department of Education, although *Gaelscoil na bhFál* managed to receive funding and recognition in just under half the time it took *Bunscoil Phobal Feirste*. Still, the *Gaelscoil* had to operate for six years without government support. In Twinbrook the situation was somewhat different. Campaigners had worked for many years to raise the money to create a purpose-built Irish language nursery and education centre in their area. After succeeding in this endeavour, the prospect of another half-decade or more of fundraising and campaigning to support a primary school looked daunting indeed. Some activists feared that people were too worn out to launch such a campaign, and that local people had given all they could possibly give in terms of financial support. Their solution was temporarily to make their school a satellite of *Bunscoil Phobal Feirste*. This enabled them to receive funding as a campus of the *Bunscoil*, with the stipulation that when their numbers grew sufficiently large, they would become a separate school once again.

The campaign to obtain government funding and recognition for *Meánscoil Feirste* was in some ways unique. In spite of a certain amount of continuing disagreement and tension between the government and Irish language educationalists, the criteria needed to satisfy the Department of Education that a new Irish-medium primary school is indeed viable are reasonably well established. Whether the schools agree with the criteria or not, they are engaged in a struggle to meet them. The criteria necessary for an Irish-medium secondary school, however, had yet to be established when the idea was first mooted by Irish language educationalists in 1989.

The announcement that an Irish-medium secondary school was soon to be launched first came in the early days of that year. Initial discussion on the subject was often through the medium of Irish. For example, an article appeared in the *Andersonstown News* (21 January 1989) entitled '*Glacaimis an chéad chéim i dtreo meánscoile*' ('Let's take the first step towards a secondary school'), calling for *Gaeilgeoirí* to organize a committee to start collecting money for an Irish-medium secondary school. An editorial in Irish in the *Andersonstown News* (30 December 1989) also discussed the pressing need for an Irish-medium secondary school. At the same time, articles occasionally appeared in English as well, providing updates on the latest steps being taken in the campaign.

In February 1989, a meeting was held (largely in Irish) in the Conway Mill which was addressed by a man involved in setting up an Irish-medium secondary school in the Rath Cairn *Gaeltacht* in County Meath. Those who attended the meeting elected a committee to examine the possibilities and oversee fundraising efforts. The results of that committee's work were presented to another meeting (largely in English) held at *Bunscoil Phobal Feirste* in April 1990. A fresh committee was elected to begin work on the new secondary school which was to open in September 1991, the twentieth anniversary of the establishment of the first Irish-medium primary school. The division between organizing in Irish and organizing in English is necessitated by the fact that so few people with an interest in the language are fluent enough to converse easily in Irish. A core of activists can and do hold meetings in Irish, but when it comes time to include others, for example the parents of children attending Irish-medium schools, it becomes necessary to make the switch to English. The same applies to articles in Irish. The use of written Irish limits the audience to those fluent enough to read the article. If those with limited or no Irish are to be included, articles must also be printed in English.[7]

The issue of the Irish-medium secondary school was discussed at another public meeting on the Irish language in June 1990, and articles in support of the school continued to appear frequently in the *Andersonstown News* and, less frequently, in the *Irish News*. The tone of the discussion at this time was confident and notably lacking in antagonism towards the British government. An article in the *Andersonstown News* (8 March 1991), for example, noted that the response to negotiations with the Belfast Education and Library Board (BELB) and the Department of Education had been 'very encouraging so far'. Another article described talks between the *Meánscoil* committee and the Department of Education as 'positive', and suggested that 'conditions for Irish language education are much more favourable than those that existed when the *Bunscoil* was set up in 1971' (*Andersonstown News*, 8 June 1991).

In August 1991 a scheme was announced whereby supporters could pay five pounds a week to help support the school for the first year while they waited for the Department of Education to provide a grant. No one seemed to doubt that the support would be provided within a year or two. Future head teacher Fearghas Ó hÍr is quoted as saying:

Níl amhras dá laghad orm go n-éireoidh leis an mheánscoil go breá agus go dtiocfaidh an rialtas isteach ar an fhiontar nuair a fheiceann siad go bhfuil ag éirí leis.

(*Andersonstown News*, 31 August 1991)

[I have no doubt that the *Meánscoil* will succeed well and that the government will support the enterprise when they see that it has succeeded.]

(my translation) [Quote 8]

While they waited for the British government to come through with funding, the Irish state body *Bord na Gaeilge* provided some financial support, along with other non-governmental organizations including the Gaelic League and the Belfast-based fundraising group TACA.

In spite of such expressions of goodwill and confidence on the part of Irish language campaigners, future conflict between the Department of Education and *Meánscoil Feirste* was foreshadowed by an announcement made in May 1992, at the end of the secondary school's first year. The Department of Education informed the school that it had reduced the projected intake of pupils needed for the school to receive grant aid from 80 to 60. While the *Meánscoil* committee welcomed the announcement and expressed confidence that this target could be met, one teacher complained that the current lack of funding forced the school to restrict its intake, creating a sort of 'Catch 22' – without funding intake could not be increased without damaging the quality of education, but unless intake was increased dramatically, funding would not be forthcoming. This situation would eventually lead to an impasse and a worsening of relations between the Department of Education and *Meánscoil Feirste*.

By the middle of the school's second year, the strain was beginning to show. The school had initiated action in the European Court of Human Rights against the British government on the grounds that it was not being treated equally with Welsh language schools, and the discourse of the campaign began to change. The chairman of the school's Finance Committee, a long-time Irish language activist in Belfast, vented his anger in an article about growth in the school's annual intake of new pupils:

The attitude of the Education Authorities in the North towards Irish language education has been nothing less than scandalous ... Despite irrefutable evidence over a 25-year period that education through the medium of the Irish language is an excellent way to educate children, the authorities only give assistance when dragged kicking and screaming to do so.

(*Andersonstown News*, 22 January 1993) [Quote 9]

Representatives of the school argued that the school had doubled its intake each year for the three years it was open – nine pupils in 1991, 17 in 1992, and 35 in 1993. In the first few years pupils were drawn solely from *Bunscoil Phobal Feirste*, the only Irish-medium primary school with children ready to enter secondary school, but from 1993 children would also be leaving the second primary school, *Gaelscoil na bhFál*, and in another few years, children would be leaving the newer schools as well. They argued that two-thirds of eligible children were already signing up to attend the *Meánscoil*, and when funding was granted numbers would surely grow, as they had at each primary school after government funding came through. The Department of Education responded by saying that the school's enrolment had not increased to meet Department requirements that a secondary school must have 300 pupils on its rolls, meaning that the school must have an intake of 60 pupils each year, a position they would stick to rigidly in the years to come.

At the start of the 1993 school year campaigners for the *Meánscoil* appear to have made a conscious decision to change tactics. In Scott's (1990) terms, the hidden transcript of the *Meánscoil* campaigners was suddenly made public:

'We have had plenty of nice words but not so much as a brass penny,' said Mr Ó Cairealláin. 'The time for nice words is now over. We have two additional teachers to employ this September because the school is expanding at breakneck speed. The government must fund the *Meánscoil* immediately' ... 'The need for the *Meánscoil* is obvious and the Department of Education has had plenty of time to get its act together. It is time that the historic prejudice against Irish medium education which has permeated the Department of Education for so long was finally flushed away.'

(*Andersonstown News*, 21 August 1993) [Quote 10]

The words of this prominent Irish language campaigner signalled the end of one strategy and the launching of another. For two years campaigners had largely accepted the 'public transcript', to borrow Scott's terminology, of fairness and equal treatment in the dealings between Irish-medium schools and the Department of Education, not contesting the Department's claim that they were adhering to rules and regulations which were applied to all schools without discrimination or special treatment. Now the 'hidden transcript' which alleged bigotry and bias on the part of the Department of Education, simmering so close to the surface all along, was brought out into the open once again.

The change in tactics also reflects a switch between two familiar types of protest discourse as described in the last section of Chapter 2. In some instances, the Irish are portrayed as a 'risen people', emphasizing their strengths, virtues and victories, while in others the focus is on the oppression of the Irish people and their suffering at the hands of the British. Both types of protest discourse can be seen in the *Meánscoil* campaign.

In the first part of the campaign for *Meánscoil Feirste*, the emphasis was on the first type of Nationalist discourse. The talk was of how the Irish language movement went 'from strength to strength', and every minor success or sign of progress was celebrated. The British government, in the form of the Department of Education, were portrayed as neutral negotiating partners, willing to help the school but bound by the rules and regulations. Towards the end of the second year, the emphasis began to shift. While there was still some positive talk reminiscent of the first year of the campaign, activists increasingly began to draw upon the discourse of the victim, emphasizing the discriminatory practices of the Department of Education in the past and accusing them of continuing this policy in the present.

By the middle of the school's third year, the anger and frustration seems to burst forth, and the hidden transcript comes fully out into the open. The chairman of the Finance Committee, speaking at a *Meánscoil* awards ceremony where 26 pupils aged 13 and under were presented with certificates for passing the GCSE[8] Irish exam, again criticized the Department of Education:

I have no doubt that if the same results were achieved in any other sector of education the Department of Education would be rushing to emulate it, yet they continue to prevaricate on Irish language education ... This, I believe, is due to ignorance on the one hand and blind prejudice on the other ... If the Department of Education want a few hints on how to improve the plummeting standard in much of the state sector, we will be only too glad to show them how. In the meantime I would suggest that they give these children the funding they are entitled to.

(*Andersonstown News*, 12 February 1994) [Quote 11]

Attacks on the government and arguments in favour of funding Irish-medium education came on a number of different fronts during this year. As well as highlighting the high standard of education and exam results obtained in the *Meánscoil*, comparisons with the status of Welsh become increasingly common. Funding for the *Meánscoil* also became an issue in Anglo-Irish relations when the school was raised by then *Tanaiste* Dick Spring during Anglo-Irish Conference discussions with then Secretary of State Patrick Mayhew. It was suggested that supporting the school would be a positive and powerful demonstration of the government's commitment to parity of esteem in Northern Ireland.

In late 1994, a press conference was held to announce the start of a 'pro-active campaign to highlight the anti-Irish sectarianism of the Department [of Education]' (*Irish News*, 24 November 1994). A key part of the campaign centred on the notion of parity of esteem for all traditions in Northern Ireland. A parent of one of the children attending the *Meánscoil* read a statement saying,

> Even the Department has had to admit that the school's record of achievement is second to none. We believe that the decision not to fund *Meánscoil Feirste* was in fact an attack on the whole idea of an independent Irish-medium secondary level sector to the education system here. It is also a clear signal to all concerned that the idea of equality and parity of esteem for all traditions has not yet been embraced by the British government [Quote 12]

Anna Eagleson, principal of *Bunscoil Phobal Feirste*, wrote a letter of protest to the Department of Education stating that

> the principle of recognizing both traditions lies at the heart of all aspirations in our community. Financial considerations are only one factor in deciding how to achieve this recognition and to create institutions that embody such community values ... Education and language cannot be marginalised – they lie at the heart of culture.
>
> (quoted in *Andersonstown News*, 3 December 1994) [Quote 13]

An editorial in the *Andersonstown News* (2 April 1994) suggested that the Irish language could be seen as a litmus test to gauge the sincerity of the Downing Street Declaration:

> The government had a unique opportunity this week to take the first step in the implementation of one of the very few positive nationalist aspects of the Downing Street Declaration when the education minister met a deputation from the North's only Irish language

secondary school, *Meánscoil Feirste*. ... That they haven't [funded the school] shows just how little interest they have in the stated aims of the Declaration. ...

That the hostile approach of the British establishment in the North towards that section of the population who profess an Irish identity was a prime cause of the conflict here can hardly now be disputed. Nevertheless, the government can't take the first baby step to remove one sign of that antipathy by recognizing the legitimacy and worth of *Meánscoil Feirste*.

In a way this issue is the litmus test for all the other proposed changes that are supposed to flow from the Declaration and usher in an equitable settlement of the conflict. If the government doesn't come through on this one, then we wouldn't hold out much hope for the Declaration as a whole. [Quote 14]

A columnist for the *Andersonstown News* dedicated a number of his articles to the issue of the *Meánscoil*, rights for Irish speakers and the peace process. In one column he writes:

Dá mbeadh Meánscoil Feirste suite i nDún Dealgan, Dún Éideann nó i nDyfedd na Breataine Bige bheadh sé státmhaoinithe. Sea, agus bheadh an Roinn Oideachais ag déanamh a mhór de ar fud an domhain. Anseo, ar ndóigh, táimidne fós gafa ag biogóideacht na nAontachtaithe agus leatrom rialtas na Breataine in éadan na Gaeilge agus an phobail a bhfuil meas acu uirthi.

(*Andersonstown News*, 5 February 1994)

If *Meánscoil Feirste* was located in Dundalk, Edinburgh or Dyfed in Wales it would be state-supported. Yes, and the Department of Education would be making a big deal about it all over the world. Here, however, we are still in the grip of Unionist bigotry and British government oppression against Irish and the community which values it.

(my translation) [Quote 15]

In another, he warns that Irish speakers must show the British government that they are a community worthy of recognition, otherwise the authorities may think that a small grant for the *Meánscoil* and an Irish language event held in Belfast City Hall are enough. Full equality of treatment would have to be fought for:

Ach is féidir bheith cinnte fá rud amháin – ní bheidh féiríní ó neamh ar bith ann do náisiúnaithe na Sé Chontae sna míonna agus sna blianta romhainn amach. Agus is lú arís na bronntanais a dháilfear ar lucht na Gaeilge.

Má tá fúinn cothrom na féinne a bhaint amach beidh orainn troid fhíochmhar a chur suas ar a shon. Má tá ciall ar bith le bheith leis an sos lámhaigh, is é go mbeidh deis againn ár gcearta a bhaint amach.

(*Andersonstown News*, 3 September 1994)

But it is possible to be certain about one thing – there will be no gifts or any kind of heaven for Six County nationalists in the months and years ahead of us. And smaller still will be the rewards distributed to Irish speakers.

If we want to achieve parity of esteem we will have to put up a ferocious fight for it. If there is a good reason for the ceasefire, it is that we will have the opportunity to get our rights.

(my translation) [Quote 16]

Aside from focusing on the issue of parity of esteem, the new campaign was to include extensive lobbying in the *Dáil* and the House of Commons, publicity in the United States,[9] and high profile protests. The first of these protests was held in front of the Department of Education headquarters in Bangor, when parents, teachers and pupils from the *Meánscoil* handed in a letter of protest and left a pile of tally sticks[10] which the students had been wearing on the front doorstep. A Christmas fast was also held at the front of Belfast City Hall to bring the issue to public attention.

Just before Christmas, *Taoiseach* John Bruton asked John Major to reverse the Department of Education's decision not to fund the *Meánscoil*, pointing out again that it would be a practical example of parity of esteem between the two communities in Northern Ireland. SDLP leader John Hume also raised the issue on a number of occasions with government officials, including Education Minister Michael Ancram. In January 1995 parents and staff of the *Meánscoil*, along with west Belfast MP Joe Hendron, met Mayhew at Stormont Castle. The meeting was hailed as an important success. Mayhew promised to lift the ban on funding for the school and made a commitment to look through other departmental budgets to find other sources of funding. It fell short of campaigners' demands for full recognition and funding, and it remained to be seen how much would be granted and when, but it was seen as progress nevertheless.

Meanwhile, Ancram was caught in a television interview claiming that he was recognizing parity of esteem by *not* funding the *Meánscoil*. According to his logic, treating the school equally alongside other schools meant not funding it. In an opinion piece for *The Irish News* (8 February 1995), SDLP politician Brian Feeney attacked Ancram for making a 'complete mess' of funding Irish-medium schools:

> Parity of esteem in any field needs special funding to enable it to be visible and functioning. You have to pay for a diverse culture .... What Ancram was saying was that parity of esteem means you get no money because you're the same as everyone else. It's the opposite of his government's stated policy. Because everyone is NOT the same in a divided society, he should be providing extra money to enable parity of esteem AND to compensate for the anti-Irish discrimination his department practiced for decades. ... As it is, funding will come by the back door. That's parity of esteem NIO style. [Quote 17]

A one-off grant of £100,000 was made available to the *Meánscoil* in time for the start of its fifth year in 1995. In July of that year, the High Court ruled that the Department of Education was not acting illegally by refusing to fund the *Meánscoil*. However, the judge praised the commitment and dedication of the people involved with the school, and suggested that the Department should make an exception in this case and make provision for it. Irish language activists were clearly heartened by the ruling, in spite of it going against them in the short term (*Andersonstown News*, 22 July 1995). In October, a pupil from the *Meánscoil* addressed the Forum for Peace and Reconciliation in Dublin. Speaking to the forum in Irish, she called the government's refusal to recognize the school 'discriminatory and vindictive', and asked the Department of Education to fund the *Meánscoil* and provide Irish language versions of the GCSE examinations (*Andersonstown News*, 14 October 1995). *Meánscoil Feirste* finally received government funding and recognition in 1996.

The campaign for *Meánscoil Feirste* moved from positive, relatively subdued tactics which emphasized cooperation with the authorities in the early years, to a more confrontational, oppositional stance in later years. One prominent campaigner suggested to me that the *Meánscoil* wished to give the Department of Education the opportunity to respond positively to the opening of the school, hoping for a new era of better relations between this branch of the British government and Irish language campaigners. Another campaigner said that he never dreamed the campaign for funding would extend beyond two years, considering the government's apparent willingness to fund Irish-medium primary

schools and the somewhat less hostile atmosphere between government and Irish language activists which began to take hold after 1991.
While hopes were high, campaigners accepted the public transcript
dictated by the Department of Education regarding quotas and regulations, while at the same time hoping that behind the scenes negotiations might lead to an exception being made. When after two years
the Department of Education and the British government continued
to deny funding, sticking to the demand for a yearly intake of 60 pupils,
the thinly veiled hidden transcript was made public once again.

In private, and usually in Irish, I heard people involved with the
Meánscoil express doubts about the government's willingness or ability
to provide official recognition and adequate funding for the Irish
language. The transcript which Irish speakers temporarily tried to keep
'hidden' included fears about the genuineness of government officials,
a belief in the inherent bigotry of the Northern Irish Civil Service and
the belief that the British authorities harboured deeply rooted pre-
judices against Irish people in general and the Irish language in particular. Since just about everyone, including the NIO, has heard this
transcript at some point, it was not completely hidden in the sense
that Scott uses the term. However, a concerted effort was made on
the part of campaigners not to use this transcript publicly during the
early years of the campaign. Some believed in a conspiracy against
the language, others that sheer ignorance played a big role. One long-
time Irish language activist commented that the Irish language
revival movement was like the civil rights movement of the 1960s,
in that the Unionist-dominated state would be shown to be incapable of providing equality of treatment for Nationalists within Northern Ireland, proving once again that the state was illegitimate and
ungovernable.

While much of this 'hidden' transcript is regularly revealed in
other Irish language campaigns and contexts, it is significant that the
Meánscoil campaigners chose, at least temporarily, to submerge the
hidden transcript and accept the public transcript in the interest of
obtaining funding for the secondary school, and perhaps, to help
encourage less acrimonious relations with the government. When this
strategy failed and the hidden transcript surfaced once again, the
discourse of the campaign came to draw heavily on rights discourse,
in fact contributing a great deal to its development.

While rights discourse clearly dominated the *Meánscoil* campaign,
decolonizing discourse also features occasionally, particularly after the
new phase of the campaign was launched. In an article for *Lá*, school

principal Ó hÍr writes:

Cuirtear an argóint chun tosaigh in amanna nach dtuigeann na Sasanaigh tábhacht na Gaeilge don phobal Náisiúnaíoch anseo agus gur sin an fáth nach riarann siad mar is ceart ar thionscnaimh Ghaeilge. A mhalairt ar fad atá fíor. Tuigeann na Sasanaigh, níos fearr b'fhéidir ná aon chine eile, tábhacht teanga i smachtú intinn an dream is mian leo a choinneáil faoi chos pholaitiúil.

I ngach tír riamh ar chuir siad faoi smacht d'fheach siad lena dteanga féin a bhualadh anuas ar an dream faoi chos le iad a choinneáil faoi chos go buan. ...

Is gairid gonta mar a chuir Edmund Spenser, cosantóir ghábhail na dTúdarach ar Éirinn, síos ar: '... ós í an Ghaeilge an teanga, is Gaelach a bheidh an croí.'

Rómhaith a thuigeann na Sasanaigh tábhacht na Gaeilge, agus an bhagairt dá leas fadtéarmach a bheadh in athbeochan na Gaeilge – níos fearr ná a thuigeann a lán Éireannach.

The argument has occasionally been put forward that the English do not understand the importance of Irish to the Nationalist community here and that that is the reason they do not provide properly for Irish institutions. Quite the opposite is true. The English understand, better perhaps that any other race, the importance of language in controlling the minds of people they want to keep politically suppressed.

In every country they ever controlled they saw that their own language was forced on the suppressed group in order to keep them suppressed permanently. ...

As Edmund Spenser, defender of the Tudor invasion of Ireland, incisively puts it: '... since Irish is the language, the heart must be Irish.'

The English understand too well the importance of Irish, and the threat in the long term of the benefits of the Irish revival – better than many Irish people understand.

(*Lá*, 1 December 1994) (my translation) [Quote 18]

This portrayal of the Irish language as being intentionally suppressed by the British government because of the threat it poses to their power is more typical of decolonizing discourse than rights discourse.

For the most part, though, rights discourse dominates. Recognition for the Irish language, both in the form of funding and in the formation of supportive institutions, is a central theme (see Chapters 3 and 6). The issue of rights for Irish speakers comes up often in this discourse, an issue which is inherently political and tends not to appeal to those who favour the ideology of cultural discourse. At the same time, those who favour the ideology of decolonizing discourse would be wary of the idea of rights for Irish speakers, because it assumes a certain degree of acceptance of British authority, since they would be the ones granting any such rights.

Comparisons with the position of Welsh in Wales and Scots Gaelic in Scotland increasingly become a part of rights discourse during the *Meánscoil* campaign, developing especially out of comparisons in the provision of education (for example, how many pupils are needed to start a Welsh or Scots Gaelic-medium school in comparison to an Irish-medium school in Northern Ireland), and the funding made available for publishing and the arts. Such comparisons tend not to be made in decolonizing discourse because, again, they imply a degree of acceptance of the current constitutional position of Northern Ireland. Comparisons with the status of Irish in the South are made less frequently, not only because such comparisons will not carry much weight with the British authorities which people are trying to influence, but also because many believe that the status of Irish in the South is far from ideal.

The position taken by *Meánscoil* campaigners by making such comparisons may imply a certain acquiescence to the constitutional status quo, but it is also an ambiguous position which allows for any contingency. The position of the Irish language must be made secure no matter what constitutional arrangement may eventually be reached. Although it is clear that the great majority of campaigners would prefer some form of union with the South, they do not want to secure the future of the language to any one potential political future.

'Parity of esteem' became a key phrase in Irish language circles after the launch of the Downing Street Declaration. This, too, brings the language into the political arena by identifying it with the status of Nationalists in Northern Ireland. While talk of parity of esteem may occasionally be a feature of decolonizing discourse, it is primarily characteristic of rights discourse for the reasons outlined above.

Although the notion of parity of esteem, comparisons with Wales and bringing of cases against the government in British courts feature strongly, the *Meánscoil* campaigners have not limited themselves to the British context. Intervention by the Dublin government in negotiations over the *Meánscoil* also implies a lack of acceptance of the Northern Irish state and British authority as it stands.

The campaign for *Meánscoil Feirste* provides a number of good examples of rights discourse in practice. Although decolonizing discourse makes an appearance occasionally, and cultural discourse could be used in the support of the campaigns to obtain funding for Irish-medium schools, rights discourse dominates the campaign and has been largely shaped by it. Drawing on both decolonizing and cultural discourses, and other discourses as well, rights discourse creates and reflects a different ideology and a different perspective on the Irish language which is neither apolitical, nor narrowly attached to a single political perspective such as Republicanism.

The demonstrations, press conferences and even the *Meánscoil* pupil addressing the Forum for Peace and Reconciliation in Dublin can be understood as part of a valuation strategy on the part of Irish language campaigners, designed to increase the profile and status of the language as a symbol of Nationalist identity, as that identity is defined in rights discourse. Campaigning for recognition for Irish-medium schools can also be seen as part of a proprietary contest, implicitly staking a claim in the language and seeking to define its meaning as a symbol. When this claim is seen to be ignored or devalued by the British government, it is interpreted by many Irish language campaigners to mean that the government is denying their right to the Irish language (a symbolic personification of the Irish people), and therefore their right to be Irish. As Harrison argues, in a gift mode of exchange, 'the circulation of goods creates social relationships between the transactors' (1992: 234). The perceived rejection by the British government of the *Meánscoil* campaigners' claims to proprietary rights in the Irish language means that the current social relationship between the British government and language campaigners – one in which the balance of power is held by the government and in which the claim to Irish identity is devalued and delegitimized – is maintained.

CASE STUDY FOUR:
A SENSE OF PLACE: STREET SIGNS IN IRISH[11]

For many people, the Irish language is deeply connected to a sense of place and a sense of belonging to a particular geographical region, whether that is Ireland as a whole, or a specific area, town or city within it. One of the first stories I ever heard about the Irish language, soon after my arrival and long before I began my research, was that in ancient times when the people still spoke Irish, every geographical feature on the island – every rock, beach, glen, section of river, grove and hill – had a name and a story associated with it. This story was to be repeated to me by a number of different people over the years, usually while travelling in the countryside, and often with a sense of awe and mystery. The people belonged to the land, and the land belonged to the people, and all Irish people are still a part of that, however far they may have come from the days when the landscape spoke to those who lived in it.

While conducting interviews a number of years later, a teacher in his forties told me:

> Any language is more than a means of communication or a sign. It contains within it a whole web of cross-references, symbols, things which we in this community understand simply because we are from this community. If you lived here all your life, I could say something to you in English which someone from London would not understand. Spread out through the community those differences in meaning can have some sort of significance, if you spread that back through generations and through history, and if you take cognizance of the fact that the language would contain within it references to historical facts, geographical locations, places, street names, town names, whatever, that the language contains within it a whole system of understanding this place where we are, our spot, more than any other language. Just because we happen to live here. Belfast English is different from London English or American English because it contains all those references. Irish, in so far as it is indigenous to this area, all the street names, all the townlands, all the mountains, all the rivers are actually Irish names, and also because it goes back longer than English, it contains all that almost undefinable, you can't put your finger on what it is, but there's all those sort of references coming through it, which actually makes sense of people's living here. This is where we live, this is the bit of ground on which we've lived for generations back, and it is the language which contains all of that, our culture. Therefore it is central to our sense of identity. This is where we live, where our people are from. I think the language brings all that together. [Quote 19]

The belief that the landscape of Ireland 'speaks' is reflected in the somewhat less mystical interest in Irish place names. Many learners and speakers of Irish express an interest in the meanings of the original Irish names of the towns and townlands of Northern Ireland, so much so that a 'cultural map of Irish place names' was recently produced by the Ordnance Survey of Northern Ireland, with the help of the Department of Celtic studies at the Queen's University of Belfast and the Ordnance Survey, Dublin. Two west Belfast conservation groups have also produced a number of posters with the names of local flora and fauna given bilingually. Another manifestation of this interest is the translation and posting of street signs in Irish in many towns and cities in Northern Ireland in recent years.

It is significant that the only piece of legislation explicitly against the use of Irish in Northern Ireland prohibited its use in street signs (in an amendment to the Public Health and Local Government Act 1949). It was passed after Nationalist councils in Newry and Omagh erected Irish language street signs in parts of the towns in 1948. During the debate that preceded the vote on this issue, future Prime Minister Brian Faulkner stated that the naming of streets by certain local authorities in County Down, 'in a language which is not our language', should not be allowed (Maguire 1991: 11).

Ironically, the continued existence of this law on the statute books seems to have encouraged the erection of street signs in Irish, particularly in the late 1970s and 1980s. Hundreds of signs were unofficially erected throughout Northern Ireland. In spite of the occasional threat, however, no legal action was taken against the various groups and individuals involved. Repeated calls to repeal the legislation were largely ignored until recently. In December 1992, Sir Patrick Mayhew declared the government's intention to remove the ban on street names in Irish. No action was taken at that time, however. In 1994, the NIO again promised the repeal of the legislation. Finally, in February 1995 the Local Government (Miscellaneous Provisions) (NI) Order (1995) was approved by the House of Lords, allowing street signs to be erected in both Irish and English.

A number of different groups have been involved over the years in the campaign to erect street signs in Irish. In fact, it has been not so much a single, organized campaign as a collection of campaigns, some neighbourhood-based, others taken on by various Irish language organizations. In 1979 a west Belfast branch of the Gaelic League announced that a campaign to have street signs erected in Irish was being launched, beginning with streets in the Lenadoon and Glen Road area. In 1981, Irish street signs were put up in the Twinbrook estate on the outskirts of west Belfast, along with a sign at the entrance of the estate reading *Fáilte go Cill Uaighe* ('Welcome to Twinbrook'). The unveiling ceremony was attended by members of *Cluain Ard*. In 1983, Irish street signs were erected in Ballymurphy,[12] and Sinn Féin became involved in the campaign for Irish street names. Door-to-door surveys to assess the level of support for the campaign were carried out by both Sinn Féin and the Gaelic League in most areas of west Belfast.

Glór na nGael became involved in erecting Irish street names as well. They also launched a campaign to encourage shopkeepers in the area to put up bilingual signs. The result is an increase in the number of shops with Irish in the sign over the door, as well as some shops which use Irish on labels and notices inside. For example, one shop on the Falls has a bilingual Irish/English sign near the till notifying the public that they do not sell alcohol to people under the age of 18, and a few shops sport *'fáilte'* and *'slán'* signs on their doors.

The idea behind this and the street signs campaign was to get people interested in the language by increasing its visibility. As a strategy it is meant to work against the tendency for things to be 'out of sight and out of mind'. Another aspect of the campaign was an attempt to convince shopkeepers that it was worth their while to cater for the Irish-speaking community in west Belfast, however small it might be. This in turn has to be understood in the context of a wider strategy to bring Irish out of the classroom (and in some instances the home) into all spheres of life, both public and private.

Part of the downfall of Irish, it is believed, was that it was not seen as a language of commerce or of the cities. To counter its rural, backward or even 'quaint' image, some people believe that it is important for it to be possible to say all things and to carry out all types of activity through the medium of Irish. Irish is not just a language used in school, nor simply a language of poetry and traditional music, but a language suitable for business and for things modern, like computers and pop music. Trivial as the use of Irish in a shop sign might seem, it is a small aspect of a much deeper and more complex set of beliefs about the language itself, about community and about how Irish society should be ideally.

The erection of Irish street signs has sometimes been viewed as little more than an exercise in sectarian boundary marking. Like curb painting, it has been seen as a way of indicating to the outsider that they are now entering territory clearly staked out as belonging to Nationalists (or to Unionists, in the case of red, white and blue curbs – see Jarman 1992, 1993, 1997). No doubt there is an element of this intended by some of those involved in putting the signs up in at least some areas. Such an image is perhaps reinforced by the abrupt change from English-only signs to bilingual signs when the border with the Republic is crossed. However, this is far from a complete picture.

In an area such as the Lower Ormeau Road in south Belfast, this type of interpretation is more easily arrived at. A small Nationalist community consisting of a handful of short streets running between the River Lagan and the Ormeau Road, the street signs on the corners of buildings fronting the Ormeau Road are visible to the driver or pedestrian going in or out of this main thoroughfare to the city centre. Small enough to be easily overlooked, nevertheless the signs mark out the boundary of the tiny enclave – Irish street signs are absent from streets on the far side of the Ormeau Bridge over the River Lagan, and from the opposite side of the Ormeau Road on streets which lead into the mixed university area.

In the Falls Road area of west Belfast, however, the majority of street signs, shop signs, slogans and murals containing words in Irish are well inside the accepted boundaries of the area. None is visible without significant penetration of the boundaries, and none is visible to the casual passerby. Jarman has made a similar observation with regards to Loyalist murals and physical signs of allegiance, noting that by the time one is aware of these signs, one has already crossed the boundaries (1992: 149).

Rather than simple boundary markers, Irish street and shop signs are best understood as part of an internal dialogue within the Nationalist community. The flurry of activity that surrounded the erection of Irish street signs throughout the 1980s was accompanied by numerous articles and letters to the editors of various newsletters and newspapers. An examination of these indicates a number of different interpretations of the importance of street signs in Irish. The great majority of letters and stories are really quite mundane, relating the results of neighbourhood surveys, calling for volunteers and/or financial assistance, thanking people for their help, providing translations of the Irish names, and announcing which areas were working towards the erection of Irish signs at any given time. There are a lot of positive and supportive words, and the discourse is primarily cultural.

When street signs were first erected in Twinbrook, for example, a short article appeared on the front page of the *Andersonstown News* (24 January 1981):

Organized by the local *Cumann Gaelach*, the campaign has received the overwhelming support of all the people of the Estate, who contributed very generously to defray the considerable costs involved in the manufacture of the new name plates. ...

'We have some beautiful names in this estate when translated into Irish', said a *Cumann Gaelach* spokesman, 'and as Irish is the common heritage of all the people here, no matter what religion or political persuasion, we think it will add greatly to the general atmosphere of the estate'. [Quote 20]

In 1991, a new sign entirely in Irish (with the exception of the name itself) was put up at a 7-Eleven shop on the Falls Road. It was hailed in the local press as a big boost to the Irish language. West Belfast Irish language activist Gearóid Ó Cairealláin, now president of the Gaelic League, was quoted as saying: 'It is a visible sign of the respect people here have for their native tongue and visitors particularly appreciate this' (*Andersonstown News*, 5 January 1991). He went on to say:

We'd like to thank all the shopkeepers, doctors, solicitors and others who have put up bilingual signs and we hope that this trend will continue. It costs nothing extra but it is a very important way of promoting the language. [Quote 21]

In some instances at least, the use of cultural discourse may be a strategy designed to maximize support for the street signs campaigns. The less political the campaign appears, the less divisive it will be. The Irish language is one of the few things that Nationalists of all political persuasions can support and feel good about. As such, it is not too difficult to obtain support for the language, providing too strong a political message is not attached to whatever issue is at hand. A more neutral approach allows people to read whatever meaning they wish into the campaign. For some it will be political, for others purely cultural, and perhaps for the majority, a combination of the two.

A cultural approach does not guarantee support when government agencies become involved, however. Residents of Artillery Flats in the New Lodge area of north Belfast campaigned for many months to have the names of the high-rise blocks of flats changed. Named after British war heroes and battle victories like Churchill, Dill, Alexander and Templar, the mainly Nationalist residents believe that the names do not reflect the culture and traditions of the area. While a previous campaign in the 1970s was unsuccessful, the Northern Ireland Housing Executive agreed to allow the changes as long as the local community was consulted. The Rename-Our-Flats Committee conducted a survey of residents to decide on names, and these were submitted to the Housing Executive for approval. The names put forward to the Housing Executive are drawn from Irish mythology: *Teach Grainne, Teach Cuchulainn, Teach na bhFiann, Teach Meabha, Teach Oisin, Teach Eithne* and *Teach Fionn*.

What was initially heralded as a new era of improved relations between Irish campaigners and government agencies turned sour when the Housing Executive refused the names chosen by residents on the grounds that their 'computers only accept the English language' (*Andersonstown News*, 23 September 1995). A New Lodge campaigner apparently retorted, 'that may come as some surprise to the many Maeves and Grainnes who work for the Executive or who live in Housing Executive accommodation', and it was pointed out that any computer that could accept the English alphabet could accept words in Irish. Irish language campaigners planned to seek legal advice on the matter after receiving the negative response, but the Housing Executive eventually backed down on the matter.

All of this is not to say that a political message has never been attached to the street signs campaigns. Occasionally, a particular campaign will take a more political tack. A street off the Shaws Road which runs through the Irish-speaking area was the centre of a naming controversy for over a decade. Members of the Shaws Road community have been trying since the early 1980s to have the street named in Irish. The first name they chose, *Cois Cluana*, was rejected by the city council because it was in Irish. For it to be accepted, it would have to be Anglicized. The residents posted a sign anyway.

A few years later, a new housing development was started which had only *Cois Cluana* as an access road. Residents and the housing company held a meeting and decided to give the street a new name, *Ros Goill*. When the construction company asked the council to ratify the new name, the council insisted on adding the English word 'park'. When the new development was completed in 1992, a new sign 'Rosgoill Park' was put up. In 1993, as part of the Gaelic League's centenary celebrations, it was decided to try once more to have the name changed to the correct Irish, *Ros Goill*. An article in *The Irish News* (24 February 1993), written by one of the residents of the Shaws Road *Gaeltacht*, describes the progress of the campaign over the years and the launch of the fresh campaign:

> The struggle of one west Belfast street to have its name in Irish will feature in this year's centenary celebrations of the Gaelic League. The residents of Rosgoill Park aim to use the occasion as a focus for the debate on what constitutes a legitimate Irish identity in Northern Ireland today. [Quote 22]

This campaign had a more overtly political slant to it than many of the others, though not from a decolonizing ideological perspective. Some people, however, interpret the meaning and purpose of

Irish street signs not only as an expression of Irishness, but as a state-ment against the British presence in Northern Ireland. The Upper Springfield Resource Centre is a community group which caters to the Ballymurphy, Turf Lodge and New Barnsley areas of west Belfast. One issue of their newsletter, *Resource* (Sept./Oct. 1982), offered words of praise for the increase in Irish cultural activities in the area:

> What importance or role has the Irish language, music, etc. got to play in an area like this, when we are beset by such huge social and economic problems?
>
> Firstly, it establishes an identity for our people – an Irish identity as opposed to the State's British identity. An identity as a proud, educated, civilised people, as opposed to the authorities' image of 'scrounging savages'.
>
> To those who oppose the presence of a foreign army in our streets, the language provides a wall which can be built between ourselves and the Brits. ... Why should our street names not be in Irish as well as in English; not as a token of some sympathy with Gaelic, but as a definite statement of our wish to be Irish, and our refusal to be part of the British state. [Quote 23]

Sinn Féin also became very involved in the street signs campaign, particularly during the first half of the 1980s. For the most part, they, too, took a highly political view of the putting up of Irish street signs. Drawing primarily on decolonizing discourse, a letter written by a mem-ber of the Lower Falls Martyrs Sinn Féin *Cumann* articulates their position on street signs in Irish:

> The Street Signs Campaign is part of an overall policy designed to help generate among Nationalist people, a wider and deeper interest for our language and culture, which through all the years of British attempts to eradicate it, has remained intact, instilling a deep sense of pride and courage into countless Irishmen and women who under-stood the importance of its role in the struggle for national freedom.
>
> Sinn Féin would like to extend our appreciation and thanks to all those who supported our idea. They are a clear example of the 'Living Irish Spirit' which will finally drive the British evil from our land. *Tiocfaidh an lá.* ['The day will come.']
>
> (*Andersonstown News*, 16 April 1983) [Quote 24]

The involvement of Sinn Féin in this campaign, even though they were only one organization among many who were involved over the years, sparked an interesting debate in the letters pages of the *Andersonstown*

News between February and March 1983. Over the years, many articles about Irish street signs and place names have appeared in the *Andersonstown News*, all of which were supportive of the campaign and in agreement with the erection of Irish street signs in principle. In the 19 February 1983 edition of the paper, a letter appeared in *Mála Poist*, the section for letters to the editor. Signed 'Turf Resident', it claimed that Sinn Féin and *Conradh na Gaeilge* (the Gaelic League) received support for the survey on Irish street names only because, called on 'in the dark of night', people were afraid to disagree with Sinn Féin. If you refuse to agree with the campaign, the writer states, 'you can expect trouble later on'. The writer goes on to say that it is all part of a plot – first the Irish names go up, then the English ones will come down, and finally the Irish version will be replaced with 'a well-known if not well-loved Provo name'.

Four letters appeared in the following week's issue in response – one from a Turf Lodge resident, another from a Turf Lodge resident who participated in the survey, one from a local Sinn Féin *cumann*, and one from the Sinn Féin Cultural Department written in both Irish and English. The first letter writer denies that anyone was called on in the dark of night, the survey being carried out during daylight hours. He also says that no one who refused to sign the petition has been harassed. The second writer who took part in the canvassing says no intimidation took place at the time of the survey, and that four weeks later no one who refused to sign the petition has come forward with accusations of intimidation. He also rubbishes what he calls the 'sinister plot' to put up Provo street names as nonsense. Predictably, the two from Sinn Féin members also deny the claims made by 'Turf Resident'.

A final letter on the matter appeared in the 12 March 1983 issue. Signed 'An Irishman', the writer dismisses 'Turf Resident' as a person either suffering from severe paranoia, or someone who is out to spread propaganda against Republicans. Assuming 'Turf Resident' is female, he writes 'To alleviate her distress, she should try adopting some convictions and self-respect. If she feels at home with nationalists, she should be true to her Irish heart and delight in any Irish revival.'

These letters are informative on a number of points. The views expressed by 'Turf Resident' would probably be considered by most to be somewhat exaggerated, particularly the assertion that the erection of Irish street names is part of a wider plot to eventually change the names to those of well-known IRA members. However, the letter does reflect the belief held by some people that the Irish language revival (or at least the erection of Irish language street signs) is intimately linked with Republicanism, though in this case the writer sees it as a full-blown conspiracy. 'Turf Resident' seems to accept the Republican interpretation of the importance of Irish street signs, and is not at all pleased about it. As has become apparent throughout the discussion, there is a fair amount of Republican involvement in the language. High-profile campaigns such as the one to erect street names in Irish has helped to foster this image.

The street signs campaigns show the use of cultural discourse in a context other than that which involves government-supported agencies. Instead of being used as part of the rapidly forming 'official' discourse on the Irish language, it is used to maximize support for the campaign by minimizing divisions among Nationalists. The street signs campaigns also show decolonizing discourse in use as one way of interpreting the meaning and importance of the Irish language.

Again, the point that the ability to name is a form of power (Parkin 1984) is relevant to an understanding of this particular set of campaigns. The street signs campaigns reveal the struggle over the right of Sinn Féin – and other organizations – to employ Irish as a collective symbol. Some, for example 'Turf Resident', believe that Republicans are appropriating the language as a means of promoting their own symbols and advancing their own political agenda in a covert manner. The right to stage rituals around the Irish language is also called into question, because the erection of street signs and the ceremonies which mark the event can be seen as a valuation strategy on the part of the participants. The struggle over the right to name, the right to erect signs (both in its practical and ceremonial aspects), the right to canvass for support for the language and the right to claim credit for accomplishments on that front can be seen in the letters exchanged in the pages of the *Andersonstown News*, and in the conflict between residents and the Housing Executive over efforts to change the names of the tower blocks in Artillery Flats.

CONCLUSION

In these four case studies, I have attempted to show the three discourses as they are used 'on the ground' through an examination of the sometimes acrimonious relationships between the different branches of the British government and different sections of the Irish language revival movement. The first case study focused on relations between different sections of the revival movement, and how variations in the interpretation of the meaning and importance of Irish can lead to conflict and misunderstanding. It also reveals suspicions about the British government's motivations in beginning to fund the language, and the development of an 'official' discourse and ideology which is deemed more acceptable by the government and those who control the purse strings.

The *Glór na nGael* controversy also shows the development of an officially acceptable discourse in a conflict which might be considered the low point of recent decades in relations between the British government and Irish language activists. Antagonism between the government and Irish speakers was at a high, and tensions were also evident within the revival movement. Differences in tactics and ideology are revealed by examining the discourse of the controversy, although much of this was kept 'private' by the use of the Irish language when discussing disagreements in public.

The campaign for *Meánscoil Feirste* shows the development of rights discourse, focused on parity of esteem and rights for Irish speakers, as it came to prominence in the revival movement. It also reveals the strategic use of what Scott (1990) calls the public and hidden transcripts. Finally, the street signs campaign shows the use of cultural discourse in a different context, and decolonizing discourse during what was probably its heyday in the contemporary Belfast revival, the early 1980s.

In the next two chapters, we shall leave Northern Ireland in order to gain a broader perspective on the social construction of ethnic identity. In Chapter 8, a comparison of the Irish language north and south of the border will shed more light on the shifting discourses and ideologies of the revival movement. In Chapter 9, the Irish language revival movement in Northern Ireland will be compared with McDonald's work on the Breton language revival, and Handler's work on language and nationalism in Quebec.

8 Irish Language Discourses in the Republic of Ireland

INTRODUCTION

Efforts to revive the Irish language diverged after the partition of Ireland in 1921, as did the sociopolitical context in which the revival was situated. Since language takes its meaning from particular historical, political and social situations, the meanings associated with the language began to change as well, along with its political significance and its role as part of the identity of Irish people north and south of the border. Discourses on the Irish language both north and south of the border share the same historical roots and in some instances have become linked to the same ideologies, but they have developed along different trajectories post-partition.

In the immediate aftermath of partition, *Gaeilgeoirí* in the North had to come to terms with the new Unionist administration. In the South, meanwhile, many goals of the Irish language revival movement became policy for the new government of the Free State. Irish became one of the official languages (along with English), and remains so to this day. In contrast to Northern Ireland, Irish is a required subject in all government-funded schools, though since 1973 it is no longer a compulsory subject in public examinations. Although shrinking, there are still *Gaeltachtaí* in the South containing roughly 2 per cent of the population.[1] Language attitudes research in the Republic has shown widespread ideological support for Irish, but this is tempered by a weak commitment both to actual use and to most government policies which might improve its position (Ó Riagáin 1997: 271).

Irish-medium education is one area in which Irish is experiencing a small but significant growth. A policy of 'Gaelicizing' education was put in place by the southern government in the 1920s. Schools were encouraged to introduce immersion programmes where all or part of the school curriculum was taught through the medium of Irish. At its highest point in the 1950s, just over half of state primary schools offered full or partial immersion programmes (Ó Riagáin 1997: 20–1). The policy proved unpopular with parents, however, and numbers declined throughout the 1960s and 1970s. From a high of 255 Irish medium schools outside of *Gaeltacht* areas in 1940/1, numbers sank to 24 in

1970/1. Interest in Irish-medium education has grown again in recent years, with the result that by 1990/1 there were 66 all-Irish schools in the Republic. That number had risen to 80 in 1994 (Ó Riagáin 1997: 201). The recent growth in the number of Irish-medium schools is especially significant because it is parent-led, in contrast to the government-sponsored initiatives of the past.

The Irish language has a stronger visual presence in the South of Ireland than it does in the North, due in large part to state policy. While bilingual street and road signs are the norm in the Republic, they do not hold the same significance as Irish signs in Northern Ireland. In both cases, signs in Irish are largely symbolic. In the South most people take little notice of them, aside from the tourists. In the North, signs in Irish or bilingual signs were actually illegal until very recently (See case study four, Chapter 7). Although still symbolic, street signs in Irish in Northern Ireland have a political significance that they lack south of the border. In Belfast, the presence of signs in both Irish and English can be seen as an indication of activity taking place around the language, while the same cannot be said of the South.

Research into language attitudes in the Republic shows that while a significant majority of the population make positive correlations between the Irish language and their identity as Irish people, there is a strong tendency towards pessimism about the language's future.[2] The ambiguous feelings that many people in the South feel towards Irish, and towards Nationalism, have had an impact on the formation and use of discourses about the language. Hindley (1990: 163), among others, has suggested that nationalist sentiment is important to the survival of Irish in an overwhelmingly English-speaking country. This is probably true, but it is also problematic in light of the antipathy shown towards Irish Nationalism by so many Irish people. The work of revisionist historians, along with the violence in Northern Ireland over the last 30 years, has prompted a rethink of the once sacred tenets of Irish Nationalism.

As in the North, there is no consensus in the South about the meaning and significance of the language beyond a general sense of its symbolic importance. The debate, however, takes place in a very different context than in Northern Ireland. Even though *Gaeilgeoirí* in the South often espouse beliefs with the same history and ideological roots as northern *Gaeilgeoirí*, talk about the Irish language in the South is not trapped in the political/apolitical dichotomy which continues to dominate language issues in the North. Not only does this create an environment of greater discursive freedom, it allows for a wider scope in the debate over the significance of the language.

The more flexible context in the South is apparent, for example, in a greater freedom to use different discourses in combination with each other. Strategies which combine discourses in different ways are easier to achieve, at least in part because there are not as many strong ideological contradictions as in the discourses of the North. There are limitations to the ways in which cultural and decolonizing discourse can be combined, because so much of their ideological content and political implications are in direct opposition. This does not mean that they cannot be combined, only that there are narrower limits to the ways in which they can be used together. The discourses used in the Republic tend not to be so immediately contradictory. They can therefore be combined in a greater variety of ways.

There are four main discourses relating to the Irish language which are widely used in the Republic. These are cultural discourse (south), national language discourse, minority language discourse and dead language discourse. As with the three discourses described in previous chapters, this is not meant to be an exhaustive framework. It does, however, cover the most important ideological streams of debate within the revival movement. The descriptions that follow are of necessity only brief sketches, meant to give a feel for the discourses and their related ideologies in the Republic. These are followed by short examples of how each of the discourses are used in everyday life.

CULTURAL DISCOURSE (SOUTH)

Cultural discourse in the South has the same historical roots as its Northern counterpart, and bears some similarities to the second version of cultural discourse described in Chapters 3 and 5. The focus is on the cultural value of Irish as a unique language, part of the heritage of the Irish people. This does not necessarily indicate a practical desire to learn the language to fluency, nor to see a widespread revival of its use in daily life. As with cultural discourse in the North, it is commonly used to explain an interest in the language, or an interest in having one's children learn the language. While in the North cultural discourse is often used to justify an apolitical position regarding the language, this is a less prominent feature of cultural discourse in the South.

As with cultural discourse in the North, there are certain key words and concepts that indicate its use. These include 'beautiful language', 'heritage' or 'Gaelic/Celtic heritage' and 'tradition'. A connection is sometimes made between a person's interest in the language, and history, songs and literature in Irish. There is often a distancing from Nationalism or any possible political implications of an interest in the language. Speaking Irish is generally seen as a cultural activity and may be considered a hobby or pastime.

NATIONAL LANGUAGE DISCOURSE

National language discourse is related to decolonizing discourse in its historical roots, although it has developed in quite a different direction since partition. At the start of the century the Gaelic League had two separate and sometimes contradictory emphases – the cultural independence and the political independence of Ireland (see discussion in Chapter 3). Decolonizing discourse in Northern Ireland has developed primarily from the political independence strain of Gaelic League thought, although still incorporating an idea of cultural independence. National language discourse takes more from the emphasis on cultural independence. Since Ireland has achieved its political independence, the priority has shifted towards the development and definition of a unique Irish identity and culture. However, there is still a perception among a substantial minority of the population that the Irish language makes Ireland more independent of England. This assertion was supported by between 37 and 41 per cent of respondents in each of the three language attitudes surveys conducted from 1973 to 1993 (Ó Riagáin and Ó Gliasáin 1994: 19).

Decolonizing discourse is aggressively nationalist and highly politicized, focusing on the language as a tool to achieve independence from Britain and reunification with the rest of Ireland. National language discourse focuses on developing a sense of national or ethnic identity, but not necessarily in contrast to its more powerful neighbour. Language attitudes surveys in the South have shown a strong set of opinions in relation to 'beliefs and feelings about Irish as a focus of ethnic or national identity' (Ó Riagáin and Ó Gliasáin 1994: 18–19). In earlier years, national language discourse bore a stronger resemblance to decolonizing discourse. More recently, especially since the 1980s, the two have diverged more noticeably.

Key words and concepts that indicate the use of national language discourse include 'identity', 'national' or 'ethnic identity' and 'crisis of identity'. There is sometimes an emphasis on pride in one's own culture as a prerequisite for being able to respect the cultures of others. Users of this discourse frequently talk about making Irish people the centre of their own world, and the ability of the Irish language to help achieve this. The idea that a knowledge of both Irish and English would contribute to creative solutions to Ireland's social problems is also a common theme. Finally, users of this discourse sometimes assert that Irish people have a deep-seated sense of inferiority and insecurity about their identity, and that this is related in some way to the plight of the language.

MINORITY LANGUAGE DISCOURSE

Minority language discourse has come into its own since Ireland joined the European Union. The idea of a 'Europe of the regions' appeals to many people – and to many *Gaeilgeoirí* in particular – because it offers an opportunity for the Irish language to be seen not as a backward, useless language, but as one of many minority and regional languages which are valued and protected within a united Europe. It offers a context in which small and non-universal is acceptable, even desirable. It also allows the focus to be shifted away from the English-speaking world towards a multilingual world, a world where many people speak two or more languages, often their own minority language along with a more 'universal' language such as French or Spanish.

Minority language discourse can be contrasted with national language discourse. It involves a shift not only in strategies for reviving Irish, but a change in the way the language is imagined in relation to Irish identity. While a national language needs no special protection, a minority language does. The rights of its speakers must be respected and even defended in the face of the onslaught of majority language and culture.

Perhaps for this reason, minority language discourse bears some relation to rights discourse in the North. As we have seen, reference to Irish as a minority language in the context of Europe has been used as one strategy to secure funding and equal status for the Irish language in Northern Ireland. It can serve a similar purpose in the South, and minority language discourse sometimes features in campaigns to fund Irish language projects.

An important difference between rights and minority language discourse is the status of the former as an oppositional discourse. Minority language discourse features in the literature of Irish government authorities such as *Bord na Gaeilge*, while rights discourse often involves an antagonistic stance towards the British government. Minority language discourse seeks support and protection for the Irish language in the wider context of European minority languages. Rights discourse seeks support for the language and rights for its speakers in three arenas – the United Kingdom, Ireland and Europe – depending on the context.

The emphasis on rights can be traced to the British context in which the Irish language revival in Northern Ireland operates. The movement in the North has been strongly influenced by the Catholic civil rights movement of the 1960s, as well as campaigns for the rights of Welsh and Scots Gaelic speakers. Rights for Irish speakers has been an issue in the Republic also, particularly in the *Gaeltachtaí* during the late 1960s and early 1970s, but this appears to be due at least in part to influences from the fledgling civil rights movement in the North. Kiberd (1995) suggests that both the civil rights movement in the North of Ireland and the *cearta sibhialta* movement spawned in the Connemara *Gaeltacht* were inspired by the movement for black emancipation in the United States.

The key words which indicate the use of this discourse are 'minority language', a descriptive term which is unlikely to appear in either cultural discourse (south) or national language discourse. Europe often provides the context in which the discourse is used, and Irish is frequently juxtaposed implicitly or explicitly with other lesser used or regional languages in the European Union. Practicalities tend to take precedence over intangibles – the topic of discussion is more likely to be business development than identity.

DEAD LANGUAGE DISCOURSE

Strictly speaking dead language discourse is not a discourse of the revival movement, and I shall deal with it only briefly. Based on the premise that the Irish language is beyond redemption, dead language discourse is important because it forms and expresses an ideology which *Gaeilgeoirí* in the South must oppose. There is a focus on the lack of utility of the Irish language in this discourse, particularly in light of EU membership. Other European languages are seen as more useful, particularly English which provides certain advantages in many parts of the world. Dead language discourse tends also to be profoundly anti-Nationalist, perceiving the language as part of a set of conservative forces in Ireland – extreme Catholicism, right-wing Nationalism and the xenophobic attitudes which have often accompanied the discourses of the Irish language revival in the past.

Dead language discourse is found both north and south of the border, but it is much more prevalent in the Republic. This is due at least in part to negative experiences with the language that many young people have while in school. In contrast, negative attitudes towards the language among Nationalists in Northern Ireland tend to manifest themselves as indifference rather than hostility.

THE DISCOURSES IN PRACTICE

A classic expression of cultural discourse is found in Daniel Corkery's *The Fortunes of the Irish Language*, published in 1968. Throughout the book Corkery blends cultural discourse with both decolonizing and national language discourse in a way that would now be considered controversial. His articulation of cultural discourse, however, would not be out of place in Irish language circles all over the island up to the present day. Describing Irish as an ancient language – 'the sensitive mould of a distinctive culture' – he says that:

> The tradition of the Irish people is to be understood and experienced with intimacy only in the Irish language. It would be impossible that it could be so come upon in the English language. ... To say tradition is to say language – and while this is true of every national tradition it is overwhelmingly true of ours.
>
> (Corkery 1968: 13–14) [Quote 1]

More recent examples of cultural discourse can be found in the way Irish is used in some tourist brochures, where the language is presented to the visitor as part of the heritage tourism experience. Irish is often juxtaposed with the beautiful countryside, local history, archaeological sites, Irish pubs and traditional music. Seeing the Irish language in this context is not unique to tourist literature, though. It is a quite common association. A Dublin woman described to me the years she spent learning the language. I asked her:

> **C. O'R.** Why is it so important to you to speak Irish, that you would put so much effort into it?
> **Reply** It's so rich in culture. It's not just the language, it's the music and the stories and everything about it. I think it's a whole new way of life. ... There's so many aspects to it. [Quote 2]

Another Dublin woman told me:

> You can't really separate the language from the other things – your culture and your language and your inheritance. It's all part of the one thing. Like the place names and history. You understand a lot more when you hear the original names in Irish, not the English names. Even the songs, the Irish songs they sing, would have to do with something historical. It all leads back to history, before the English language came. [Quote 3]

The ideology of cultural discourse is taken in a unique direction by a youth organization established in Dublin in 1993 called *An Ciorcal Craiceáilte* ('The Fun Circle', loosely translated). Once or twice a year, the club organizes a *Féile Craiceáilte* ('Fun Festival') which includes live music, cabaret and discos, all conducted through the medium of Irish. A membership leaflet describes the goal of the organization as follows:

> *Tá an Ciorcal Craiceáilte á bhunú sa dóigh is gur féidir linne, Gaeil óga na tíre, sult agus pléisiúr a bhaint as an teanga ar achan bhealach gur féidir.*

> *An Ciorcal Craiceáilte* was established so that we, the young Gaels of the country, could take enjoyment and pleasure from the language in every way we can.
>
> (my translation) [Quote 4]

The rules of the organization as stated in this leaflet draw on cultural discourse, but with a zany twist. For example:

- *Caithfidh suim a bheith ag na baill sa chraic, ceol agus an timpeallacht. 'Sé an chraic is tábhachtaí ar fad, dár ndóigh!*
- *Tá an Ciorcal neamhpholaitiúil go hiomlán.*
- *Caithfidh gach ball amhrán nó dán nó damhsa a fhoghlaim, sin nó a bheith an-mhaith ag caitheamh siar piontaí!*

- Every member must be interested in fun, music and the environment. Fun is the most important, of course!
- The *Ciorcal* is completely apolitical.
- Every member must learn singing or poetry or dancing, that or be very good at knocking back pints!

(my translation) [Quote 5]

Cultural discourse in the South is relatively uncontested ground in comparison with its northern counterpart, and also in comparison with other discourses used in the Republic. National language discourse in many ways reflects the rethink of nationalism currently taking place in Irish society. As part of this process, the role of the language in the collective identity of Irish people is also under scrutiny.

One notable indication of this rethinking of Irish identity and the Irish language is the essay *Why Irish?* by Tovey, Hannan and Abramson. Published by *Bord na Gaeilge* in 1989, the authors attempt to reassess the significance of the language to the Irish people. They suggest that a crisis of identity is the key to understanding Ireland's social and economic problems (unemployment, emigration and social deprivation). In an introduction to the essay, Patrick Commins describes the problem like this:

> our incapacity to cope with problems in the civic domain is traceable to our inability as a people to express a coherent and authentic sense of Irish identity, or a broadly acceptable philosophy of what it means to be Irish in today's world. ... The rhetoric and symbols of the past are no longer appropriate but we have not been able to replace them with new bondings of collective identity or allegiance which would give us a sense of common purpose
>
> (Tovey et al. 1989: i) [Quote 6]

Tovey et al. suggest that having a sense of national identity and national pride is perfectly compatible with a respect for other cultures and other traditions, and may even enhance such a sense of respect if taught and articulated correctly.[3] They argue that ethnicity will continue to be a feature of modern life in spite of predictions to the contrary. If the ethnic label 'Irish' is inescapable, then the reconstruction of a sense of cultural and historic distinctiveness is essential, and the Irish language is the key to achieving this. Irish as a living language makes Irish history and heritage real, connecting it with the present instead of holding it at a distance.

They argue that the language issue is relevant to wider socioeconomic issues in Ireland for two reasons. First, it provides a medium for making Irish people the centre of their own world. This cannot be achieved through the medium of English, which places Irish people at the periphery of the English-speaking world, making them provincial and somehow inferior. Second, genuine bilingualism would contribute to creative problem-solving because it increases the capacity to move between different points of view, enriching Irish people's abilities to find creative solutions to the dilemmas of their society (Tovey et al. 1989: 32).

The idea that the Irish language is the key to solving Ireland's problems is not a new one. Back in the 1960s, de Fréine attributed the 'Irish condition' – emigration and 'disintegrating tendencies' – to anomie caused by the loss of Irish. He argues that once the language was lost by the majority of the population, there was a subsequent inability to express and develop norms and traditions, and to create new institutions to 'restate and transmit the values of the community' (de Fréine 1968: 109). If you accept that this is the case, it is logical to conclude that a revival in the use of Irish would be a positive step towards solving Ireland's social problems – as suggested by Tovey and her co-authors. They are not the only ones currently arguing along these lines. The prominent Irish historian Professor Joseph Lee, among others, has made a correlation between a sense of self-confidence, a secure Irish identity, a healthy enterprise economy and the Irish language.

While Tovey and her co-writers are professionals in the use of discourse, it is significant that much of what they say is echoed in discussions I have had with people involved with the Irish language in Dublin. It is difficult to say whether this is because the ideas they express have filtered out into the wider world, or because they do a good job of articulating the beliefs and attitudes of the 'non-professionals' (or most likely, both). In any case, it is clear that many people feel a deep-seated sense of insecurity, and even inferiority, in their identity as Irish people. The Irish language is seen by at least some people as a means of reclaiming or strengthening their national or ethnic identity. Among *Gaeilgeoirí* there is a widespread belief that the benefits of knowing and using 'our own language' extend beyond the individual. If Irish becomes more widely used, and if attitudes towards the language can be developed along more positive lines, they believe that this will have far-reaching implications for Ireland as a whole.

Placing the Irish language in a European context, rather than simply the national context, has become increasingly common in the discourse of professionals and non-professionals alike. For example *Comhar*, an Irish-medium magazine, often examines the language in a European context. *Bord na Gaeilge* recently promoted participation in a European Commission competition called Euroblas, designed to encourage the use of lesser-used languages in the private sector. Minority language discourse has become quite prominent in *Bord na Gaeilge* literature, often appearing alongside national language discourse:

> In calling for a refurbishing of Irish identity we suggest that the Irish language has an integrating and stimulating role to play. This is by no means a plea for a return to the outlook of the narrow nativistic ideology of the revivalists, current in the early 20th century. Neither is it to favour Irish as opposed to English; indeed we are fortunate in having one of the major languages of the world. Rather it seeks for a sense of confidence in our uniqueness within a polyethnic Europe. A process of revitalising Irish identity could perhaps espouse a new and serious political neutrality, reflect a sophisticated distrust of modern hidden imperialisms, show solidarity with the Third World, show a strong tendency towards humanism and egalitarianism, and, in re-examining Irish history, transcend any myopic preoccupation with the grievances of the past. In any event the construction of a modern Irish identity should affirm those values and outlooks which are positive, universal and liberating and be seen as a positive contribution to the evolution of the community of nations.
>
> (*Bord na Gaeilge* 1988: xxxiv–xxxvi) [Quote 7]

This passage begins with a plea for a 'refurbished' Irish identity. Drawing on national language discourse, the Irish language is seen as vital to achieving this. Irish is then tied in with Ireland's place as part of a 'polyethnic Europe'. The wording is self-consciously liberal, juxtaposing this new Irish identity with neutrality, humanism, and an ability to transcend the past – probably a veiled reference to the revival movement's former preoccupation with Ireland's colonial past, and the tendency to see the Irish language and Irish identity primarily in contrast with the English language and English identity. At the end of the passage, the Irish language is seen as playing a key role in establishing a new Irish identity which will shape Ireland's place in the 'community of nations'.

Imagining Irish within the wider framework of Europe is a common theme in the discussions I have had with individuals involved with the language in Dublin. People often talk about Irish as a minority language within Europe, sometimes with a sense of pride at their status as minority language speakers. Occasionally, people feel the need to defend the importance of Irish when they talk about Europe. A popular argument against the teaching of Irish in schools is that other European languages such as German or French would be much more useful for a child to learn. It is fairly common to hear Irish speakers bring this point up, even unsolicited. Generally speaking they acknowledge the importance of these other languages, but then make a plea for the necessity of a strong Irish identity lest Ireland be overshadowed by its larger and more powerful European neighbours. In the words of one Dublin resident:

> I don't honestly hold a hope of Ireland returning to a Gaelic speaking nation, but I think in recent years ... there's an upsurge of people wanting to learn it [Irish], especially in working class areas – a kind of 'go back to their roots' type of thing, because they're afraid that their identity is going to be lost in the European Community, that everybody else has their identity, where's the Irish going to be? It's creating an upsurge back towards Irish and the whole cultural aspect. [Quote 8]

An *Irish Times* journalist investigating the rise in popularity of Irish-medium education in Dublin received some similar responses. As one person told her:

> It's because of multi-channel television ... It's because we're in the EC. They see that other people speak their own languages. So why not us?
>
> (*Irish Times* 13 September 1993) [Quote 9]

CONCLUSION

The highly politicized context of Northern Ireland has had a significant impact on the discourses of the North and their associated ideologies. Yet it is clear that *Gaeilgeoirí* both north and south of the border draw on the same historical and ideological material in the formation of discourses on the Irish language, resulting in some similar features.

Making a clear distinction between northern and southern discourses is not always an easy matter. I have already commented on the similarities between cultural discourse north and south, and the common use of Europe as a context and framework. At times, the distinction between decolonizing discourse and national language discourse is blurred as well. The following passage from a Dublin interviewee, for example, clearly contains elements of both:

> There are different Irish identities ... [but] these are all reactive sorts of Irishness, reactive to the colonial situation. The Irish personality is in fact formed in response to English pressures. I think it's

a personality with some strengths, but an awful lot of weaknesses. The lack of self-confidence, the negativity, the lack of an ability to involve themselves in serious entrepreneurship, that failure at the commercial level, are all part and parcel of the colonized Irish identity. The alternative is to have a different sort of Irish identity, hegemonized by the Irish language but made up of elements which would be, if you like, a decolonized Irish identity. ... I would argue for the centrality of the language in establishing a decolonized Irish identity, and the establishment of this identity as essential for economic survival and dignity in the future. [Quote 10]

In spite of their common historical roots, the discourses have developed in distinct directions as the social and political contexts in the North and South of Ireland diverged post-partition. The result is that although they have certain common features, the discourses are now characterized by different ideologies and tend to be used in different ways. Changes which have affected both parts of Ireland have had different effects on the discourses of the revival, for example the increasing economic and political importance of Europe.

In Northern Ireland the discourses have developed in the context of a direct political relationship between Irish people in the North, the Unionist population and Britain. A segment of the Nationalist population in the North believe that learning and speaking Irish underlines their distinct identity in open contrast to British cultural and political hegemony.

Although political ties between Britain and the Republic of Ireland have been largely severed, many people in the South still feel the need to heal wounds they perceive as being inflicted by the English in the past, most especially the loss of the Irish language.[4] There may be no direct British political presence to struggle against, but some Irish people believe that England's cultural and economic influence in Ireland is still strong. The 'inferiority complex' or 'weakness' that so many Irish speakers in the South refer to seems to be the southern counterpart of the northern desire to underline their Irishness in the face of British cultural and political hegemony.

In the absence of direct political domination by Britain but in light of continuing economic and cultural influences, and in the context of Ireland's changing position in Europe and the wider world, southerners have become engaged in a collective ethnic reassessment. For some, the relevance of the Irish language is a key part of this reassessment.

9 Northern Ireland, Brittany and Quebec

Ethnonationalist movements have become a familiar phenomenon throughout the western world over the last few decades. Many of these are associated with movements to restore or protect minority or lesser-used languages. In this broader context the situation in Northern Ireland is not entirely unique. So far we have looked at the Irish language revival in relation to the conflict in Northern Ireland, and as a product of Irish historical, political and social developments. In this chapter, I shall examine two anthropological studies of ethnonationalist linguistic revivals which offer particularly relevant comparative insights, Handler's (1988) study of the 'politics of culture in Quebec' and McDonald's (1989) study of language, culture and identity in Brittany.

Comparison between Handler's and McDonald's work and my own research is hampered by our different analytical approaches. My own focus on discourse as a tool of analysis has led to the use of large sections of text taken directly from the source, while Handler and McDonald rely very little on the direct quotation of texts. It is clear, for example, that some of the discourse of the Breton militants resembles decolonizing discourse,[1] but without the words of the militants themselves it is impossible to make a comparison on this basis. What all three works do have in common is a focus on the politics of language, and on the social construction of identity. It is in these areas that I will attempt to draw out common themes and conclusions.

McDonald (1989) carried out field research in Brittany during the late 1970s and early 1980s. Her analysis of the Breton language revival movement looks at both the Breton language 'militants' – non-native speaking activists – and native Breton-speaking peasants in rural Brittany.[2] Her work with the militants is of particular relevance here, since they are (loosely) the Breton equivalents of Irish language activists in Northern Ireland.

In Handler's study of the social construction of national identity, he examines three metaphors for the nation: the individual as a member of the nation, the nation as a collective individual and the metaphor of the national species. The second and third are biological metaphors which suggest that the nation is a bounded, homogeneous and histori-cally continuous entity. In Cohen's (1994) words, the individual is seen

161

as 'the nation writ small'. Handler conducted his field research during roughly the same period as McDonald, but mostly in the urban areas of Quebec City and Montreal. Although he did talk to politicians and other political experts, the people Handler spoke to were not necessarily part of any political or linguistic movement.

French is the dominant language of Quebec, but it is a minority language in the context of Canada and North America as a whole. It is spoken both in rural areas and in the cities, although some English is spoken in Montreal (much to the dismay of Quebec nationalists). Most consider the French language to be an essential part of Québécois identity, and it does not appear to be in imminent danger of decline. In Brittany there are approximately 500,000 Breton speakers, mostly peasants, fishermen and their families (McDonald 1989: 7). However French is now commonly spoken throughout Brittany, and the Breton language is in a state of serious decline. French has come to dominate the public sphere, and Breton is now rarely spoken even as a language of the home (Kuter 1989: 85–6).

CONTEXTS

The relative strength of Breton, Irish in Northern Ireland and French in Quebec is quite varied. In each region there is a distinct relationship between the dominant and minority language, and there is a different balance within each movement between revival and survival tactics. French in Quebec is in a relatively strong position compared with many minority and lesser-used languages. It is spoken in both the public and private spheres in a wide variety of contexts, and it is protected by strong laws which favour French over English in public life. In Quebec, language revival is not a key issue. The focus is on survival and protection.

Breton and Irish are much weaker in relation to the dominant languages of their respective regions. Breton is still spoken as a native language in parts of Brittany, but shows signs of very serious decline. There are no historically native Irish-speaking areas within Northern Ireland, but in the context of island as a whole there are still small communities of native speakers. In both Brittany and Northern Ireland the focus is on language revival, although the preservation of currently native-speaking areas is also seen as important.

The sociopolitical context of each region varies as well, of course. In Northern Ireland the violent political conflict of the last few decades has had a profound impact, and as we have seen in previous chapters, the language revival is now primarily associated with the Catholic minority and the history of discrimination against this group. While there has been some political violence in Brittany since the late 1960s, it is on a much smaller scale. Aside from the more obvious issue of political violence, there are other important contrasts between the three regions.

Quebec is a province with a considerable amount of autonomy. Canada officially recognizes the uniqueness of French language and culture in the region. According to Handler, most Québécois feel some ambivalence about the idea of complete independence from Canada, a feeling which is reflected in part through voting behaviour, but also through differing philosophies of national culture.[3] Although French has the power of institutionalization behind it, there is still a sense of threat to the survival of the language – and therefore the nation – which is expressed through fears of 'contamination' and 'pollution'.

Brittany's regional status and its degree of political autonomy has varied over the centuries.[4] France maintains a strong central government with relatively little regional autonomy. Breton receives some official backing from the French government, but not unambiguously.[5] The French language became politicized during the 1789 revolution, and as the 'language of liberty' it has maintained a central place in French identity. French embodied the ideals of the Republic, and was to be the common language which bound together the citizenry. Regional languages such as Breton were in many ways seen as a threat. The ongoing preoccupation with the French language has created a context which is quite different from that in Northern Ireland, where almost the reverse has occurred. The dominant English has become naturalized and the minority Irish politicized – a topic of heated debate, as we have seen.

Similar to the Irish language revival movement, the Breton language revival has had to contend with a right-wing, conservative, Catholic history. During the period described by McDonald, however, the dominant self-image of the Breton language revival movement was left wing. A shift to the left seems to have occurred during the 1960s in both Northern Ireland and Brittany, particularly after the events of 1968 in France, and the growth of the civil rights movement from 1968–9 in Northern Ireland. However, the association with left-wing politics has not developed to the same extent in Northern Ireland as in Brittany.

As with the French language in Quebec, political associations with the Irish language revival movement tend to be nationalist and not necessarily left-wing. Still, there is a greater divide between nationalist politics and the language revival in Northern Ireland than in Brittany. In fact, as we have seen, any connection at all between politics and the Irish language is contentious in the North. In Brittany, by contrast, there is a much stronger connection between political organizations seeking autonomy or independence for Brittany and the language movement. McDonald writes:

> Since the Breton language is of prime importance, learning Breton is an important part of becoming a Breton militant. You may learn Breton dances (in a *Cercle celtique*) or blow up the palace of Versailles (like the FLB[6]) and call yourself part of the Breton movement; you will not always be taken seriously, however, by those who now dominate the movement, if you do not speak, or at least seriously aspire to speak, Breton. (1989: 87)

This is not the case in Northern Ireland. Republican organizations, most notably Sinn Féin, may claim to support the Irish language, but there is no requirement to speak it. It is possible to become quite prominent in the party without speaking a word of Irish. There are only a handful of serious *Gaeilgeoirí* in the Republican movement.

In addition, there is comparatively little centralization in the Irish language revival movement. McDonald describes large meetings of Breton militants organized to debate policy and the philosophy of the movement, and mentions an umbrella organization, *Le Front Culturel Progressiste Breton* ('The Breton Cultural Progressive Front'). She also describes mass events and the writing of militant histories and manifestos. None of these is characteristic of Northern Ireland's Irish language revival, where decentralization is usually seen as one of the movement's strengths. No one has much interest in attending meetings or writing manifestos. There are rarely large demonstrations. Those that are held tend to be of limited scope, aiming to make a symbolic statement.[7] When a few *Gaeilgeoirí* get an idea, they tend to gather only as many people as are necessary to get the project off the ground. Once it is up and running, others may decide to participate – or not. There is a saying from the revival movement of the 1960s: *na habair é, déan é* ('don't talk about it, do it'). Although not widely referred to today, it is still an accurate reflection of the underlying philosophy of the Irish language revival in the North.

These differences are due in part to timing – I witnessed the Irish revival in the 1990s, while McDonald's research was conducted in the late 1970s and early 1980s when left-wing politics had a higher profile in many parts of Europe. They are also due to the divergent goals of the two movements. The Breton movement is closely associated with left-wing politics and employs mass political tactics. The Irish language revival is not geared towards starting a mass movement, nor is it particularly concerned with broader left-wing politics. While some of the individuals involved have left-wing sympathies and links have been drawn with environmental issues such as mining on Belfast's Black Mountain, these remain for the most part personal rather than organizational concerns.

CONCEPTUALIZING ETHNIC IDENTITY

The assertion that nations and ethnic groups are created entities is now widely accepted. It is a generalization which is affirmed by the work of both Handler and McDonald. McDonald points out that the modern idea of the nation had a key developmental moment in the French revolution, tying the idea of the French language and nation especially close together and having important implications for the development of Breton identity.

She argues that Brittany has been conceptualized as a separate locality in relation to France in different ways throughout history. It was a duchy from the tenth to the sixteenth century, and a province of France from the sixteenth century to the revolution, when it was officially abolished along with all the old provinces to be replaced by *départements*. From that point, Brittany remained a 'folk' classification without official status. Since the 1970s, *départements* have been regrouped under the names of many of the old provinces. Brittany has once again become a recognized government category, this time in the form of a 'region'.

McDonald suggests that a modern Breton identity came to be constructed only through Brittany's incorporation into the wider French world (1989: 14). One of the most quoted theorists of ethnicity in the anthropological tradition, Fredrik Barth (1969), has suggested that ethnic groups are formed in the process of social interaction. Ethnic boundaries are defined in opposition to outside groups, Breton in relation to French, Irish in relation to English, and so on. A modern concern for the loss of Breton identity has led militants to construct their own histories which emphasize the autonomy and independence of Brittany in the past. The writing of these 'oppositional' histories is a key activity of the revival movement. The histories not only define a Breton identity in opposition to French identity, but create a Breton heritage with links to other 'oppressed' Celtic countries, including Wales, Ireland, Scotland and Cornwall. Handler, too, highlights the importance of history to the construction of Québécois identity. The search for an authentic 'folk' society and 'folk' tradition is part of the pursuit of an identity sufficiently rooted in history to be considered 'genuine'.

The use of history in the creation of Breton ethnicity is a key point in McDonald's argument. At times, however, McDonald strongly relates ethnicity to race, a conflation which is not helpful to her attempt to understand the construction of a militant Breton identity. She suggests that while modern militants no longer make reference to 'race' because it is considered to be old-fashioned and reactionary, 'within the uncritical positivism that marches language and culture and blood and kin back together into history, however, "ethnicity" is no more and no less than racialism' (McDonald 1989: 116). This reductionist approach to race and ethnicity takes little account of the large amount of literature which addresses the relationship between these two concepts.

In a review of McDonald's book, Badone (1992) acknowledges that she successfully documents the process whereby cultural identities are constructed by the Breton language militants. Badone is critical, however, of McDonald's failure to 'penetrate the seriousness of the motivations underlying this search for authenticity' (1992: 808). McDonald tends to trivialize the interests and pursuits of the militants. Her account is full of irony, but does little to illuminate how and why the symbolic universe of the language militants is meaningful (Badone 1992: 809). Breton language and culture are seen by the militants as the means to creating an alternative lifestyle, a point which McDonald could have investigated more thoroughly.

While the Breton identity espoused by the Breton language revival movement is the more recent construction, it is wrong to assume that the beliefs and motivations of the militants are somehow less genuine for this. In their efforts to seek an alternative way of life, perhaps the Breton revivalists have failed to see the reality of the Breton world as it is lived by native-speaking peasants, seeing instead the 'myth' of the Celt,[8] but an understanding of this process is still relevant for an investigation into ethnic identity.

One of the ways in which Handler investigates the creation of ethnicity is by looking at the fear of linguistic pollution in Quebec, revealing a fundamental insecurity about ethnic identity. As the key component of Québécois identity, French distinguishes Quebec from the rest of

North America, and to the extent that Québécois French is considered distinct from the French language of France, it makes Quebec unique. Handler suggests that the English language in Quebec threatens the collective self. The collapse of cultural and linguistic boundaries, it is believed, will lead to the death of the nation. The fear that the French language of Quebec is being corrupted by contact with English has led to an ongoing campaign to 'purify' it. National identity can be defended through the protection of the language which embodies that identity.

This poses an interesting contrast to the Irish language in relation to Irish identity in Northern Ireland. As a minority language in continuous contact with English, Irish is losing much of its unique syntax and idioms. Even in the *Gaeltacht*, Gaelicized English, Anglicized Irish and direct borrowings from English have replaced Irish in certain contexts.[9] Northern *Gaeilgeoirí* try to avoid this tendency. In part, this avoidance is the result of 'book Irish' and the learning of Irish from other non-native speakers. The use of dictionaries and grammar books to learn unknown vocabulary may limit the use of English loan words and Gaelicized English, but it tends to encourage Anglicized Irish and discourage the use of idiomatic expressions. Both of these tendencies are lamented by *Gaeilgeoirí* who turn to *Gaeltacht* Irish in pursuit of a 'richness' considered to be lacking in much 'learned' Irish. In this sense, the pursuit of linguistic purity bears some similarity to Quebec. McDonald, too, has observed debates over the purity of Breton. There is some argument over which version of Breton is most 'authentic', the book version or the version spoken by the 'peasantry'.

There is, however, a marked difference in attitudes towards bilingualism in Quebec and Northern Ireland. Handler reports negative associations with bilingualism in Quebec nationalist ideologies, including the belief that a second language inhibits the ability to think clearly if learned too early, that a second language would hinder socialization into a French world-view and cause confusion, and that bilingual individuals suffer from mental deficiency, maladjustment and an inadequate command of both languages.

All of these beliefs have also been associated with a *lack* of support for the teaching of Irish to children, and have been used in Ireland in the past to justify a shift from Irish to the dominant English. As has already been seen, Irish language campaigners today tend to have a positive view of bilingualism. They suggest that it enhances a child's ability to learn other languages and to think creatively, is pedagogically beneficial to the learning environment, and contributes to the development of tolerance and positive attitudes to cultural difference.

Instead of being a threat to the collective self and the cause of cultural and linguistic collapse, Northern Irish speakers tend to see bilingualism as a route into an enhanced or strengthened Irish identity. The difference is probably due to the relative strength of the two languages in question. French in Quebec is not in a serious state of decline, while Irish is. With no chance of reviving Irish as the dominant language of the majority of Irish people, bilingualism is perhaps the only hope of avoiding the complete loss of Irish as a living, spoken language. Although linguistic contact and 'contamination' are seen as a threat to both languages, in the case of Quebec they are also interpreted as threats to national identity. In Northern Ireland, they are seen as the regrettable side effects of efforts to protect or enhance Irish identity through the promotion of the Irish language.

History and language are key elements in the conceptualization of ethnic identities. In Brittany, Quebec and Northern Ireland alike, history is constructed in ways that justify the existence of the ethnic group and reinforce its boundaries. For some people in each of these regions, the history they construct is used to ground an argument for national autonomy. Language is not only a key element in the conceptualization of ethnic identity, it is a metaphorical gauge of the health of the ethnic group. Preservation or purity of language is equated with the survival and integrity of the ethnic or national group.

SELF-CONSCIOUS CULTURE AND THE SEARCH FOR AUTHENTICITY

Since Hobsbawm and Ranger's (1983) seminal work on the invention of tradition, the notion that tradition can be 'created' has been affirmed many times over. The creation of tradition and the search for authenticity figure prominently in the work of both Handler and McDonald. Handler describes the search for an 'authentic' folk society as part of the creation of a 'traditional' Quebecois culture from which present-day Quebec is seen to have sprung. True authenticity is sought in the traditions of the countryside, from farming implements to folk dances. Handler describes a folk dance exhibition held in a hockey arena, the stage designed to resemble the interior of a farmhouse complete with a larger-than-life fireplace. The audience is meant to feel part of a rural tradition of visiting and festivities, to witness the roots of a unique Québécois culture which unites the nation. Authenticity is claimed and expressed through the objectification and reification of culture.

In Northern Ireland, *Gaeilgeoirí* often gauge authenticity in relation to an idealized image of the Gael. The *fíor-Gael* ('true Gael') is Irish-speaking, devoutly Catholic, nationalist in political orientation, a player of Gaelic sports, preferably a rural dweller and generally of high moral character. This idealized image has its roots in the turn-of-the-century Irish revival, but with the growth of the Irish language movement and the return of the language to the centre of the political arena, the image of the *fíor-Gael* has once again come to the fore. Though the stereotype of the *fíor-Gael* has less currency than it once did, there are still those who adhere to it as an ideal. Of the elements that define a *fíor-Gael*, some are more important than others. In Northern Ireland today, the most essential elements are to be a Nationalist, to be dedicated and to have good Irish.

This makes an interesting contrast with the Breton language revival in Brittany. McDonald (1989) describes how the modern, urban and intellectual Breton language militants seek authenticity in the world of native Breton-speaking peasants. The rural harvest festival has been recreated into the *fest-noz* to give militants and tourists alike the chance to participate in 'authentic' Breton life (McDonald 1989: 144). Romantic associations between language, the soil and rustic, peasant living which are still current in the Breton revival are reminiscent of an earlier emphasis on rural idyll in the Irish language revival. However, the current revival movement in the North has embraced urban living. The centre of the revival is in Belfast, and although many *Gaeilgeoirí* enjoy waxing lyrical about the countryside for a time, they are more than happy to return to their urban lives at the end of their *Gaeltacht* holiday. For the majority of *Gaeilgeoirí*, authenticity is sought elsewhere.

'Good Irish' is perhaps the most important determinant. While there seems to be no shortage of dedicated people to tirelessly carry out the work of the revival, a good command of the language requires many years of study and effort to attain, especially considering that very few Irish language activists are native speakers. Achieving a high level of fluency is the next best thing to being a native speaker in terms of a claim to authenticity.

Bowie (1993) makes some similar observations about the importance of the Welsh language to an authentic Welsh identity. She argues that there are essentially three different Waleses, divided by language, geography and history. The native Welsh speakers of Gwynedd and parts of Dyfed tend to consider themselves the only true Welsh. 'Welsh Wales' encompasses West and Mid-Glamorgan and part of Gwent, and although English-speaking, the residents strongly resent the implication that they are not truly Welsh. 'British Wales' is more Anglicized. According to Bowie, identity is seen as problematic in all parts of Wales – 'it needs to be fought for and over, talked about and defended, defined and rejected' (1993: 170). The question of to what extent the Welsh language can be taken as the primary mediator of Welshness and the main criterion of nationhood is at the heart of Welsh identity, and at the core of deep divisions in Welsh society (Bowie 1993: 169).

What I call the *fíor-Gael* has been described as 'a spectacularly dramatic example of internalised colonialism' by Mac Póilin (1994: 20). The ideal image created in nineteenth-century Ireland had very little to do with the *Gaeltacht* and existing native speakers of the language at the time, still less to do with *Gaeltacht* or Irish life today. It could be argued that the ideals enshrined in this image were not those of the Gaelic way of life of any period. Mac Póilin suggests that 'the ideals were, in fact, those of Victorian England, filtered through French Jansenism, with a touch of theocracy, and embodied in an extreme form the convergence of Victoria's England with ultra-montaine Ireland' (Mac Póilin 1994b: 20).

Chapman (1982, 1992) has examined portrayals of the 'Celt', particularly the impact of outsiders' perceptions on a group's self-ascribed identity. He argues that since classical times, the Celt has been described as 'unreliable, moody, evasive, uncertain, incompetent and selfish', or, alternatively, as 'excitable, high-spirited, eloquent, subtle, independent and individualist' (Chapman 1982: 129). These images contrast with how writers of both the classical era and eighteenth- and nineteenth-century Europe characterized themselves, as 'ordered, rational, civilized and right'. Chapman suggests that 'the Celt served them both as a figure of opposition, a mythical alter-ego which they used in pursuit of their own self-definition' (1982: 129).

This caricatured image of the Celt has strongly influenced conceptualizations of identity in the 'Celtic fringe'. McDonald notes that the stereotype of the Breton 'other' as emotional, free and irrational appealed to the militants who conceptualized Breton identity as an alternative to being French. Along with the social and historical forces described by Mac Póilin, the stereotype of the Celtic 'other' has had a profound influence on the creation and re-creation of the *fíor-Ghael* over the last century. It is ironic that Breton authenticity and Irish authenticity are now judged in relation to an idealized identity which has its roots in outsiders' romanticized and stereotyped visions of the Celt as 'other'.

One of the consequences of the search for tradition and authenticity is a degree of self-consciousness about, and objectification of, culture. People 'have' a culture which they can stand back from and examine as an entity separate from themselves (Handler 1988: 14). 'Authentic' traditions are recreated as cultural spectacles, like the *fest-noz* in Brittany or the folk dance exhibition in Quebec. The act of witnessing or participating in these events creates a self-conscious sense of belonging.

In all three cases – Northern Ireland, Quebec and Brittany – authenticity is at least partially equated with rural ways of life. Urban dwellers can attain this sense of belonging by participating in an objectification of country life. *Gaeilgeoirí* from Northern Ireland travel to the *Gaeltacht* to speak and learn Irish in an authentic surrounding. Breton language militants move to rural Brittany in order to experience an authentic Breton lifestyle. In Quebec, one can take a holiday in a farmhouse and participate in traditional Québécois country activities.

The cultural objectification described by Handler is a prerequisite for nation-building. It is also a prerequisite for language revival. It takes a certain degree of cultural self-consciousness to convince adults to undertake the task of learning a new language on the grounds that it *should* have been their native tongue, or that they will 'lose' their culture and identity if they allow the indigenous language to slip away. The ideal of the *fíor-Gael* is part of an attempt to create self-consciousness about what it means to be Irish in Northern Ireland today. Breton militants feel the need to raise people's consciousness, and see the use of French by Breton peasants as an indication of their 'alienation' from their own culture. The paradox is that the search for authenticity and tradition inevitably leads to sociocultural change – change in the name of continuity.

CHANGE OR CONTINUITY?

The search for authenticity presupposes a certain degree of continuity with the past, the foundation on which tradition is constructed. But the search for authenticity is generally part of a larger exercise in ethnic group formation or nation-building, processes which involve social change. In the case of ethnic revivals, change is cloaked in the discourses of heritage and tradition to create the illusion of reclaiming the past or revitalizing fading customs. The revival of a language, for example, requires tremendous change, yet it is perceived by those involved in terms of tradition and historical continuity.

M. E. Smith (1982) offers a way of understanding this paradox. She argues that tradition and change are not separate phenomena, but interpretive constructs. They should be viewed as two manifestations of the process of sociocultural continuity. Continuity, she says, can be defined 'as a synthetic phenomenon with the property of appearing flexible and adaptive under some conditions and persistent and self-replicating under others' (Smith 1982: 127). Change is in fact continuous, an integral part of social processes. However, under some circumstances people tend to interpret these processes in terms of change, while under others the perception is of long-term stability.

This conceptual framework is particularly useful when looking at the process of ethnic or linguistic revival movements. All identities, Smith points out, are made up of altered, rearranged, freshly understood or even newly created events and cultural artifacts (1982: 135). An interesting feature of cultural revivals is that they emphasize both the traditional and historically deep, and the novel and freshly adapted. The perception that something lost or abandoned is being reclaimed is often accompanied by an acknowledgment that this cultural item or event is newly valued and reinvested with meaning relevant to present day circumstances. Identity is both reaffirmed and readjusted to suit people's needs. Change can even be welcomed as a means of *preserving* a durable, long standing identity.

A sense of continuity is sought through change, but a particular sort of change that emphasizes reclamation or revitalization. At times this can be quite self-conscious, as with the folklore *spectacle* described by Handler, the *fest-noz* in Brittany described by McDonald, or the yearly pilgrimage to Irish-speaking areas of Donegal undertaken by *Gaeilgeoirí* from Northern Ireland. Cultural objectification of this sort could be seen in part as the result of perceptions of undesired change – a type of social engineering which attempts to correct a shift away from 'tradition' by capturing and reifying the 'disappearing' cultural artifact.

CONCLUSIONS

In this chapter I have taken a brief comparative look at the social construction of ethnic identity and the politics of language in Quebec, Brittany and Northern Ireland. A number of common themes arise from this comparison. The first relates to the creation of ethnicity as an oppositional identity. Like the Gael who seems to have been in the process of disappearing for centuries,[10] ethnic revivalists tend to perceive their culture as continually in imminent danger of extinction, under threat from the dominant group and language to which it is juxtaposed. This is the case regardless of the relative strength of the minority language or ethnic group in question. Both the ethnic group itself, and the relationship of threat and opposition are conceptualized through versions of history, linguistics and tradition.

Ethnic identities are not monolithic, nor are they understood in the same terms even by those who claim membership of the group. It has been said before, but it is worth reiterating that ethnic boundaries are fuzzy and ambiguous, while the cultural 'content' which they enclose is contested and in a continual state of flux. Handler's discussion of the three philosophies of national culture which have developed over the last few decades in Quebec's political circles is an example of the type of struggle which occurs over the construction of ethnic identities, as is my own account of the three discourses of Northern Ireland's Irish language revival movement. McDonald's conclusion about the different values invested into French and Breton by militants and peasants is another example (McDonald 1989: 279). The struggle over which construction will dominate is more than a simple debate over words or different versions of the same story. It is essentially a struggle for power, because the ability to name, define and objectify is at the root of the exercise of power (Parkin 1984).

A second theme has been the search for tradition and authenticity. Cultural objectification is a prerequisite for ethnic and linguistic revival, an integral part of the creation of tradition. The work of Handler and McDonald exposes a paradox – the search for authenticity, folk customs and 'genuine' Québécois (or Irish, or Breton) culture leads to sociocultural change rather than any true continuity with the past. M. E. Smith's framework for understanding sociocultural continuity provides us with a useful way of looking at language and ethnic revivals. Revivalists tend to juggle the interpretive constructs of 'tradition' and 'change' in such a way that the desired cultural transformations appear in the guise of heritage and the reaffirmation of tradition, rather than innovation or a break with the past. The term 'tradition' has come to carry considerable symbolic capital, bestowing legitimacy and meaning onto just about any cultural or social practice.

Breton militants appropriate something they perceive as belonging to another, alternative world of which they want to be a part. They justify this desire by using discourses of opposition, authenticity, and reclamation. *Gaeilgeoirí* become involved in creating something they already perceive to be theirs, a lost heritage that lies dormant within them – a belief which is typified by the phrase 'our own language'. Both the Breton movement and the Irish language revival in Northern Ireland are about the reinvention of heritage and tradition, although these are constructed through different idioms. The Québécois nationalists, on the other hand, maneuver to protect and to reimagine what they already have – protect it from contamination by the English-speaking world, and reimagine it into a cohesive whole that is independent, or at least more autonomous. All three are about the politics of language and culture in pursuit of power and a political voice.

10 Conclusion

The phrase 'our own language' has come to symbolize the importance of the Irish language to Irish identity for *Gaeilgeoirí* in the North. The passion and conviction of a handful of Irish speakers has filtered out into the wider community in the form of a generalized, positive feeling about the language. In fact, the Irish language has become one of the few issues which can unite the majority of Nationalists of all political descriptions. A number of different campaigns have mustered fairly widespread support, including the putting up of Irish street signs and, especially, Irish-medium education. A picture of unity and agreement is only the surface image, however. Individuals and different interests compete to have their version of the meaning and significance of the Irish language accepted, with consequences for the shape of Irish identity and for power relations at all levels in Northern Irish society.

As Handler and McDonald also point out, language and ethnicity can be constructed as part of an oppositional identity. This is conceptualized through different versions of history, language and tradition, including both versions that contest dominant ideological constructions, and those that compete with other oppositional constructions. The appropriation of history, or the assertion of alternative histories, is an important means of challenging or subverting dominant discourses, while the links between history and language provide new opportunities to reinvent identity. In Northern Ireland, competing versions of the significance of Irish, both within the Nationalist community and between Nationalists and government institutions, are part of an ideological struggle to define Irish identity, and to have this identity officially recognized.

The Irish language has become an alternative point of political access for many Nationalists. It provides a means of accumulating political, symbolic and cultural capital both within the Nationalist community and in the wider political field. In the context of political strife and the historical repression of Irish identity in the North, the Irish language offers an opportunity for people to assert their sense of Irishness. For many, it is also a chance to make a compelling but non-violent statement about being Irish in a situation where opportunities to do so have been severely limited by prejudice and violence. For those whose access to economic, educational and social resources has been limited, Irish can offer fresh opportunities.

As such, Irish has become an important tool of political organiza-tion in Northern Ireland. In an 'abnormal' political situation, the Irish language revival movement has become a meaningful mode of political expression and participation. There are a number of reasons why this is so. The history of inequality and lack of political representation for the Catholic minority in the North has left its legacy, and even though much has been done to address Catholic grievances, inequality still exists. The violence and civil unrest which have characterized most of the history of Northern Ireland, especially the last 30 years, have severely limited possibilities for political participation for most people. The political structures that do exist offer few opportunities for par-ticipation or expression and very little real power for either Catholics or Protestants. And finally, the dominant British ethos of the state continues to stifle political and cultural expressions of Irishness, even with the limited progress made in recent years as a result of new policies intended to nurture the 'two traditions', and rhetoric about 'parity of esteem'.

With an increasingly high profile, the Irish language revival can no longer be ignored by the authorities. Different government agencies and representatives, from the CCRU to DENI, and from civil servants to the Secretary of State, have had to engage with the revival movement and its representatives, particularly over issues of expenditure on the language. They have adopted aspects of cultural discourse to do this, exerting control by requiring conformity to a government ideology on the language which emphasizes cultural identity and delegitimates the use of Irish in a political context.

Criteria for funding in many agencies favour projects which are accessible to people from outside established Irish language circles, rather than those that cater solely to the Irish-speaking community. In fact, much funding is contingent on a cross-community aspect to the proposed project. Both of these criteria require at least partial use of the dominant languge, English. The funding agency is in a position to determine if the group requesting money is legitimate and respon-sible, and whether the proposed project is financially viable. The onus is on the group requesting funding to demonstrate these things, which means conforming to state policies on the promotion of Irish and approaching the agency via the appropriate discourse. To use Frazer and Cameron's terminology, cultural discourse has become part of the 'language of power' in relation to the Irish language in Northern Ireland.

As a vehicle for ideology, discourse is used to communicate belief and define the acceptable. As the exercise of ideological and symbolic power, discourse influences and alters social relations. According to Frazer and Cameron, a language of liberation makes available meanings which are not articulated in competing discourses, meanings which may be considered illegitimate in circles of power. Languages of liberation may carry prestige in some contexts, but they lack the power of dominant discourses. To the extent that the discourses of the Irish language revival movement challenge dominant discourses associated with institutions of power, they could be considered languages of liberation. Decolonizing and rights discourses in particular might be seen in this light. Alternative discourses such as these are handled by institutions of authority in different ways. Sometimes they are suppressed, either directly (for example, removing funding from a controversial organization such as *Glór na nGael*), or indirectly (by attempting to delegitimate a particular discourse or certain aspects of it). There is also the option of simply ignoring an alternative discourse, hoping that it will lack the power, or that its users will lack the stamina, to press forward their ideological position.

Calls to 'depoliticize' the Irish language in practice often mean efforts to disassociate it from Nationalism and/or Republicanism. The depoliticization of the language would have consequences both for the way Irish identity is imagined in relation to it, and for the use of Irish as a political tool. It would mean giving up this point of access, which many would not be willing to do in the absence of alternative means of legitimate political expression which acknowledge and incorporate their claim to an Irish political and cultural identity. Yet blocking off this point of access to political expression is precisely what some aim to achieve by calling for depoliticization, including some government authorities. By favouring a version of cultural discourse which labels the language as a purely cultural pursuit, the language is associated with a cultural rather than a political identity, and its value as a political tool is diminished.

The Irish language movement has become an important avenue for demands that an Irish political and cultural identity be recognized by the state. Users of all three discourses participate in this struggle to a greater or lesser degree, but as I have shown in Chapters 3–7, they place their emphases in different areas and interpret the significance of the language in different ways. As an Irish identity becomes increasingly legitimate in Northern Ireland, the question becomes which version – or versions – of this identity will dominate, and who will control or influence its shape. Funding and other forms of official recognition can be used to manipulate this process. Ideologies can be promoted through the adoption of certain discourses by institutions of power, or delegitimized through strategies such as the 'depoliticization' of the Irish language.

We saw that most people mix or switch between discourses in the course of everyday speech. This accomplishes a number of different things. For some individuals, the mixing of discourses creates a hybrid that suits their own idiosyncratic or ambiguous beliefs about the language. Consistency is not obligatory in human belief systems. In fact, a lack of consistency can be a strength in many ideologies. Mixing or switching discourses can also be a strategy, conscious or otherwise, to get the most out of a situation. When dealing with discursive constraints such as the preference for cultural discourse found in many funding agencies, switching from, say, rights discourse to cultural discourse can be a means to an end. Another example would be the use of decolonizing discourse in order to be intentionally confrontational. Switching discourses may also simply reflect the prominence of different ideas at different times or in different contexts.

Although cultural discourse is strongly favoured by funding agencies, in other contexts government authorities seem to be more willing to consider the Irish language as part of Nationalist identity. During the peace process of the last few years, the treatment of the language has come to be seen as a sort of litmus test for parity of esteem for Nationalists in Northern Ireland (O'Reilly 1996). This has had real consequences for how the relationship of language to identity is conceptualized, and for the shape of a negotiated settlement in the North.

During the all-party talks in Castle Buildings at Stormont, some members of Sinn Féin, the SDLP and representatives of the southern government conversed in Irish in the halls and over lunch. Although at an unofficial level, it is significant that Irish was spoken at the talks on a daily basis between those people who are fluent in the language. The language was promoted by both Sinn Féin and the SDLP as part of a package for official recognition of Irish identity in the North. Both parties continue to link recognition for the Irish language with parity of esteem, as does the Dublin government. When the talks finally came to an end and the Good Friday agreement was published, the Irish language figured prominently under the heading 'Rights, Safeguards and Equality of Opportunity'. For the first time the British government have made a commitment to promote the language 'where appropriate and where people so desire it'. The Irish language has been transformed over the last two decades from a marginal and eccentric activity into the key cultural point for Nationalists on the peace agenda.

All of these things contribute to the association of Irish with a Catholic/Nationalist cultural package. This will have consequences for Protestants interested in the language, as the discourse of 'two traditions' comes to dominate over that of 'common heritage', and the Irish language returns to a solid position in the Nationalist cultural and political repertoire. It also appears that rights discourse is becoming increasingly powerful in terms of its ability to influence government policy towards the language, competing more successfully with cultural discourse for an institutional position.

Macdonald suggests that the task of those with an interest in ethnicity and identity is to map out the 'creation and appropriation' different models of identity as they are lived in everyday life, both in terms of generalities and the specifics of particular situations (1993: 22). This volume is intended to be just such a contribution, illuminating general processes in the politics of language and identity as well as the particular intricacies of the Irish language revival in Northern Ireland. In spite of Hindley's (1990) 'qualified obituary' of the language, as long as it remains part of the politics of culture and identity, it is not time to bury Irish yet.

Appendix I
Timeline of Some Important Events in Northern Ireland's History

1886, 1893

Home Rule Bills are proposed in the British Parliament. Both are defeated amidst strong hostility from Ulster Unionists.

1912

A third Home Rule Bill is proposed and passed, and goes on the statute books in 1914. An amendment is proposed to temporarily exclude the nine counties of Ulster. This is eventually pushed back to the six counties which currently make up Northern Ireland. Counties Donegal, Monaghan and Cavan, all of which have significant Protestant populations, are sacrificed in order to create what is considered to be a governable state with a two-thirds Protestant majority.

1913

In January, Unionist leaders Edward Carson and Sir James Craig, later to become the first Prime Minister of Northern Ireland, found the Ulster Volunteer Force in order to resist, if necessary, the imposition of home rule. In response the Irish Volunteers are founded in November to support home rule. The implementation of the Home Rule Bill is suspended during the First World War. Nationalists are divided on the issue of whether or not the Irish should fight on the side of the British, an issue which results in a split into John Redmond's National Volunteers and Eoin MacNeill's Irish Volunteers. The Irish Republican Brotherhood (IRB) join forces with MacNeill.

May 1915

The IRB start plans for a military uprising, to take place at Easter in Dublin.

April 1916

The 1916 Easter Rising lasts just five days. Those leaders who did not die in the fighting are later executed.

1920

Under the Government of Ireland Act 1920, parliaments are established in Dublin and Belfast with powers of local self-government. Ireland is partitioned along the six county border, with the possibility of the future unification of Ireland if both parliaments agree to it.

1921

After years of violence which pitted the IRA against the British army and the special police force known as the Black and Tans, Éamon de Valera's government sends a delegation to London for a conference with the British. Faced with the ultimatum of 'war within three days' issued by British Prime Minister Lloyd George, the Irish delegation sign a treaty on 6 December 1921 which confers dominion status on the Irish Free State and provides for a border commission to consider the status of the 'temporary' six county boundary. Conflict over the Treaty results in a split in the IRA into anti- and pro-Treaty factions. A bitter civil war is ultimately won by the pro-Treaty faction.

1922

The Border Commission which was provided for in the Government of Ireland Act meets for the first time. The status quo prevails, and the boundary remains more or less as it was originally drawn in 1920.

1923

Local boundaries within Northern Ireland are redrawn. Gerrymandering is rife. Before partition, Nationalists won control of 26 councils (Farrell 1980: 25). After the 1924 elections, Nationalists control just two (Farrell 1980: 84–5).

December 1948

The *Dáil* pass a bill declaring Ireland to be a Republic.

1949

In February, a general election is held in Northern Ireland. The Anti-Partition League contest the elections and do well. However, there is still no universal suffrage in Northern Ireland. Voting rights are restricted to ratepayers, and with the so-called 'company vote', company directors could exercise up to six votes, depending on the rateable valuation of the company (Farrell 1980: 85). In May, the London government passes the Ireland Bill, clause 1(1) of which effectively strengthens the union with Britain.

1955

The IRA launch the most serious physical force campaign against the northern state since partition. Known as the 'border campaign', it is a largely military offensive which will last over five years. Internment and arrests break the campaign by 1960, and it is officially called off in 1962.

1963

Terence O'Neill is chosen to succeed Lord Brookeborough as Northern Ireland's Prime Minister. He institutes a number of reforms designed to include more Catholics in the running of the state, but they are not far-reaching enough for most Nationalists.

1966

The Ulster Volunteer Force, named for the UVF of the 1912–22 period, initiate an assassination campaign against Catholics. On 27 May, John Scullion is shot on Clonard Street in west Belfast, and later dies from his wounds. On 26 June, three Catholics are shot as they leave a bar on the Shankill Road. One of the men, Peter Ward, dies.

1967

The Northern Ireland Civil Rights Association (NICRA) adopts a programme which includes 'one man [*sic*], one vote in local elections; no gerrymandering of constituency boundaries, fair distribution of local council houses, the repeal of the Special Powers Act, the disbanding of the B Specials, and a formal complaints procedure against local authorities' (Lee 1989: 420). (Formed in October 1920 as part of the Ulster Special Constabulary, the B Specials were a part-time, armed, 100 per cent Protestant police force. Known for their brutality and sectarianism, they were especially hated and feared by Catholics.)

1968

The first of the civil rights marches, from Coalisland to Dungannon in County Tyrone, is held in August to protest at discrimination in housing. Another march, scheduled for Derry in October, is blocked when the Minister for Home Affairs prohibits all marches. When the organizers defy the order there is a confrontation between the RUC and marchers. The police brutality and riots which follow are televised worldwide. Civil rights marches and protests continue to be held throughout October and November. On 22 November, O'Neill announces further reforms to try to calm the situation, but they do not include universal suffrage, a key demand of the civil rights campaigners.

1969

A month-long moratorium on marches is called by the Derry Citizens Action Committee for January. People's Democracy do not heed the moratorium, however, and organize a four-day march from Belfast to Derry starting on 1 January. The marchers are met with harassment by Loyalists along the route, and are attacked in an organized ambush at Burntollet Bridge, near Claudy, on 4 January. The RUC, who had been accompanying the march, do little or nothing to stop the attack by around 200 Loyalists wielding bottles, stones, cudgels and iron bars. It was later discovered that off-duty members of the B Specials were among the attackers. When the march finally enters Derry there is further confrontation, and riots ensue between the RUC and youths from the Catholic Bogside district. O'Neill announces a commission of inquiry into the Derry disturbances, and in an attempt to resecure his position, calls a snap general election for February. While he wins a majority, O'Neill's authority is seriously undermined.

April 1969

Universal suffrage is finally conceded by a 28 to 22 vote. One of O'Neill's Ministers, Major James Chichester-Clarke, resigns in protest. In the same month there is a series of explosions at electricity and water installations. They are attributed to the IRA, but it is later discovered that the bombs were planted by the UVF in an attempt to destablize O'Neill's administration and end the programme of reforms (Bew and Gillespie 1993: 14). On 28 April, O'Neill resigns and is succeeded by Chichester-Clarke. Following the resignation, radical Unionist Ian Paisley wins a by-election for the Bannside seat, signalling a further shift away from reformist and towards more extremist politics.

July 1969

Samuel Devenney, considered to be the first victim of the Troubles, dies on 16 July as the result of a beating by police which took place in his Derry home on 19 April (Bew and Gillespie 1993: 16–17). During the summer marching season, there are serious riots throughout Northern Ireland.

August and September 1969

3,500 families are driven from their homes in Belfast, 3,000 of them Catholic. That same number again would be driven from their homes over the next four years (Lee 1989: 429). 10,000 British troops are dispatched to the North, arriving in Derry on 14 August and in Belfast on 15 August. Catholics are relieved to see them, seeing them as protectors.

1970

In January, the Republican movement splits after a conference in Dublin. The smaller faction, who favour a return to a military strategy, call themselves the Provisional Army Council, nicknamed the 'Provos' or 'Provies'. The larger Official IRA adopt a Marxist ideology and continue to favour political participation. The split precipitates a violent feud in the North in which many people die. Although initially smaller, the Provisionals build up their support and ultimately are more successful at obtaining arms than the Officials.

July 1970

The British army institute a 36-hour curfew in the Catholic Falls Road area of west Belfast to facilitate arms searches. It proves to be a turning point in Catholic attitudes towards the army. Five lives are lost during the curfew, and membership of the IRA mushrooms. Meanwhile, the British government brings in series of reforms designed to address the issues originally raised by the civil rights campaigners.

1971

In 1971 alone, the British army search 17,262 houses (Lee 1989: 433). The searches involve the destruction of Catholic homes in armed midnight raids. Floorboards are pulled up, cupboards emptied, soft furniture cut open, holes knocked into the walls, and private papers read in an effort to uncover hidden arms. Between November 1971 and January 1972 only 47 of the 1,183 houses searched produce arms (Lee 1989: 433).

In March, Chichester-Clark resigns as Prime Minister of Northern Ireland, and is succeeded by Brian Faulkner. In August, Faulkner introduces internment without trial. The majority of internees are Catholic, although some Protestants are also interned. At 4:00 a.m. on 9 August, Catholic areas are sealed off while paratroopers smash down doors and drag men out of bed. Intelligence is poor, and few senior IRA members are caught in the net. Many innocent people with no political involvement are interned. There are reports of the use of selective torture on internees (Lee 1989: 439). By 12 August, 22 people have been killed in the violence sparked off by internment, including Belfast priest Father Hugh McMullan, who is shot dead while administering the last rites to an injured man. 2,000 Protestants are left homeless as the result of arson and intimidation, and 2,500 Catholics leave Belfast for refugee camps set up along the border by the Dublin government.

1972

On 30 January, 13 unarmed men are shot dead by paratroopers after a march in Derry. The events of 'Bloody Sunday' cause a wave of anger in the Catholic community north and south of the border, and provoke international condemnation. The Irish ambassador to Britain is recalled to Dublin in protest. On 2 February, a crowd of 20,000 demonstrators attack the British embassy in Dublin, burning it to the ground. On 24 March, Conservative Prime Minister Edward Heath announces the suspension of the Stormont government and the introduction of direct rule. A two-week IRA truce in June comes to nothing. 1972 proves to be the most bloody year in the history of the Troubles with 467 deaths, 10,628 shootings and 1,853 bombs planted (Bew and Gillespie 1993: 57).

1973

Government proposals for a new power-sharing assembly for the North lead to elections in June. Faulkner's Unionists, who support the new power-sharing proposals, gain 26.5 per cent of the vote, while hard-line Unionists (including Paisley's Democratic Unionist Party and Craig's Vanguard Party) gain 35 per cent. Of the other parties, Alliance receive 9 per cent, and the SDLP 22 per cent (Lee 1989: 443).

On 9 December, the Sunningdale Agreement is announced, after the first conference since 1925 where heads of government from Britain and both parts of Ireland are present. The main result is an agreement to set up a Council of Ireland with representatives from both Northern Ireland and the Republic, including a Consultative Assembly consisting of 30 members from the Northern Ireland assembly and 30 members from the *Dáil*, and a Council of Ministers made up of seven ministers from the NI executive and seven members of the Irish government.

1974

On 15 May, the Ulster Workers' Council (UWC) calls a general strike to protest against the Sunningdale Agreement and the existence of the power-sharing executive. Armed Loyalists block roads and harbours. Factories close, and electricity, water and petrol supplies are in the control of the strikers. Two days into the strike, Loyalists plant three no-warning car bombs in Dublin and one in Monaghan which explode during rush hour, killing 33 people and injuring over 120. Although the new Prime Minister Harold Wilson condemns the UWC strike in a BBC broadcast on 25 May, the government refuses to move against the strikers. The power-sharing executive resigns on 28 May, and London once again resumes direct rule, finally ending the UWC strike.

1976

In May, the withdrawal of special category status for prisoners convicted of crimes relating to the Troubles leads to protests by Republican prisoners. Initially they refuse to wear prison clothing, because under special category status they had been allowed to wear their own clothes. Instead, they wear only blankets. When they are refused permission to leave their cells without wearing the prison uniform, the prisoners embark on the 'dirty protest', refusing to wash or to 'slop out' waste from their cells. By 1978, more than 300 Republican prisoners are participating in the protest.

1980

On 27 October, seven Republican prisoners commence a hunger strike to push for a return to special category status. There is widespread support for the hunger strikers among Catholics, and by November there are marches larger than any held by Nationalists since the early 1970s. The hunger strike is called off on 18 December, partly because the prisoners believe an agreement with the British government has been reached, and partly because one hunger striker is on the verge of death.

1981

Agreement had not been reached, however, and IRA prisoner Bobby Sands commences a second hunger strike at the beginning of March. Over a period of months he is joined by other Republican prisoners, one by one. In April, Sands wins the Westminster seat for Fermanagh-South Tyrone with 30,000 votes, but Margaret Thatcher's government still refuses to negotiate with the hunger strikers. On 5 May, Sands dies in the 66th day of his protest. Widespread rioting follows his death both north and south of the border. The second hunger striker, Francis Hughes, dies on 12 May. Rioting which has been almost continuous since Sands' death intensifies. In all, ten men die before the families of the remaining hunger strikers intervene. The protest is officially called off by the prisoners on 3 October. Three days later, Thatcher's government concedes one of the prisoners' five demands, allowing them to wear their own clothes. Partial concessions are also made on the other demands.

The hunger strikes are another important turning point in the history of the Troubles. The civil unrest which accompanied them seriously threatened the stability of both Northern Ireland and the Republic, and the standing of Republican prisoners in the Catholic community was elevated considerably. Sinn Féin enjoyed unprecedented electoral success after the hunger strikes, gaining 13.4 per cent of the vote in Northern Ireland by June 1983, compared to the SDLP's 17.9 per cent (Bew and Gillespie 1993: 156; Lee 1989: 455).

1985

On 15 November, the Anglo-Irish Agreement is signed by British Prime Minister Margaret Thatcher and *Taoiseach* Garret FitzGerald at Hillsborough Castle, County Down. The Agreement establishes an Inter-Governmental Conference concerned with relations between the two parts of Ireland. Its remit is to deal on a regular basis with security, political and legal matters, and the promotion of cross-border co-operation. Unionists react to the Agreement with fury. They protest against it in the House of Commons, make a number of attempts to challenge its legality through the courts and hold numerous large demonstrations in protest. One such demonstration at Belfast City Hall attracts by various estimates between 100,000 and 200,000 people (Bew and Gillespie 1993: 192).

Article 5(a) of the Agreement states that the Inter-governmental Conference will consider measures which will recognise and accommodate the rights and identities of the two traditions in Northern Ireland, to protect human rights and to prevent discrimination. This part of Article 5 is of particular significance for Irish language activists, many of whom believe that British attitudes towards funding for the language softened after the signing of the Agreement.

1986

Protests against the Agreement continue. Unionists adopt the slogan 'Ulster Says No' in January's Westminster by-elections. On the first anniversary of the signing of the Anglo-Irish Agreement up to 200,000 Unionists attend a protest rally at Belfast City Hall, which is followed by two days of rioting in Protestant areas (Bew and Gillespie 1993: 202).

1988

In January, Hume begins talks with Sinn Féin president Gerry Adams in order to find common ground on the conditions for an all-Ireland settlement.

1989

The IRA renews its bombing campaign in July with a massive 1,000 pound car bomb at the Belfast High Court. This was followed by three other large explosions during the year. In December the IRA announces a three-day Christmas truce for the first time in 15 years.

1990

Secretary of State for Northern Ireland Peter Brooke initiates another attempt at all-party talks, with the exception of Sinn Féin. Strand One of the talks is meant to deal with the internal government of Northern Ireland, Strand Two the relationship between Ireland north and south, and Strand Three the relationship between Britain and Ireland. By the end of December, Brooke admits that the talks process has so far failed to produce any answers, but insists that there has been 'real advances' in thinking and in the analysis of goals in the context of the 1990s (Bew and Gillespie 1993: 242).

1991

In February, the IRA launches a mortar bomb which lands in the garden of 10 Downing Street, just 15 yards from a room where John Major is meeting with the Gulf War cabinet. Brooke pre-empts the total breakdown of the talks by calling a temporary end to Strand One in July. Sectarian attacks by Loyalist paramilitaries increase. In a dramatic upsurge in violence, 20 people are killed by Loyalist and Republican paramilitaries in a five-week period in October–November, seven of them in just two days (Bew and Gillespie 1993: 252).

1992

For the first time since the 1970s, Loyalist paramilitaries murder more people than the IRA (Bew and Gillespie 1993: 270). The IRA bombing campaign continues, with bombs in London and Manchester as well as in the North. Strand Two of the Brooke talks begins in June, even though Strand One is deadlocked. Strand Three starts later in the month, but the talks ultimately fail.

1993

Tensions are at their worst since the 1970s after Loyalist mass murders in pubs in Greysteel and Loughinisland over the summer, an IRA bomb on the Protestant Shankill Road in Belfast in October, and a wave of sectarian killings. The IRA explode more massive bombs in Northern Ireland and increasingly in Britain as well, with a number of high-profile attacks in London. At the same time, talks start once again between Sinn Féin's Gerry Adams and the SDLP's John Hume to find a way forward out of the political stalemate. They issue a joint statement after two weeks of official talks in April, but it is later revealed that negotiations between the two men had been taking place in secret for some time. The Hume/Adams talks eventually lead to the issuing of a joint statement to the British and Irish governments, the full text of which has remained secret. On 15 December, the *Downing Street Declaration* is issued jointly by Prime Minister John Major and *Taoiseach* Albert Reynolds. The document underlines the principle of consent to any future political arrangements, but also guarantees equality for both traditions in Northern Ireland, coining the phrase 'parity of esteem'.

1994

On 31 August the IRA calls a ceasefire which is met with jubilation in the Nationalist community, but scepticism from other quarters. In 13 October the Combined Loyalist Paramilitary Command, an umbrella group for the UDA/UFF and UVF, also declares a ceasefire. Before long, however, frustration and anxiety set in at the semantic wrangling and lack of political progress in the wake of the ceasefires. For many months there are arguments over the precise meaning of the word 'permanent', and then a long debate over the precise meaning of 'a complete cessation of military activity', as stated in the IRA's ceasefire announcement. The battle over words is eventually put aside in favour of an argument over the decommissioning of arms.

1995

In February, the British government issue a document entitled *Frameworks for the Future*, intended to stimulate discussion in advance of inclusive talks. The deadlock over talks between Sinn Féin and the British government continues, stuck primarily on the issue of the surrender of IRA arms. In July the RUC prevents Orangemen from marching through the Catholic Garvaghy Road in Portadown, resulting in a stand-off. 10,000 Orange supporters clash with 1,000 police. There is widespread rioting and protest in Protestant areas during the confrontation, and threats of more serious violence if the parade is not allowed to go ahead. The three-day stand-off ends when the government backs down and allows the Orange march to go ahead. There are accusations of heavy-handedness when the RUC forcibly removes Nationalists who are sitting in the road in protest at the march going forward.

1996

After nearly 18 months with no tangible progress towards inclusive talks, the IRA break their ceasefire in February 1996 with a massive bomb at Canary Wharf in London. Confrontation between Loyalists and the RUC over the re-routing of Orange marches away from Catholic areas once again leads to widespread rioting, arson attacks and intimidation over the summer. Many commentators, including spokespersons for the RUC, say it is the worst period of civil disturbance since 1969, and for a few months Northern Ireland seems to teeter on the brink of civil war.

1997

A Labour government headed by Tony Blair is elected in May. The new Secretary of State for Northern Ireland Mo Mowlam takes a hands-on approach, visiting the North soon after her appointment and meeting with community groups from both sides. In July, the IRA declares a second ceasefire in spite of widespread violence and rioting which accompanies the Orange marching season. All-party talks on the future of Northern Ireland begin on 7 October, including Sinn Féin and the 'fringe' Loyalist parties the UDP and PUP (both of which are associated with the Loyalist paramilitaries). Violence from fringe paramilitaries on both sides who are against the ceasefires (the Republican INLA and the Loyalist LVF) threaten the talks process.

1998

A 'Heads of Agreement' document is put forward as the talks resume after the holidays. The document is welcomed by the UUP, but met with scepticism by Nationalists. There is a wave of sectarian killings in January and February carried out by the INLA and the LVF. When it comes to light that the UFF was involved in a number of the random murders of Catholics, their political wing, the Ulster Decmocratic Party, leave the talks to pre-empt a decision by Mowlam to force them out. In February the IRA ceasefire appears to be on shaky ground. Mowlam excludes Sinn Féin from the talks for a period of two weeks.

Both parties eventually return to the discussion table, and the talks continue throughout March. As the 10 April talks deadline arrives, discussion goes on late into the night. On Good Friday it is announced that an agreement has been reached. The agreement includes a new Northern Ireland assembly, new cross-border bodies, and a Council of the Isles. On 22 May, a referendum is held simultaneously on both sides of the border. The South overwhelmingly votes to allow Articles 2 and 3 of the Constitution to be changed, removing a key obstacle to Unionist agreement to the settlement. In the North, a simple yes or no referendum results in 71 per cent voting in favour of the Good Friday agreement.

Elections for the new assembly are held on 25 June. For the first time in the history of Northern Ireland, a Nationalist party, the SDLP, receives a majority of first preference votes. After transfer votes are taken into account, the final results are: UUP 28 seats, SDLP 24 seats, DUP 20 seats, Sinn Féin 18 seats, Alliance 6 seats, UK Unionists 5 seats, independent Unionists 3 seats, Women's Coalition 2 seats, and PUP 2 seats. Ulster Unionist leader David Trimble becomes the Assembly's First Minister, with the SDLP's Seamus Mallon as the Deputy. It is a victory for the parties which support the Good Friday agreement, but anti-agreement candidates make a good showing, holding a total of 28 seats (DUP, UK Unionists, and the independent Unionists are all anti-agreement). Anti-agreement members of the Assembly hope to block the setting up of cross-border bodies, and if they receive support from any of the more hard-line unionists in David Trimble's camp, they may succeed.

Appendix II
Funding Criteria for Independent Schools

There has been considerable confusion about the exact policy of the government with regards to funding Irish-medium schools. Some Irish language campaigners have complained that the Department of Education keeps 'moving the goal posts', and that they treat Irish-medium schools differently that they treat other independent schools seeking funding, especially integrated schools.

Department of Education for Northern Ireland spokesperson Brian Hill told me in a telephone interview that the government takes a number of criteria into account when deciding whether or not to fund Irish-medium schools, as with other independent schools. The key factor is enrolment. A primary school must demonstrate the ability to achieve an eventual overall enrolment of 100 pupils. This means that the school's yearly intake must reach 14–15 pupils before funding will be granted (seven groups with 15 pupils in each adds up to about 100 pupils overall). A secondary school must demonstrate the ability to achieve an overall enrolment of 300 pupils (five groups of 60 pupils). Other factors which are taken into consideration are the distance of the school from other similar schools, the standard of education, and the overall cost of funding the school.

Hill told me that 'the criteria is exactly the same, and has to be seen to be the same, for Irish-medium schools and integrated schools'. He added that the argument that integrated schools get preferential treatment is a mistaken perception. There is legislation which requires DENI to facilitate the provision of integrated education, but Hill says that the criteria for financial support is still the same for both types of schools. Official DENI policy is to encourage the establishment of Irish-medium units, attached either to English-medium schools or as satellites to other Irish-medium schools, rather than free-standing schools. *Scoil na Fuiseoige*, for example, is a satellite campus of *Bunscoil Phobal Feirste*. St Patrick's, an English-medium primary school in Armagh, has an Irish-medium unit, and *Bunscoil Cholm Cille* in Derry became independent after many years as a unit of the English-medium Steelstown Primary School. However, an application made to establish a school in the Lower Ormeau of south Belfast as a satellite of *Gaelscoil na bhFál* was recently denied.

Irish language campaigners have some reservations about DENI's claims. Many disagree with the Department's policy to promote units, particularly those attached to English-medium schools, for a number of reasons. First of all, in principle they believe that the government has an obligation to support Irish-medium education in the same way as it supports Welsh-medium education in Wales. Second, there is a strong desire to promote an Irish language ethos both inside and outside the classroom. They argue that a small Irish-medium unit attached to a much larger English-medium school suffocates such an ethos, and it has been shown that under such circumstances, the language of the playground and of non-academic activities tends to revert to the dominant English. Finally, in a unit attached to an English-medium school, the language of administration is necessarily English, limiting the opportunities for teachers to use Irish and setting a poor example for the children, who learn that Irish is a language of the classroom only.

There is also disagreement over the criteria used to determine which schools will be funded. According to *Gaeloiliúint* spokesperson Cathal Ó Donnghaile, what the Department of Education says in public is not the same as what it says in private to Irish language educationalists. He says that at first, they were told that Irish-medium schools would be treated the same as integrated schools, but that DENI later retracted on this. First, the Irish-medium schools organization was told that an enrolment of 14–15 pupils was needed in order to receive funding and government recognition. However, Ó Donnghaile points out that in 1995–6 *Bunscoil an tSleibhe Dhuibh* had already met this target, and *Bunscoil Bheann Mhadagáin* fell only one pupil short, yet both were denied funding that year in spite of official reports of an excellent standard of education and an enrolment at Irish-medium nursery schools which suggests an increasingly large demand in the years to come. Ó Donnghaile claims that DENI now speak of a 'pattern' of such an intake being established over a few years in order to prove future viability. When asked to put this in writing in order to clarify what they meant by a 'pattern' of enrolment, he says that DENI officials refused. Ó Donnghaile and other supporters of Irish-medium education are vehement that DENI does not treat Irish-medium schools and integrated schools equally in practice, in spite of official statements to the contrary.

Notes

1 INTRODUCTION

1. Except, perhaps, by immigrants to the city arriving from Irish-speaking parts of the countryside during the nineteenth century.
2. See Moerman (1988), Grillo (1989a), Carrithers (1992).
3. See Eriksen (1993), Romanucci-Ross and DeVos (1995), Banks (1996) and Jenkins (1997) for some recent examples.
4. 'What I am proposing is that nationalism has to be understood by aligning it not with self-consciously held political ideologies, but with the large cultural systems that preceded it, out of which – as well as against which – it came into being' (Anderson 1983: 19). Nationalism, according to Anderson, is more usefully thought of along the same lines as kinship or religion rather than ideologies like liberalism or fascism. If one lives in a kinship centred society, one does not need to be a 'kinshipist' in order to view the world in a way which is profoundly shaped by kinship. In the same way, we live in a world which is largely structured by nations and the idea of nation; we do not have to subscribe to the ideology of nationalism in order to have our worldview shaped by this fact.
5. See Mouzelis (1995).
6. See Grillo (1989a, 1989b), Frazer and Cameron (1989), Fairclough (1989, 1992) and Bourdieu (1991).
7. First used around the time of the Downing Street Declaration, the term 'parity of esteem' was quickly adopted by Irish language activists, who saw the treatment of Irish as a sort of litmus test for its complete implementation.
8. For rural studies, see Brody (1973), Harris (1972), Leyton (1975), Buckley (1982), Glassie (1982), Scheper-Hughes (1979) and Taylor (1995). For urban studies in other disciplines, see Boal (1970, 1976, 1981, 1982), Burton (1978) and Maguire (1991).
9. See especially Curtin et al. (1993).
10. See Sluka (1989), Feldman (1991), Jarman (1992, 1993, 1997), Cecil (1993), O'Connor (1993) and McCormick (1996).
11. See also McCann (1987).
12. See, for example, Harris (1972), Leyton (1974), Glassie (1982), Larsen (1982a), Larsen (1982b), Buckley (1982), Bufwack (1982).
13. Not all studies in Northern Ireland have focused solely on the Troubles and related issues. Howe (1990) produced an illuminating investigation into class and unemployment, and Bell (1990) and Jenkins (1982; 1983) have also investigated class. Curtin et al. (1993) have produced a collection of Irish urban ethnographic studies covering a variety of different issues in relation to the construction and reproduction of urban culture. Researchers from other disciplines have also written important ethnographic studies (Nelson 1984, on Loyalism; Brewer 1990, on policing in the North).
14. See, for example, Ó Cuív (1969), *Bord na Gaeilge* (1989), Tovey, Hannan and Abramson (1989), Hindley (1990), Ó Riagáin (1997). Ó Huallacháin

(1994) is one exception, taking a historical look at the Irish language in both Northern Ireland and the Republic.
15. See Ó hAdhmaill (1985), Sweeney (1987), and Andrews (1991, 1993).

2   LANGUAGE AND CULTURE IN NORTHERN IRELAND: THE BACKGROUND TO THE IRISH LANGUAGE REVIVAL MOVEMENT

1. See, for example, O'Connor (1993: 21).
2. See, for example, McDonald's (1989) discussion of militant histories of Brittany.
3. See O'Reilly (1993) and Andrews (1997) for some of this history.
4. See Maguire (1991) for an interesting analysis of the Shaws Road *Gaeltacht*.
5. See Maguire (1991) and Ó Huallacháin (1994).
6. Grillo (1989b), Chapter 5 provides an interesting comparison.
7. See McKee (1995) for a comparison of the politics of the Gaelic language in Scotland and Northern Ireland.
8. See Jenkins (1986), Harries (1986) and Griffiths (1986a, 1986b) for a discussion of the development of Welsh-medium education.
9. In this case, the Irish word *cumainn* refers to Sinn Féin party organization at the smallest level, groups of party activists based on the neighbourhood. *Cumann* means society or association.
10. Before 1971, there were no children being educated through the medium of Irish in Northern Ireland. Until 1987, the numbers remained below 300. In the last ten years numbers have more than quadrupled. Since two-thirds of the primary schools have opened their doors only within the last five years, I expect that the number of pupils in Irish-medium education should continue to increase.
11. See Malcolm (1997).
12. See Mac Póilin (1997).
13. Nationalism and the role of Hyde in the Gaelic League will be discussed in greater detail in section two of Chapter 3.
14. There are no precise figures for the number of Protestants taking up the language, and it is difficult to say how many of them are Nationalist or Unionist. McCoy, however, notes that 46 per cent of his Protestant informants were Unionists, 31 per cent Nationalist, while the rest declined to state their political views (1997: 134).
15. Bowie (1993) reports a similar sentiment in parts of Wales. In native Welsh-speaking areas, at least, there is a sense that learning and speaking Welsh makes a person a fuller member of the community, enhancing their claim to a Welsh identity. Most people in west Belfast, however, are perhaps more like the inhabitants of 'Welsh Wales' – English-speaking, and potentially resentful of any suggestion that they are not Irish for not being competent or native speakers of the indigenous language.
16. While the dominant ethos of the Northern Irish state is British, nevertheless, Catholics have always had an Irish identity, although what this means

Notes

has varied over time and is still heavily contested. The relationship of those
with an Irish identity to the state has also varied. Kachuk suggests that
'the subordinate culture' – meaning Catholic, Irish culture – 'possesses
neither autonomy nor its own hegemonic position in Northern Ireland'
(1994: 137). This a truism, but it also underestimates the strength of Irish
identity and its position as a counter-hegemonic culture throughout the
history of Northern Ireland. Protestant identity has also undergone considerable change over the last few decades, as Unionist hegemony in
Northern Ireland has been increasingly undermined and challenged.
17. Maguire (1991), Chapter 12, discusses some of these changes.
18. While it might be possible to identify a residual category of other discourses
about the Irish language used in west Belfast, the majority of talk about
Irish can be placed in one of the three categories I describe here.

3 IDENTIFYING THE THREE DISCOURSES

1. In this case, the speaker is using 'military' to refer to the Republican 'armed
struggle' rather than the Irish or British army.
2. *Tiocfaidh ár lá* is Irish for 'Our day will come', a common Republican
slogan which has become most familiar in its Irish form.

4 DECOLONIZING DISCOURSE

1. TOMÁS attended a Christian Brothers Grammar School which is well
known for the teaching of Irish and the interest the Brothers take in passing
on the language.
2. Quote 5, for example, starts with a rather unassuming 'I think you would
find', and he characterizes Republican interest in the language as 'a fairly
steady line'. In Quote 7, however, the language is more forceful. He makes
a direct statement which warns against contradiction, 'the reality is …',
and then follows this with a series of clauses delivered in a powerful
'one-two' punch style.
3. On one occasion, for example, Sammy Wilson called Irish a 'leprechaun
language' (*Irish Times* 3 November 1987).
4. Ian Adamson is a Unionist politician. He is the author of a somewhat
fantastic book on the 'original' inhabitants of what is now Northern Ireland
(Adamson 1974).
5. Bobby Sands was an IRA prisoner who went on hunger strike for political
status in 1981. He was the first of ten men to die in succession before the
protest was ended.
6. The full quote reads 'Everyone, Republican or otherwise, has his or her
part to play'.
7. PÓL prefers to use republican with a small 'r', because, he says, he is a
republican, but not a member of the Republican movement or Sinn Féin.
He pointed out to me that he is not against Sinn Féin, but that he does

not agree with them on all points. He also pointed out that they are an English language organization, and for him the Irish language comes first.
8. PÓL asked me to emphasize here that while for him these things are intimately linked, he does not necessarily believe that this is so for everyone, nor that it should be.

5   CULTURAL DISCOURSE

1. ULTACH is an acronym for Ulster Language, Traditions and Cultural Heritage. Ultach is also the Irish word for a native of Ulster.
2. McDonald (1989) and Handler (1988) also note a similar characterization among language activists and nationalists of Breton and Québécois French as particularly beautiful and poetic languages.
3. Kuter (1989) makes a similar observation in relation to Breton and French. She identifies three oppositions in play between the two languages: politically, French is symbolized as a 'national' language, while Breton is a 'regional' language; socio-economically, French is symbolized as the language of progress and civilization, while Breton is a 'backward' language of the past; culturally, French is symbolized as an international, urban language, while Breton is associated with a uniquely local, rural identity (Kuter 1989: 76).
4. *Dúchas* is an Irish word with no precise English equivalent, but it can mean 'heritage,' 'native place' or 'natural affinity'. Dr Roger Blaney of the CTG suggests that the English word 'roots' might be a suitable equivalent (CTG 1994: 4).
5. These terms carry a similar ambiguity when used in the context of other discourses. For example, the two traditions idea meshes well with the concept of parity of esteem and the assertion made by many Nationalists that Irish is 'our own language'. On the other hand, the common heritage idea meshes with the often made assertion that the language belongs to both Protestants and Catholics. Aodán Mac Póilin of the ULTACH Trust argues that most Nationalists do not think through the implications of this terminology. For example, he suggests that the term 'our own language' actively excludes non-Catholics and non-Nationalists (Mac Póilin 1989; ULTACH Trust 1991).
6. The proceedings of this conference were published – see Crozier (1989).
7. *'Cumann Chluain Ard ... Its History, its Purpose'*, *circa* 1950s, written by Seán Mag Aonghusa. The pamphlet was also published at a later date as an article in the *Andersonstown News* (30 July 1977).
8. 'Provies' and 'Provos' are nicknames for the Provisional IRA, so called since a split in the organization in the mid-1970s. The other faction in the split became known as the Official IRA.
9. The 'blanket protest' was part of an effort by Republican prisoners to regain political status in the late 1970s. New prison regulations specified that they had to wear prison uniforms instead of their own clothing, as they had done previously. Rather than wear the uniform they refused to wear any clothing at all, wrapping themselves in blankets instead.

6 RIGHTS DISCOURSE

1. Republicans and some Nationalists call Northern Ireland 'the Six Counties' to emphasize its partial nature and a desired connection to the South. In this discourse, the Republic of Ireland is 'the Twenty-Six Counties'. Only the island as a whole is called 'Ireland' – all 32 counties together.
2. 'Fenians' is a derogatory term for Catholics. Originally it was the nickname of the Irish Republican Brotherhood (IRB), the group which was largely behind the Easter Rising in 1916.
3. IAIN's difficulty in dealing with the idea that a Unionist with a British identity might want to learn Irish is not unusual. McCoy (1997: 133) points out that many Protestant Nationalists who are interested in Irish do not see how a Protestant could learn Irish and *not* be a Nationalist.
4. Adamson (1974) argues that the Cruthin are a distinct ethnic group, occupying Scotland and Ulster since biblical times, who were eventually conquered by the Celts.
5. Potential audiences might include the government/political parties or groups; Unionists/Protestants; other *Gaeilgeoirí*; other Nationalists; people from the south of Ireland; other minority language speakers/groups; outsiders including the media; and European Community agencies. When speaking or writing, all of these perceived audiences can influence choice of discourse. Audience is also controlled by choosing to write or speak in English or Irish.

7 THE DISCOURSES IN PRACTICE: FOUR CASE STUDIES

1. See, for example, the comments made by DUP politician Willie McCrea in the House of Commons. He complained about the 'constant bombardment' from a 'foreign' Irish culture, and argued that the British government should help promote Ullans – a dialect of English unique to the northeast of the island – to counteract the influence of the Irish language in Northern Ireland (*Irish News* 22-3-96).
2. Mac Póilin told me that this was an off-the-cuff remark made at a conference which was picked up by the newspaper's editor.
3. In fact, 50 per cent of the Trust's funding goes towards the support of Irish-medium education.
4. There has been some debate in both academic and Irish language circles about just how important a role Sinn Féin have played in the revival movement. Kachuk (1994), for example, tends to over-privilege the contribution of Sinn Féin, to the extent of rendering other perspectives nearly invisible.
5. The *Dáil* is the Parliament of the Irish Republic.
6. See The Political Vetting of Community Work Working Group (1990).
7. In fact, the *Andersonstown News* often prints the same information in two different articles, one in each language, when the widest possible audience is sought.

8. GCSE (General Certificate in Secondary Education) examinations are normally taken at age 16.
9. Sinn Féin president Gerry Adams raised the issue of funding for the Irish language in general, and the *Meánscoil* in particular, at a meeting in the White House in December 1994.
10. The tally stick, or *bata scór*, is a wooden stick which was placed around the neck of Irish-speaking school children in the nineteenth century. A notch was placed on the stick every time the child spoke Irish instead of English, and an equivalent number of slaps were administered at the end of the day. See Chapter 9 for a discussion of the symbolic importance afforded to the tally stick and its equivalent in Brittany.
11. Parts of this section are taken from O'Reilly (1998).
12. At the time of writing, all street signs in Ballymurphy are in Irish. The English versions were painted over or removed long ago, reportedly to confuse patrolling British soldiers and the RUC. It is also pretty hard on visitors who are unfamiliar with the area.

8   IRISH LANGUAGE DISCOURSES, NORTH AND SOUTH

1. A substantial minority of *Gaeltacht* residents do not use Irish – see Ó Riagáin (1997).
2. Research over the last two decades has shown many ambiguities in people's attitudes towards Irish. See Ó Riagáin (1997), especially Chapter 6, for an overview of relevant attitudes research.
3. Handler (1988) makes a similar observation regarding nationalist ideology in Quebec. Nationalists there argue that a healthy national culture is important because it enables the national culture to make contributions to humanity as a whole – an idea which Handler attributes to Herder's distinction between national and universal culture.
4. Blame for the loss of the language is allotted in different proportions by different people. Some blame the English directly for intentionally destroying the language. Others see the loss of Irish as an indirect product of the colonial experience. Still others blame the Irish themselves, whom they see as all too willing to abandon the language once it came to be seen as a hindrance to individual success or advancement.

9   NORTHERN IRELAND, BRITTANY AND QUEBEC

1. For example, McDonald reports that one militant manual bears the title *The Breton language in the face of its oppressors.*
2. McDonald also provides a detailed account of the development of Breton schools. A comparison between Breton-medium schools and Irish-medium schools in Northern Ireland would be an interesting one, but is far too complex to be dealt with adequately here.
3. See Handler (1988), especially Chapter 4.

4. See McDonald (1989: 12–16).
5. The varying degrees of support for Breton in the schools is one example – see McDonald (1989) Part One, especially Chapter 3. There have been feelings of ambiguity towards the language not only from the government, but from native Breton speakers as well.
6. The *Front de Libération de la Bretagne*, or the 'Breton Liberation Front', is an openly 'terrorist' organization which has been outlawed since 1974 (McDonald 1989: 79).
7. One such demonstration is described in Chapter 7, where the children from *Meánscoil Feirste* left 'tally sticks' on the doorstep of the Department of Education for Northern Ireland to protest at the lack of government funding for their school. Another symbolic demonstration involved two *Gaeilgeoirí* fasting at Christmas in support of Irish medium schools. They held a vigil in front of Belfast City Hall for 24 hours on Christmas day to publicize the fast and their protest at lack of funding.
8. See Chapman (1992).
9. Gaelicized English words are sometimes created and used in place of Irish equivalents. For example, *Gaeltacht* speakers might ask, '*Ar enjoyal tú an oíche aréir?*' ('Did you enjoy the evening last night?), a Gaelicization of the English word 'enjoy' in a sentence with Anglicized syntax. An Irish equivalent is '*Ar thaitin an oíche aréir leat?*' (more like 'Did you get pleasure from the evening last night?). An example of straight borrowing from English is the tendency to use the English words for the months of the year in some *Gaeltacht* areas, even when the rest of the sentence or conversation is in Irish.
10. See Chapman (1992), especially Chapter 8. 'The disappearance of ancient tradition, in this sense, is continuous; its last vestiges are *always* on the point of dying out, but in practice never actually do so, for the content of 'ancient tradition' is redefined in every generation. Nothing, indeed, more characterises the lament for dying Celtic traditions, than its evergreen poignancy' (Chapman 1992: 97).

Bibliography

Adamson, I. 1974. *Cruthin: the Ancient Kindred*. Newtownards, Northern Ireland: Nosmada Books.

Anderson, B. 1983. *Imagined Communities: Reflections on the Origin and Spread of Nationalism*. London: Verso.

Andrews, L. S. 1991. The Irish language in the education system of Northern Ireland: some political and cultural perspectives. In *Motivating the Majority: Modern Languages in Northern Ireland*, ed. R. Pritchard. London: The Centre for Information on Language Teaching and Research and Coleraine: University of Ulster.

——1992. BBC Northern Ireland and the Irish language: the background. In *BBC agus an Ghaeilge*/BBC and the Irish Language, eds. A. Mac Póilin and L. Andrews. Belfast: *Iontaobhas ULTACH*/ULTACH Trust.

——1993. *The Irish Language in Northern Ireland: the Training of Primary and post-Primary Teachers*. Ljouwert/Leeuwarden, the Netherlands: Fryske Akademy.

——1997. 'The very dogs in the streets will bark in Irish': The Unionist government and the Irish Language 1921–43. In *The Irish Language in Northern Ireland*, ed. A. Mac Póilin. Belfast: *Iontaobhas ULTACH*/ ULTACH Trust.

Arensberg, C. M. and S. Kimball, 1968 (1940). *Family and community in Ireland*. Cambridge, MA: Harvard University Press.

Badone, E. 1992. The construction of national identity in Brittany and Quebec. *American Ethnologist*. 19 (4), 806–17.

Banks, M. 1996. *Ethnicity: Anthropological Constructions*. London: Routledge.

Barth, F. 1969. Introduction. In *Ethnic Groups and Boundaries: The Social Organization of Culture Difference*, ed. F. Barth. London: Allen & Unwin.

——1987. *Cosmologies in the Making: a Generative Approach to Cultural Variation in Inner New Guinea*. Cambridge: Cambridge University Press.

Bell, D. 1990. *Acts of Union: Youth Culture and Sectarianism in Northern Ireland*. London: Macmillan.

Bew, P. and G. Gillespie, 1993. *Northern Ireland: a Chronology of the Troubles 1968–1993*. Dublin: Gill & Macmillan.

Blaney, R. 1996. *Presbyterians and the Irish Language*. Belfast: The Ulster Historical Foundation and the ULTACH Trust.

Boal, F. 1970. Social space in the Belfast urban area. In *Irish Geographical Studies*, eds. N. Stephens and R. E. Glasscock. Belfast: Queen's University.

——1976. Ethnic residential segregation. In *Social Areas in Cities: Spatial Processes and Form*, ed. P. A. Compton. Belfast: Queens University, Institute of Irish Studies.

——1981. Residential segregation and mixing in a situation of ethnic and national conflict: Belfast. In *The Contemporary Population of Northern Ireland and Population-related Issues*, ed. P. A. Compton. Belfast: Queens University, Institute of Irish Studies.

——1982. Segregation and mixing: space and residence in Belfast. In *Integration and Division: Geographical Perspectives on the Northern Ireland Problem*, eds. F. Boal and J. N. H. Douglas. London: Academic Press.

Bord na Gaeilge 1988. *The Irish Language in a Changing Society: Shaping the Future*. Dublin: The Advisory Planning Committee.

Bourdieu, P. 1991. *Language and Symbolic Power*, ed. J. B. Thompson. Oxford: Polity Press.

Bowie, F. 1993. Wales from Within: Conflicting Interpretations of Welsh Identity. In *Inside European Identities*, ed. S. Macdonald. Oxford: Berg.

Brewer, J. 1990. *Inside the RUC: Routine Policing in a Divided Society*. Oxford: Clarendon Press.

Brody, H. 1973. *Inishkillane: Change and Decline in the West of Ireland*. Harmondsworth: Penguin.

Brow, J. 1990. Notes on community, hegemony, and the uses of the past. In *Tendentious Revisions of the Past in the Construction of Community*, eds. J. Brow and T. Swedenburg. *Anthropological Quarterly* 63 (1), 1–6.

Buckley, A. 1982. *A Gentle People: a Study of a Peaceful Community in Ulster*. Cultra: Ulster Folk and Transport Museum.

Bufwack, M. S. 1982. *Village without Violence: an Examination of a Northern Irish Community*. Cambridge, Mass.: Schenkman.

Burton, F. 1978. *The Politics of Legitimacy: Struggles in a Belfast Community*. London: Routledge and Kegan Paul.

Cameron, D. 1986. *Feminism and Linguistic Theory*. London: Macmillan.

Carrithers, M. 1992. *Why Humans have Cultures: Explaining Anthropology and Social Diversity*. Oxford: Oxford University Press.

Cathcart, R. 1984. *The Most Contrary Region: the BBC in Northern Ireland 1924–1984*. Belfast: Blackstaff Press.

Cecil, R. 1993. The marching season in Northern Ireland: an expression of politico-religious identity. In *Inside European Identities: Ethnography in Western Europe*, ed. S. Macdonald. Oxford: Berg.

Chapman, M, 1982. 'Semantics' and the 'Celt'. *Semantic Anthropology*. ASA Monograph 22. London: Academic Press.

——1992. *The Celts: the Construction of a Myth*. London: Macmillan.

Charsley, S. 1987. Interpretation and custom: the case of the wedding cake. *Man* 22, 93–110.

Cohen, Anthony, 1982. Belonging: the experience of culture. In *Belonging: Identity and Social Organization in British Rural Cultures*, ed. A. P. Cohen. Manchester: Manchester University Press.

——1985. *The Symbolic Construction of Community*. London: Routledge.

——1994. *Self Consciousness: an Alternative Anthropology of Identity*. London: Routledge.

Connor, W. 1978. A nation is a nation, is a state, is an ethnic group, is a ... *Ethnic and Racial Studies* 1 (4), 379–88.

Corkery, D. 1968. *The Fortunes of the Irish Language*. Cork: The Mercier Press.

Crozier, M. 1985. *Patterns of Hospitality in a Rural Ulster Community*. Unpublished PhD dissertation, Queen's University of Belfast.

——(ed.) 1989. *Cultural Traditions in Northern Ireland: Varieties of Irishness. Proceedings of the Cultural Traditions Group Conference*. Belfast: Queen's University, Institute of Irish Studies.

——(ed.) 1990a. *Cultural Traditions in Northern Ireland: Varieties of British-ness. Proceedings of the Cultural Traditions Group Conference*. Belfast: Queen's University, Institute of Irish Studies.

Cultural Traditions Group. 1994. *Giving Voices: the Work of the Cultural Traditions Group 1990–1994*. Belfast: Community Relations Council.

Curtin, C., H. Donnan and T. Wilson (eds.) 1993. *Irish Urban Cultures*. Belfast: Queen's University, Institute of Irish Studies.

De Fréine, S. 1968. *The Great Silence: the Study of a Relationship between Language and Nationality*. Dublin & Cork: The Mercier Press.

Donnan, H. and G. McFarlane, 1986a. Social anthropology and the sectarian divide in Northern Ireland. In *The Sectarian Divide in Northern Ireland*, eds. H. Donnan, G. McFarlane and R. Jenkins. London: Royal Anthropological Institute Occasional Paper 41.

——1986b. 'You get on better with your own': social continuity and change in rural Northern Ireland. In *Ireland: a Sociological Profile*, eds. P. Clancy, S. Drudy, K. Lynch and L. O'Dowd. Dublin: Institute of Public Administration.

Dunleavy, J. E. and G. W. Dunleavy, 1991. *Douglas Hyde: a Maker of Modern Ireland*. Oxford: University of California Press.

Edwards, J. 1984. Language, diversity and identity. In *Linguistic Minorities, Policies and Pluralism*, ed. J. Edwards. London: Academic Press.

——1985. *Language, Society and Identity*. Oxford: Basil Blackwell.

English, R. 1994. 'Cultural traditions' and political ambiguity. In *A Northern Change? Politics and Culture in the North. The Irish Review* 15, 97–106. Belfast: Queen's University, Institute of Irish Studies.

Eriksen, T. H. 1993. *Ethnicity and Nationalism: Anthropological Perspectives*. London: Pluto Press.

Fairclough, N. 1989. *Language and Power*. Harlow: Longman.

——1992. *Discourse and Social Change*. Cambridge: Polity Press.

Farrell, M. 1980. *Northern Ireland: the Orange State*. London: Pluto Press.

Feldman, A. 1991. *Formations of Violence: the Narrative of the Body and Political Terror in Northern Ireland*. Chicago: University of Chicago Press.

Foucault, M. 1972. *The Archaeology of Knowledge*. London: Tavistock.

——1982. The order of discourse. In *Language and Politics*, ed. M. Shapiro. Oxford: Basil Blackwell.

Frazer, E. and D. Cameron, 1989. Knowing what to say: the construction of gender in linguistic practice. *Sociological Review Monograph*. Vol. 36, 25–40.

Gellner, E. 1972. Nationalism. In *Thought and Change*. Chapter 7. London: Weidenfeld and Nicolson.

——1973. Concepts and society. In *Cause and Meaning in the Social Sciences*. London: Routledge & Kegan Paul.

——1983. *Nations and Nationalism*. Oxford: Basil Blackwell.

Giddens, A. 1976. *New Rules of Sociological Method*. London: Hutchinson & Co.

——1984. *The Constitution of Society: Outline of the Theory of Structuration*. Cambridge: Polity Press and Oxford: Basil Blackwell.

Glassie, H. 1982. *Passing the Time in Ballymenone: Culture and History of an Ulster Community*. Philadelphia: University of Pennsylvania Press.

Goody, J. 1987. Foreword. In F. Barth. *Cosmologies in the Making: a Generative Approach to Cultural Variation in inner New Guinea*. Cambridge: Cambridge University Press.

Griffiths, M. 1986a. Introduction. In *The Welsh Language in Education*, ed. M. Griffiths. Adran Gymraeg: Cyd-Bwyllgor Addysg Cymru.

——1986b. Central government policy. In *The Welsh Language in Education*, ed. M. Griffiths. Adran Gymraeg: Cyd-Bwyllgor Addysg Cymru.

Grillo, Ralph, 1989a. Anthropology, language, politics. In *Social Anthropology and the Politics of Language*, ed. R. Grillo. Sociological Review Monograph 36. London: Routledge.

——1989b. *Dominant Languages: Language and Hierarchy in Britain and France*. Cambridge: Cambridge University Press.

Halliday, M. A. K. 1978. *Language as Social Semiotic: the Social Interpretation of Language and Meaning*. London: Edward Arnold.

Handler, R. 1984. On sociocultural discontinuity: nationalism and cultural objectification in Quebec. *Current Anthropology* 25 (1), 55–71.

——1988. *Nationalism and the Politics of Culture in Quebec*. Madison and London: University of Wisconsin Press.

Harries, B. D. 1986. The teaching of Welsh as a second language in schools. In *The Welsh Language in Education*, ed. M. Griffiths. Adran Gymraeg: Cyd-Bwyllgor Addysg Cymru.

Harris, R. 1972. *Prejudice and Tolerance in Ulster*. Manchester: Manchester University Press.

Harrison, S. 1992. Ritual as intellectual property. *Man* 27, 225–244.

——1995. Four types of symbolic conflict. *J. Roy. Anthrop. Inst.* 1, 1–18.

Hindley, R. 1990. *The Death of the Irish Language: a Qualified Obituary*. London: Routledge.

——1990. *Nations and Nationalism since 1780*. Cambridge: Cambridge University Press.

Hobsbawm, E. and Ranger, 1983. *The Invention of Tradition*. Cambridge: Cambridge University Press.

Howe, L. 1990. *Being Unemployed in Northern Ireland: an Ethnographic Study*. Cambridge: Cambridge University Press.

Hutchinson, J. 1987. *The Dynamics of Cultural Nationalism: the Gaelic Revival and the Creation of the Irish Nation State*. London: Allen & Unwin.

Hyde, D. 1986 (1892). The necessity for de-Anglicising Ireland. In *Language, Love and Lyrics*, ed. B. Ó Conaise. Blackrock: Irish Academic Press.

Iontaobhas ULTACH tuairisc bhliantúil/ULTACH Trust Annual Report 1990–91. 1991. Belfast: ULTACH Trust.

Iontaobhas ULTACH: an dara tuairisc/ULTACH Trust: Second Report 1991–93. 1994. Belfast: ULTACH Trust.

James, A. 1993. Eating green(s): discourses of organic food. In *Environmentalism: the View from Anthropology*, ed. K. Milton. London & New York: Routledge.

Jarman, N. 1992. Troubled images. *Critique of Anthropology* 12 (2), 133–65.

——1993. Intersecting Belfast. In *Landscape: Politics and Perspectives*, ed. B. Bender. Oxford: Berg.

——1997. *Material Conflicts: Parades and Visual Displays in Northern Ireland*. Oxford: Berg.

Jenkins, G. 1986. The Welsh language in education: an historical survey. In *The Welsh Language in Education*, ed. M. Griffiths. Adran Gymraeg: Cyd-Bwyllgor Addysg Cymru.

Jenkins, R. 1982. *Hightown Rules: Growing up in a Belfast Housing Estate*. Leicester: National Youth Bureau.

——1983. *Lads, Citizens, and Ordinary Kids: Working Class Youth lifestyles in Belfast*. London: Routledge & Kegan Paul.

——1993. Beyond ethnography: primary data sources in the urban anthropology of Northern Ireland. In *Irish Urban Cultures*, eds. C. Curtin et al. Belfast: Queens University, Institute of Irish Studies.

——1997. *Rethinking Ethnicity: Arguments and Explorations*. London: Sage.

Kachuk, P. 1994. A resistance to British cultural hegemony: Irish language activism in west Belfast. *Anthropologica* XXXVI, 135–54.

Kedourie, E. 1960. *Nationalism*. London: Hutchinson.

Kiberd, D. 1995. *Inventing Ireland*. London: Jonathan Cape.

Kuter, L. 1989. Breton v. French: language and the opposition of political, economic, social, and cultural values. In *Investigating Obsolescence: Studies in Language Contraction and Death*, ed. N. Dorian. Cambridge: Cambridge University Press.

Larrain, J. 1983. *Marxism and Ideology*. London: Macmillan.

Larsen, S. A. 1982a. The two sides of the house: identity and social organisation in Kilbroney, Northern Ireland. In *Belonging: Identity and Social Organisation in British Rural Cultures*, ed. A. P. Cohen. Manchester: Manchester University Press.

——1982b. The Glorious Twelfth: a ritual expression of collective identity. In *Belonging: Identity and Social Organisation in British Rural Cultures*, ed. A. P. Cohen. Manchester: Manchester University Press.

Lee, J. J. 1989. *Ireland 1912–1985: Politics and Society*. Cambridge: Cambridge University Press.

Leyton, E. 1975. *The One Blood: Kinship and Class in an Irish Village*. St John's: Institute of Social and Economic Research.

MacDonagh, O. 1983. *States of Mind: a Study of Anglo-Irish Conflict 1780–1980*. London: Allen & Unwin.

Macdonald, S. 1993. *Inside European Identities: Ethnography in Western Europe*. Berg Ethnic Identities Series. Oxford: Berg Publishers Ltd.

Mac Póilin, A. 1989. *Presentation on the Theme of Cross-cultural Connections*. Learning Links Communities, NICEA Conference, 24 June 1989. Unpublished.

——1994a. *The Background to the Irish Language Revival in Northern Ireland*. Speech delivered to the International conference on Language in Ireland at the University of Ulster, Jordanstown, 24 June 1994. Unpublished.

——1994b. 'Spiritual beyond the ways of men': images of the Gael. *The Irish Review* 16, autumn/winter, 1–22. Belfast: Queen's University, the Institute of Irish Studies.

——1995. *Aspects of the Irish Language Movement in Northern Ireland*. Unpublished paper presented at Language Policy and Planning in the European Union Conference, Institute of Irish Studies, University of Liverpool, 29 April.

——1997. *Plus ça change*: The Irish Language and politics. In *The Irish Language in Northern Ireland*, ed. A. Mac Póilin. Belfast: *Iontaobhas ULTACH*/ULTACH Trust.

Mag Aonghusa, S. *circa* 1950. *Cumann Chluain Ard*: its History, its Purpose. Pamphlet.

Maguire, G. 1991. *Our Own Language: an Irish Initiative*. Multilingual Matters 66. Clevedon: Multilingual Matters.

Mahmood, C. and S. L. Armstrong, 1992. Do ethnic groups exist? a cognitive perspective on the concept of cultures. *Ethnology* 31 (1), 5–12.

Malcolm, I. 1997. Living with Irish. In *The Irish Language in Northern Ireland*, ed. A. Mac Póilin. Belfast: *Iontaobhas ULTACH*/ULTACH Trust.

McCann, M. 1987. '*Tribal Northern Ireland*': an Analysis of a Stereotype. Paper presented to conference on Ireland and the Irish: a study of stereotypes. Youngstown, Ohio, 25–26 April 1987.

McCormick, M. 1996. Avoiding violence and reconciliation in Northern Ireland. In *Cultural Variation in Conflict Resolution: Alternatives for Reducing Violence*, eds. K. Bjorkvist and D. Fry. Mahwah, New Jersey: Lawrence Erlbaum.

McCoy, G. 1991. *Social Change and the Decline of the Irish Language in Rosguill, County Donegal*. Unpublished BA dissertation, Queen's University of Belfast.

——— 1996. *Protestants and the Irish Language in Northern Ireland*. Unpublished PhD thesis, Queen's University of Belfast.

——— 1997. Protestant learners of Irish in Northern Ireland. In *The Irish Language in Northern Ireland*, ed. A. Mac Póilin. Belfast: *Iontaobhas ULTACH*/ULTACH Trust.

McDonald, M. 1989. *We are not French! Language, Culture and Identity in Brittany*. London: Routledge.

McKee, V. 1995. Contemporary Gaelic language politics in Western Scotland and Northern Ireland since 1950: comparative assessments. *Contemporary Politics* 1 (1), 92–113.

McMinn, J. 1992. Language, literature and cultural identity: Irish and Anglo-Irish. In *Styles of Belonging: the Cultural Identities of Ulster*, eds. J. Lundy and A. Mac Póilin. Belfast: Lagan Press.

Mertz, E. 1989. Sociolinguistic creativity: Cape Breton Gaelic's linguistic 'tip'. In *Investigating Obsolescence: Studies in Language Contraction and Death*, ed. N. Dorian. Cambridge: Cambridge University Press.

Milton, K. 1993. Belfast: whose city? In *Irish Urban Cultures*, eds C. Curtin et al. Belfast: Queen's University, Institute of Irish Studies.

——— 1996. *Environmentalism and Cultural Theory*. London: Routledge.

Moerman, M. 1988. *Talking Culture: Ethnography and Conversation Analysis*. Philadelphia: University of Pennsylvania Press.

Mouzelis, N. 1995. *Sociological Theory: What Went Wrong? Diagnosis and Remedies*. London: Routledge.

Nairn, T. 1977. *The Break-up of Britain: Crisis and Neo-nationalism*. London: New Left Books.

Nelson, S. 1984. *Ulster's Uncertain Defenders: Loyalists and the Northern Ireland Conflict*. Belfast: Appletree Press.

Nic Craith, M. 1995. The symbolism of language in Northern Ireland. In *Landscape, Heritage, and Identity: Case Studies in Irish Ethnography*, ed. U. Kockel. Liverpool: Liverpool University Press.

Ó Conaise, B. (ed.) 1986. *Language, Love and Lyrics*. Blackrock: Irish Academic Press.

206   *The Irish Language in Northern Ireland*

O'Connor, F. 1993. *In Search of a State: Catholics in Northern Ireland*. Belfast: The Blackstaff Press.
Ó Cuív, B. 1969. *A View of the Irish Language*. Dublin: The Stationery Office.
Ó Donnaile, A. 1997. Can linguistic minorities cope with a favourable majority? In *The Irish Language in Northern Ireland*, ed. A. Mac Póilin. Belfast: *Iontaobhas ULTACH*/ULTACH Trust.
Ó Fiaich, T. 1969. The language and political history. In *A View of the Irish Language*, ed. B. Ó Cuív. Dublin: The Stationery Office.
Ó hAdhmaill, F. 1985. *Report of a Survey Carried out on the Irish Language in West Belfast in the Winter of 1984/5*. Belfast: *Glór na nGael, Coiste Bhéal Feirste Thiar.*
Ó hAilín, T. 1969. Irish revival movements. In *A View of the Irish Language*, ed. B. Ó Cuív. Dublin: The Stationery Office.
Ó Huallacháin, C. (Fr.) 1994. *The Irish and Irish: a Sociolinguistic Analysis of the Relationship between a People and their Language*. Dublin: Irish Franciscan Provincial Office.
O'Leary, P., J. MacNeill, P. O'Daly and S. Barrett. 1905. *Connradh na Gaedhilge: Letter to the Irish of America*. Dublin: The Gaelic League.
Ó Muilleoir, M. 1995. Correspondence with Sir Patrick Mayhew, Secretary of State for Northern Ireland, 20 June 1995.
O'Reilly, C. 1993. The development of the Irish language in Belfast: a brief historical background. *Ulster Local Studies* 15 (1), summer, 72–79.
——1996. The Irish language – litmus test for equality? Competing discourses of identity, parity of esteem, and the peace process. *Irish Journal of Sociology* 6, 154–78.
——1998. The Irish language as symbol: visual representations of Irish in Northern Ireland. In *Symbols in Northern Ireland*, ed. A. Buckley. Belfast: Cultural Traditions Group.
Ó Riagáin, P. and M. Ó Gliasáin, 1994. *National Survey on Languages 1993: Preliminary Report*. Research Report 18. Dublin: Institiúid Teangeolaíochta Éireann.
Ó Riagáin, P. 1997. *Language Policy and Social Reproduction: Ireland 1893–1993*. Oxford: Oxford University Press.
Ó Ríordáin, S. 1987. *Brosna*. Dublin: *Sáirséal Ó Marcaigh.*
Paine, R. 1981. *Politically Speaking: Cross-cultural Studies of Rhetoric*. Newfoundland Institute of Social & Economic Research. Philadelphia: ISHI.
Parkin, D. 1984. Political language. *Annual Review of Anthropology* 13, 345–65.
Peace, A. 1993. Environmental protest, bureaucratic closure: the politics of discourse in rural Ireland. In *Environmentalism: the View from Anthropology*, ed. K. Milton. London & New York: Routledge.
The Political Vetting of Community Work Working Group 1990. *The Political Vetting of Community Work in Northern Ireland*. Belfast: Northern Ireland Council for Voluntary Action.
Purvis, T. and A. Hunt. 1993. Discourse, ideology, discourse, ideology, discourse, ideology … *British Journal of Sociology* 44 (3), 473–99.
Rogers, S. 1995. Correspondence on behalf of Secretary of State for Northern Ireland Sir Patrick Mayhew, to Máirtín Ó Muilleoir, Sinn Féin Councillor, 15 May 1995.

Romanucci-Ross, L. and G. DeVos. (eds.) 1995. *Ethnic Identity: Creation, Conflict and Accommodation*. London: Altamira Press.
Ruane, J. and J. Todd, 1991. 'Why can't you get along with each other?': culture, structure and the Northern Ireland conflict. In *Culture and Politics in Northern Ireland 1960–1990*, ed. E. Hughes. Milton Keynes: Open University Press.
——1992. Diversity, division and the middle ground in Northern Ireland. In *Irish Political Studies* 7.
Scheper-Hughes, N. 1979. *Saints, Scholars and Schizophrenics: Mental illness in Rural Ireland*. Berkeley: University of California Press.
Scott, J. C. 1990. *Domination and the Art of Resistance: Hidden Transcripts*. New Haven & London: Yale University Press.
Seidel, G. 1989. 'We condemn apartheid, BUT …': a discursive analysis of the European Parliamentary debate on sanctions (July 1986). In *Social Anthropology and the Politics of Language*, ed. R. Grillo. Sociological Review Monograph 36. London: Routledge.
Sinn Féin. 1984. *Learning Irish: an Instruction and Information Booklet*. Belfast: Sinn Féin.
Sluka, J. 1989. *Hearts and Minds, Water and Fish: Support for the IRA and INLA in a Northern Irish Ghetto*. London: JAI Press.
Smith, A. D. 1981. *The Ethnic Revival*. Cambridge: Cambridge University Press.
Smith, M. E. 1982. The process of sociocultural continuity. *Current Anthropology* 23 (2), 127–42.
Spencer, J. 1990. Writing within: anthropology, nationalism, and culture in Sri Lanka. *Current Anthropology* 31 (3).
Sweeney, K. 1987. *The Irish Language in Northern Ireland 1987: Preliminary Report of a Survey of Knowledge, Interest and Ability*. Policy Planning and Research Unit, Occasional Paper No. 17. A Government Statistical Publication.
Taylor, L. J. 1995. *Occasions of Faith: an Anthropology of Irish Catholics*. Dublin: Lilliput Press.
Thompson, J. 1991. Introduction. In P. Bourdieu. *Language and Symbolic Power*. Oxford: Polity Press.
Todd, J. 1987. Two traditions in unionist political culture. *Irish Political Studies* 2, 1–26.
Tovey, H., D. Hannan and H. Abramson 1989. *Why Irish? Irish Identity and the Irish Language*. Dublin: Bord na Gaeilge.
ULTACH Trust annual report/*Iontaobhas ULTACH tuairisc bhliantúil 1990–91*. 1991. Belfast: ULTACH Trust.
ULTACH Trust: second report/*Iontaobhas ULTACH: an dara tuairisc 1991–93*. 1994. Belfast: ULTACH Trust.
Wardaugh, R. 1987. *Languages in Competition: Dominance, Diversity and Decline*. Oxford: Basil Blackwell.
West Belfast Economic Forum. July 1993. Briefing paper no. 1. *The 1991 Census Results*.

Glossary

ACE – Action for Community Employment, a government employment scheme

Alliance – a middle ground party which supports the union with Britain as long as the majority in Northern Ireland continue to support it. Alliance is perceived by Nationalists as a moderate Unionist party.

Béal Feirste – Belfast

BIFHE – Belfast Institute of Further and Higher Education

Bord na Gaeilge – An Irish government agency which funds and supports the Irish language

bun rang – beginners Irish class

bunscoil (pl. *bunscoileanna*) – 'primary school'

Bunscoil an tSleibhe Dhuibh – 'Black Mountain Primary School', Belfast's fourth Irish medium primary school, located in Ballymurphy, west Belfast

Bunscoil Bheann Mhadagáin – 'Ben Madigan Primary School', Belfast's fifth Irish medium primary school, located in Ardoyne, north Belfast

Bunscoil Phobal Feirste – 'Belfast Community Primary School', the city's first Irish medium primary school, located off the Shaws Road, Andersonstown, west Belfast

CAJ – Committee on the Administration of Justice, a human rights organization

Catholic – In Northern Ireland, the religious label serves as a marker of ethnic identity or community membership. The term 'Catholic' generally implies an Irish identity and is usually synonymous with Nationalist. For a discussion of the complexities involved in such labels, see Ruane and Todd (1991, 1992).

Comhaltas Uladh – the northern branch of the Gaelic League

Conradh na Gaeilge – 'the Gaelic League'

CRC – Community Relations Council

CRD – Centre for Research and Documentation, an organization dedicated to the comparative study of development in Ireland and the Third World

CTG – Cultural Traditions Group, a committee of the Community Relations Council

Cultúrlann McAdam-Ó Fiaich – bilingual cultural centre which houses an Irish language bookstore, cafe, *Lá*, a variety of offices, and *Meánscoil Feirste*

cumann (pl. *cumainn*) – 'society' or 'association'

Cumann Chluain Ard – ('Clonard Society') formerly a branch of the Gaelic League, a well known Irish language club and teaching organization in west Belfast

Cumann Gaelach – ('Gaelic Society'), an Irish language club at Queens University of Belfast. Other universities have clubs of the same name.

Dáil – the Irish parliament

DENI – Department of Education for Northern Ireland

DUP – Democratic Unionist Party

fainne (pl. *fainní*) – ('ring') a symbol in the form of a circular lapel pin, worn to indicate a knowledge of the Irish language

FAIT – Families Against Intimidation and Terror

fíor-Ghael (pl. *fíor-Ghaeil*) – 'true Gael'

GAA – Gaelic Athletic Association

Gaeilgeoir (pl. *Gaeilgeoirí*) – an Irish speaker or learner; Irish language enthusiast

Gael-Linn – Irish language fundraising body

Gaelic League (*Conradh na Gaeilge*) – an organization founded in 1897 to promote the Irish language

Gaeloiliúint – an organization which promotes Irish-medium education

Gaelscoil na bhFál – 'Irish School of the Hedgerow' or 'Falls Irish School', Belfast's second Irish-medium primary school, located in the lower Falls

Gaeltacht (pl. *Gaeltachtaí*) – an Irish-speaking area

Glór na nGael – ('Voice of the Gael'), throughout Ireland, a competition for the area or town which has done the most to promote the Irish language each year. It is also the name of the west Belfast organization which oversees the district's entry into the competition, and which campaigns on behalf of Irish.

INLA – Irish Nationalist Liberation Army, a paramilitary group which split from the Official IRA in the 1970s

Iontaobhas ULTACH – see **ULTACH Trust**

IRA – Irish Republican Army

Lá – ('Day') an Irish-medium newspaper produced in Belfast

Loyalist – Those people, mostly Protestant, who wish for Northern Ireland either to remain a part of the United Kingdom or to become an independent state. Usually, the term Loyalist refers to someone who supports or justifies the use of violence to obtain these goals. Generally more radical than Unionists – see Todd (1987) for a detailed discussion of the complexities of Unionist politics and identity.

meánscoil (pl. *meánsoileanna*) – secondary school

Meánscoil Feirste – 'Belfast Secondary School', the first Irish medium secondary school in Northern Ireland

naíonra (pl. *naíonraí*) – nursery school

Nationalist – Those people, mostly Catholic, who wish to see some form of a united Ireland, but who generally support constitutional means of obtaining this goal (see Ruane and Todd 1991, 1992).

NICVA – Northern Ireland Council for Voluntary Action

NIO – Northern Ireland Office

NUPE – National Union of Public Employees

Orange Order – a Protestant organization formed to protect and promote Protestant ascendancy in the North

People's Democracy – a civil rights organization active in the late 1960s and early 1970s

PUP – Progressive Unionist Party, one of the 'fringe' Loyalist parties, associated with the Ulster Volunteer Force (UVF)

Protestant – As with the term Catholic, the religious label serves as a marker of ethnic identity or community membership. The term 'Protestant' generally implies a British or Ulster Irish identity, and is usually synonymous with Unionist (see Ruane and Todd 1991, 1992).

Republican – Those people, mostly Catholic, who wish to see a united Ireland as an immediate political goal, and who generally (but not always) support Sinn Féin. Usually, the term Republican refers to someone who supports or justifies the use of violence to obtain this goal.

Roinn na Gaeltachta – 'Department of the Gaeltacht', an Irish government agency responsible for development and Irish language issues in the *Gaeltachtaí*

RUC – Royal Ulster Constabulary, the police force in Northern Ireland, which is over 90 per cent Protestant in membership

RVH – Royal Victoria Hospital, located on the Falls Road in west Belfast

Scoil na Fuiseoige – 'School of the Lark', Belfast's third Irish medium primary school, located in Twinbrook, west Belfast

SDLP – Social Democratic and Labour Party (a Nationalist political party)

Sinn Féin – ('Ourselves') the Republican party generally associated with the IRA

TACA – an Irish language fundraising body based in Belfast

UDP – Ulster Democratic Party, one of the 'fringe' Loyalist parties associated with the UFF

UFF – Ulster Freedom Fighters, a Loyalist paramilitary group associated with the Ulster Defense Association (UDA) and the 'fringe' Loyalist party the UDP

ULTACH Trust – (***Iontaobhas ULTACH***) an organization which funds and supports the Irish language

Unionist – Those people, mostly Protestant, who wish for Northern Ireland to remain part of the United Kingdom, but who generally support constitutional means of maintaining this connection (see Todd 1987).

UUP – Ulster Unionist Party (also known as the OUP, Official Unionist Party)

UVF – Ulster Volunteer Force, a Loyalist paramilitary group associated with the 'fringe' Loyalist party the PUP

Index